IN THE GROOVE

IN THE
GROOVE

The People Behind the Music

TED FOX

St. Martin's Press
New York

Design by Paolo Pepe

Library of Congress Cataloging-in-Publication Data

Fox, Ted, 1954–
    In the groove.

    1. Music, Popular (Songs, etc.)—United States—
History and criticism. I. Title.
ML3477.F7   1986   780'.42'09   86-13812
ISBN 0-312-41166-9

First Edition
10 9 8 7 6 5 4 3 2 1

Contents

JOHN HAMMOND:

He's the grand old man of the business—a talent scout, A&R man, and producer. He "discovered" Billie Holiday, Count Basie, Aretha Franklin, George Benson, Bob Dylan, and Bruce Springsteen, among others. He has also produced some of the greats of classical music at Vanguard and Columbia Masterworks. A pioneer, and outspoken critic, his influence becomes more apparent as his name comes up again and again in several of these interviews.

MITCH MILLER:

Everyone remembers his TV show and records, but he was also the most important man in the record business throughout the fifties as the head of A&R for Columbia Records. With his roster of middle-of-the-road discoveries such as Frankie Laine, Rosemary Clooney, Johnny Mathis, and Ray Conniff, he has probably produced more hits than any other producer ever will. He also worked with Sinatra, Charlie Parker, and Mahalia Jackson. He was a true studio pioneer, a great classical musician, childhood friend of Alec Wilder, and on and on.

MILT GABLER:

Through his world-famous Commodore Music Shop he set up the first independent jazz record company, and released the first jazz reissues. He produced jazz greats like Billie Holiday, Lester Young, and Eddie Condon. He also founded a legendary series of jam sessions on 52nd Street. At Decca he worked with Ella Fitzgerald, Brenda Lee, Louis Jordan, The Weavers, and made the first rock 'n' roll smash hit, "Rock Around the Clock," with Bill Haley and the Comets. He is one of the classic record men.

CLIVE DAVIS:

PHIL RAMONE:

CHRIS STRACHWITZ:

CHRIS BLACKWELL:

viii   CONTENTS

NILE RODGERS:

He's probably the hottest young producer on the scene today. Start-
ing with his own group, Chic, he produced top disco acts like Sister
Sledge, and he has a lot to say about disco's reception in America.
His career really heated up with his production of David Bowie's
Let's Dance. He has also produced Diana Ross, Debbie Harry,
Duran Duran, Jeff Beck, The Thompson Twins, Madonna's smash
hit album, and co-produced Mick Jagger's solo debut. A highly
intelligent, thoughtful, and articulate man.   **325**

Index   **348**

Acknowledgments

These interviews were originally conducted for *Audio* magazine—the best periodical of its kind, I think. Gene Pitts saw their potential when other editors would not have, and he published them in an absolutely first-class manner. I'm thankful for his vision, constant support, and his great skill with a pencil. I'd also like to acknowledge the others at *Audio* who helped make these interviews happen: Kay Blumenthal, Elise Marton, Andrea Lynne Hecker, and Linda Zerella. Special thanks to art director Cathy Cacchione, who continued to outdo herself to make the magazine pieces look better than I ever thought they could.

Thanks to Bob Miller at St. Martin's, my agent, Perry Knowlton, and my friends Marcy Guth and Joe Rosen.

I also want to thank those who gave up their valuable time to be interviewed, and those who were really responsible for making the interviews happen: Jenny Trent, Sue Jacobs, Mikey Harris, Joe D'Ambrosio, Olga Kovacs, Deborah Radel, Rose Gross-Marino, Simo Doe, Bud Tunick, Karen Rooney, and Bob Golden.

Finally, to my true friend Doc Pomus—Jewish blues shouter . . . record producer . . . writer of "Save the Last Dance for Me," "Viva Las Vegas," "Teenager in Love," and so many other classic tunes—thanks.

Preface

The men in this book discovered, nurtured, advised, recorded, and presented the artists who have shaped our lives with their music. Along the way many of these same people virtually invented the recording industry—creating a new art form, and a form of commerce with a profound effect upon our culture and society.

They are fascinating characters. I hope what emerges from these interviews, in addition to some great stories and information, is the give and take of good conversation. I tried to be the dutiful representative of music fandom in my talks, but I also found myself responding directly to my subjects as interesting people as well as sources.

It takes a great deal of self-confidence, and a strong ego, to impose your musical tastes on great artists and the public. That is one thing that cannot fail to come through in the interviews. In most cases, though, these men have remained behind the scenes. Artists must project themselves physically, outwardly, but the work of the men behind the music remains largely unseen, trapped in vinyl.

I have looked upon the interviews in this book as my subjects' opportunity to tell their stories. I have tried to prod and challenge them, but others will undoubtedly have different memories of the same events—just as some of the men in this book contradict and disagree with others in the book.

Aside from the information I learned, the *process* of doing these interviews has given me a better feeling for how records are made. Conducting and reproducing an interview is very similar to producing a record. Either way, the raw material must be there first, then one can add to it, edit it, change it around slightly. The interviewer is unable, in the question and answer format, to tell the story himself—just as the record producer cannot sing or play the tune himself. The interviewer must find a way to draw out compelling material, just as a record producer tries to elicit a compelling performance. In the end, the results must be on the page, or in the groove.

—TED FOX
New York City
May 1986

Foreword
by Doc Pomus

Last year I read *Showtime at the Apollo,* a book about the old Apollo Theater written by some guy named Ted Fox. It was so accurate and real that after a few pages I could feel and almost taste 1951 all over again. I was back in my usual seat in the rear of the theater surrounded by the "zoot suits" and short skirts of the good timin', righteous 125th Street folk. I could hear Big Joe Turner shouting "Chains of Love," while a sweet voice in the balcony hollered "You won't have to chain me, Daddy!" Gravel-voiced Moms Mabley was dishing out the dozens and Judge Pigmeat Markham was pounding his gavel and pronouncing the world guilty of not enough giggles and smiles. I could see Porto Rico with his outlandish, rainbow-splashed costumes, running across the stage while the sirens howled and the band was blasting "Leap Frog," and the lame amateur-night loser raced for cover backstage.

I just had to get a hold of this old dude Ted Fox and hang out with him a little to trade some lies and other good stuff about what used to be. After a few false starts, I Sherlock Holmes'd him down and we got together. . . . Imagine my surprise when he turned out to be this nice, straight, thirtyish-looking white cat! He was so polite, quiet, and respectable that he seemed like the perfect candidate to date your kid sister or youngest daughter. I'm not much for the usual fast, double-talking type of journalistic hot shot, so we hit it off more than just pretty good. We went out to the Lone Star Cafe a few nights to dig some blues and zydeco sounds. We also talked on the phone a gang of times and split a couple of tasty meals sprinkled with conversations about where we were at, where we'd been, and where we were going.

One day several months later, he called up and said he wanted me to write the Foreword to a new book he was about to publish. It was to be a compilation of interviews he had conducted with famous and infamous record producers of the past and present. He perceived that these interviews would almost be a human chronology of the record industry. This idea fascinated me.

One of the central themes—the record industry's increasing

reliance on technology—seemed to me a microcosm of a world controlled more and more by computers and robotics, and less and less by the soul and the heart. In music, the idea is to get the soul of the sound into the record. Ostensibly, the more sophisticated the equipment, the better the chance of capturing the instant. But if there's an over-involvement, consciously or otherwise, with technique and technology, then the real point of making a record—the capturing of the instant—is missed. In life, the same holds true. If you use a computer or synthesizer as a substitute instead of an aid, you're missing the point of technological advancement. The soul can never be replaced.

Anyway, I told Ted that I would be pleased and honored to write the Foreword to this book. But deep down, part of me figured that it would just mean reading and writing about characters that I knew only too well, and would entail him and me wasting too much time and effort trying to get through their usual bullshit and tap-dancing.

Well, I underestimated Ted Fox. . . . That polite, seemingly innocent exterior was insidious. It worked wonders and performed major surgery on the psyches of the interviewees. Out poured a stream of consciousness of truths, revealing tantalizing glimpses of usually unexposed parts that they have kept hidden from interviewers, their public, and perhaps even from themselves . . . like a virgin giving up her chastity after being sweet-talked with a conversation that sounded to her like it had something to do with the weather. Ted reminds me of a fighter who always knocks out his opponents with a sneak punch. When the KO'd fighter comes to, he never really remembers what happened, but he's got resin on the seat of his trunks and his head's buzzing, so he knows he's been belted.

Well, Jerry Wexler, Leiber & Stoller, Phil Ramone, Chris Strachwitz, Alfred Lion, Clive Davis, etc., etc., all fell victim to Ted Fox's sneak attack. They let their guard down, but instead of getting KO'd, their hearts and souls opened up and they revealed, not only how unusually talented and intelligent they are, but how real and warm they could be if they were caught without their walls and disguises protecting them. And when they expose their shortcomings and weaknesses, they become more appealing—human, vulnerable, and lopsided like the rest of us. In each of these interviews Ted Fox gets the person to keep on talking and talking and talking. Then Ted's filtering system washes away all the extraneous bits and pieces that are hanging around just taking up space. What's finally left is the heart and guts—the essence.

Consequently, the real Phil Ramone says that he is only interested in today and tomorrow, and shuts out yesterday. . . .

Chris Blackwell confides that the future of the music business is in the fusion of films and records. . . .

Milt Gabler philosophizes that if you work for a corporation, you always end up getting fired. . . . I go way back with Milt Gabler. In the late forties and early fifties, Gabler and the late Jack Crystal (who, incidentally, was talented comedian Billy Crystal's father) ran jam sessions at the old Central Plaza on Second Avenue. I sang there many Friday and Saturday nights accompanied by jazz greats like Willie "The Lion" Smith, Roy Eldridge, Zutty Singleton, Pops Foster, etc., etc. Gabler and Crystal were warm and generous, and many times went deep into their shallow pockets to make sure we ended up with some bread.

I've known Jerry Leiber and Mike Stoller forever, and very, very well. But until I read Ted Fox's interview, I never knew the facts about their relationship with legendary record industry entrepreneur and character George Goldner. And now I also know what happened to Mike and the *Andria Doria*. . . . On the other hand I know something about Mike and Jerry that perhaps Ted doesn't know. They are the most extraordinarily generous guys with a dollar and time, for any blues or R&B talent. Early in my songwriting career they were always available with great advice and plenty of hours, and I'm proud to say we've collaborated on two songs, "Youngblood" and "She's Not You." They both have been huge hits, so we're batting a thousand together.

I knew Jerry Wexler from the first day he replaced Herb Abramson at Atlantic Records. I knew those guys when they were putting in subliminal apprenticeships with the brilliant recording engineer and producer Tommy Dowd. I've seen Jerry emerge as an upper-echelon sensitive operator at the studio board and become a major record company whiz as well. But after all these years I never knew that Wexler thought that the most talented of all the rock 'n' rollers was my wild and wooly Texas "boon," Doug Sahm. Well, whatta you know! . . .

I ain't gonna give away anything else. You've gotta read this book carefully. It's a killer!

John Hammond

J ohn Hammond has been an important presence in the record business from its very early days. His mother was a Vanderbilt, but he became a champion of the oppressed—both politically and musically. He rescued legendary black artists such as Fletcher Henderson and Bessie Smith from despair and decline. He "discovered" some of the most important stars in American popular music, including Billie Holiday, Charlie Christian, Count Basie, Bob Dylan, Aretha Franklin, George Benson, and Bruce Springsteen. More recently he helped launch the career of Stevie Ray Vaughan. He has also been a top producer of classical recordings since his days with Columbia Masterworks in the 1930s. He has been most closely associated with CBS and Columbia Records throughout his fifty-year career, but he also helped shape the catalogs of Mercury and Vanguard. In addition, Hammond was a top jazz critic, one of the first to write seriously about black jazz. On top of all of his personal accomplishments, Hammond has been a catalyst in the careers of many other seminally important people in the music business through his enthusiasm and encouragement. Indeed, his name will come up again and again throughout this book. Appropriately, this was the first interview

I conducted for *Audio*, and I have placed it first in this book, because that is where Hammond belongs historically.

Is this really something you're thinking of doing? George Benson and Stevie Ray Vaughan together?

Oh, yeah, sure, that's one thing, and the other thing is that I think we might be able to get George back to CBS. That would be wonderful. George wants to play jazz and Warner Bros. won't let him.

They're pushing him into more of a pop thing?

Oh, yes, completely. He's done some marvelous jazz things and they won't release them. They don't want to tarnish his image.

But he's got that Frank Lloyd Wright house in New Jersey, and he didn't get that playing jazz.

No. He got that from playing pop.

So isn't he kind of committed now? Doesn't he have to keep doing this?

No way. He built a $300,000 recording studio in Hawaii, and his investments have been very good.

Ah, ha. So now he's able to do what he wants to do.

Exactly.

How did you meet George Benson?

On 125th Street. I was walking to the Apollo. Nineteen years ago. And I looked in the window of the Palm Cafe, and it said, "Introducing the World's Greatest Guitar Player: George Benson." I just had a feeling I ought to go up and hear him. At the same time, I had gotten a letter, sort of an illiterate scrawl from a guy who turned out to be his manager—a great person called Jimmy Boyd. So my wife and I went over that night to the Palm Cafe. There were big signs saying GO-GO DANCING. People had described me to George so he knew what I looked like. As soon as Esmé and I walked in he drew a band signature, because they were really playing for dancing there, and the go-go girls suddenly disappeared, and George starts to play real jazz. I really hadn't heard anybody like him since Charlie Christian.

Did he remind you of Charlie Christian, who was also one of your finds?

Charlie was one of his main influences. George's father was a Charlie Christian fanatic. He built George's first guitar out of cigar boxes. George is extraordinary. I'm sure glad I was on my way to the Apollo that day. I signed him the next day to CBS.

You've been the producer of some of the most incredible sessions of the past fifty years. How would you characterize your production technique?

Well, I'm basically a one-mike mono man, you know. I make adjustments, obviously, for rock. But, I like natural sound. I hate overdubbing. Fortunately, in Stevie I have a guy who agrees with me.

How would you record someone like Stevie Ray Vaughan?

The last album we made was at the Power Station. It's a wonderful studio on West 53rd Street. I told them what I wanted. I didn't want Stevie isolated, and I wanted the impact of the group. It's only a trio, you know. We added, on some sides, his brother on another guitar, and a tenor man. Stevie, like George, accompanies himself. He doesn't overdub vocals.

But you've worked with other artists. . . .

I've worked with Lawrence Welk, if you want to call him an artist. . . .

You've worked with other artists who you'd think would want to do something simple, but ended up doing something much more elaborate.

Well, you know, stereo came in and set back the record business twenty years, I think, with isolation and all that.

You really feel that stereo set the recording business back twenty years?

Now that digital recording has come in, and Compact Discs, we're discarding all that stereo technique that was used. Because the more mikes you have open and everything, the more distortion there is. Yeah, I have my definite feelings about this.

You've said that one of your favorite sessions was a '36 session you did with Basie, and you also said that was one of your most technically inept sessions.

The studio was so terrible. It was a little second-story studio in Chicago, across from the Drake Hotel. You couldn't record the bass and the bass drum at the same time. So, Jo Jones, it was his first recording date, and Walter Page was on bass. We decided we didn't need the bass drum. We just used snares and a hi-hat. However, it was one of the few perfect recording sessions I ever had. There wasn't a reject. All perfect. It was done in the morning after the guys had gotten finished working at the Grand Terrace. It was just a little sextet. Jimmy Rushing was on vocals, and Basie, Jo Jones, Walter Page, Lester Young, and Buck Clayton had a split lip that day, so we used another trumpet player from the band, Carl "Tatti" Smith. We called it Jones-Smith Inc., because Basie had just signed that underscale Decca contract, and we couldn't use [his name].

I guess you weren't a big fan of fifties jazz, and you also said you didn't feel that it was as well recorded as classical music.

No, and that's how I got with Vanguard. The Vanguard Recording Society was started in the early fifties, after long-playing records came in. Both Seymour Solomon and Maynard Solomon were musicians, good musicians. In fact, Seymour and I had been old pupils of the same violin teacher. I wrote an article for *The New York Times* in '53, decrying modern recording techniques. So Seymour, whom I hadn't seen since he was a student, called me up and said, "John, I'm going to give you the opportunity to do exactly what you want to do." He said, "I've uncovered an incredible concert hall in Brooklyn, the Brooklyn Masonic Temple, and we can bring over portable equipment and record there. The only trouble is we have to record at night because we're right next to a school and the noise of basketball tryouts and everything is hopeless in the daytime." And I said that's fine by me. So we started going over there, and we had to haul in a Steinway grand. If we had to do it today it would cost about $500; it cost about a hundred then. I made, I still think, some of the best records, stereo and mono, that I've ever made in my life.

Which ones?

Count Basie with a fantastic all-star band. Vic Dickenson, Mel Powell—he used to be Benny Goodman's pianist—Edmond Hall, all sorts of things.

Did you do any classical recordings there?

No. They did a whole lot of chamber music, and I used to sit in on those sessions.

I guess Columbia Masterworks was the classical label you were most closely associated with.

Yeah, I guess so. Because I made my first Columbia classical records with Joseph Szigeti back in 1937. And again, one of the worst studios ever, the old Brunswick Studios at 1776 Broadway, and we made the first recordings of a recently discovered Mozart divertimento. The playing was sublime. Of course, this was years before there was tape, and Max Goberman was the conductor. Max, who was a good leftist, didn't believe in using anything but unemployed French horn players, and two of the most important French horn parts in the history of chamber music were in that divertimento. There were bloops on practically every side, and there was no way we could edit them out. So it stayed, bloops and all, and it's still in the catalog. See, tape didn't come until after World War II.

So how did that affect things, aside from obviously improving the quality of the sound?

Well, not that, because it made it possible to make more dishonest records than there had ever been, through splicing.

You've come out pretty strongly against splicing, especially in classical recording. In fact, I think you uncovered some famous overdubs that wouldn't have otherwise been known. Is that correct?

Well, I mean, for instance, Horowitz, who was a perfectionist, wouldn't allow any technical errors on his recordings when he was with Columbia. So Columbia would have to record rehearsals, you see, so that there could be splices made.

Backups?

Yeah, backups, exactly. But, the unfortunate thing was there was a famous record dealer in New York, who shall be nameless, who used to bring a little Nagra recorder to concerts and he would compare what was on the record, as a live performance, with what he had on his tape. Somehow or other it came out in *The New York Times,* about this controversy. Tom Frost nearly lost his job; he was Horowitz's producer. Horowitz figured that Tom Frost had squealed. But it wasn't; it was our friend on 43rd Street.

Playing devil's advocate: If a piece on a record is going to be played over and over again, and will stand forever, isn't it fair that the artist wants the piece to be the best it can be?

Only if you don't advertise it as the actual concert, and *that*'s where they came a cropper. Now, for instance, Glenn Gould would edit, and in his later years Szigeti had to edit. When Columbia dropped Szigeti, I got him a contract with Vanguard immediately, and he did the unaccompanied Bach sonatas. And I think there's something like eight-hundred splices on that series of six LP sides. It couldn't have been done without it.

But he wasn't advertising it as a live performance?

No way. Well, I've recorded Gieseking, and Gieseking was an honest man, and there's a wonderful story here. He was my favorite pianist, and the only record he ever made in America, I was the supervisor of: the Second Book of Debussy Preludes. I couldn't get there in the morning for the rehearsal, but I met Gieseking for lunch at Child's before the actual session started. I said, "How did it go?" He said, "John, we wasted an awful lot of time this morning." I said, "How?" He said, "Trying to get the Middle Western accent out of the Baldwin." Because Gieseking was a Baldwin artist, you see. I said, "Well, you know, Mr. Gieseking, we have the most beautiful Boston Mason & Hamlin in the studio." He said, "You *do?*" I said, "We certainly do." So we waited until the Baldwin man left. Baldwin now makes a marvelous piano since they bought Bechstein, but in those days they were made in Cincinnati and they were not what they should have been. So we waited until the Baldwin man left, and then, on this ravishing piano, Gieseking recorded the Second Book of Preludes.

He got what he wanted.

He sure did. I also found out why his records sounded so much more satisfactory than he did in person. Gieseking had terribly small nostrils, and he was a very passionate player. And you would hear [*sniffs*]. We had a regular setup for him, and it wasn't any good because all you heard was his breathing. So I started experimenting, putting the microphone further and further back. Finally, about twenty-two feet away, I said, "Now I think we've got it." Because we had the overtones from the studio and so forth. I said,

"How did you do this in Europe?" He said, "We found out it came out better when the microphone was away."

So were you able to apply what you learned from him on other sessions?

A lot. Absolutely, particularly in regard to piano sounds. This is another thing wonderful about the Vanguard studios. At the present Vanguard studios in New York, they have a nine-foot concert grand, the last made before accelerated action came in. A friend of mine who had been a chief technician at Steinway rebuilt the piano for Vanguard, and they have the best piano in New York. Accelerated action, most people think, was a step back—the way stereo was in the record business, a step back in the history of Steinway.

Frankly, I don't know what accelerated action is.

Well, nobody else does. It was a gimmick that Steinway used in 1933, and they're stuck with it.

The old ones are almost like Stradivarius violins, I guess.

Exactly. You can't improve on the original.

What was it about moving that mike back that improved the sound?

Usually, it gives more air and breath to the sound. I don't use it in every case, obviously. In the old days I used to record big bands, and I used to record them on a B44 RCA mike. I'd have the piano and vocals on one side of the mike, and the rest of the band on the other.

No twenty-four tracks? [Laughter.]

No, and no tape. We didn't start using tape until after I got out of the army in 1946. I worked first for Columbia, which didn't have any tape, and then I worked for Majestic, which didn't own any tape. But luckily, Bob Fine, who was chief engineer for Mercury, was a friend of Buzz Reeves, Hazard Reeves, who has the Reeves studio, and they had the first great tape recorders made in America, which were made by Fairchild. This is pre-Ampex. And then when Ampex came out with their line, we used Ampex. That Olympian series on Mercury, the classical series with the Chicago Symphony and Kubelik, those were all made with a one-mike technique. They were made in Chicago. The Orchestra Hall, the acoustics weren't good enough, so we went to Louis Sullivan's Auditorium Theater, which was around the corner. It just turned out beautifully.

How about when you did the From Spirituals to Swing concerts at Carnegie Hall?

That was done with two overhanging mikes. No, one overhanging mike, that's all. That was recorded by Zig Franck; this was back in '38 or '39. He owned a little studio upstairs in Carnegie Hall, and we just ran a line down from the studio.

Did you amplify those concerts in Carnegie Hall?

No, that was all acoustic. You didn't need any amplification there.

How did you get involved with Stevie Ray Vaughan?

He sought me out, if you can believe it. He sought me out because he worshipped Charlie Christian, and he knew that I was the first guy to go to Oklahoma City to find Charlie Christian and put him with Benny Goodman's sextet. He knew my son, who is a blues singer, and he figured if he met me I would understand what he was trying to do. And I did. He had already recorded some things out in L.A. but they were not well balanced, so we rebalanced his original tapes. Stevie and I got to be good friends.

Was he with Bowie when he first came to you?

No, that was before he was with Bowie. Then he went with Bowie and did that *Let's Dance* album and toured with Bowie. But Bowie was interested in Bowie, and he wasn't interested in promoting another artist.

I understand he wasn't willing to pay too much either.

No, he wasn't. But why should he? You know, he's a businessman. But Stevie is a businessman too. I got him a contract with Epic Records, and I'm amazed that I did because Epic was pretty square in those days. But there was one great A&R man, Greg Geller, and as soon as Epic signed him, Geller was fired and went to RCA. He's a good man.

When you came to them with Stevie Ray, did they say, "Oh, Jesus, another white Texas blues player"?

No, there were no white Texas blues players at that time.

Johnny Winter, and his brother Edgar.

Well, Johnny was on Columbia, not Epic, and as good as he is, Johnny was not comparable with Stevie Ray. The head of Epic is Don Dempsey, a terribly nice guy, and that's why when I'm signing people I sort of favor Epic over Columbia. They proved with Michael Jackson that they can sell more records than any other record company in history.

I want to talk for a bit about your great career. . . .

Don't let me be too libelous, because I'm likely to be libelous.

Okay, we'll stay away from that. Tell me, do you hear things no one else hears?

I don't think so.

But you've discovered so many greats.

Oh, but I've been around so long. The most important thing for me, really, is that I had a classical background. I played in a string quartet for fourteen years. I was one of the more miserable viola players in history, but at least I could play with people better than I. So I got a sense of ensemble, and of what I wanted to hear.

Okay, but for instance, you heard Basie—the famous story of you hearing Basie over your car radio from Kansas City . . .

That was a good radio.

Thank God, it was. And you then brought Benny Goodman out in the car with you to listen, and he didn't like Basie. He didn't think he was any big deal. What did you hear that he didn't?

In the first place, I had known Basie when he was a piano player with Bennie Moten's band, and then Basie used to hang out in a speak-easy in 1931 in back of the Lafayette Theater. They had an upright piano there, and I was able to hear what Basie could do. He was, aside from James P. Johnson and Fats Waller, the greatest stride piano player that ever had been.

Did you know that when you heard him in the speak-easy?

Oh, of course.

But he was just plain old Bill Basie from Red Bank, New Jersey.

No, that horrible Count thing did not get added until about 1934, '35. I heard him first with Moten's band, then Moten's band was having trouble, so Basie started a small band. Well, I just knew from the sound of the little nine-piece that I heard on the radio that day that there was no other sound like that in history.

You knew it was Bill Basie?

I sure did, couldn't help it. And he was all over the keyboard then, you know. As Basie matured, he got more economical in the sound that he had. He was a genius.

*You know, this is one criticism I've heard about Stevie Ray. Some
have said he plays too much guitar.*

Well, listen, when a guy has got overpowering technique, this
sometimes happens. They like to display it. But, we've been pretty
careful on these records. I mean, it's not display just for display's
sake. Stevie happens to be a damned good singer, which you don't
expect out of a guitar player, and he knows the sound he wants.
Also, like George Benson, he is his own ideal accompanist. George
also, as a singer, is an incredible accompanist to himself. Of course,
these commercial records he makes nowadays aren't like that.

He has a voice like Stevie Wonder, I always thought.

To a degree. No, George's idol was Nat Cole. There were other
influences in George's playing. One of them was Wes Montgomery,
but I have a feeling that as a guitar player, George far excels Wes
Montgomery. But the vocal style really came from Nat. Just two
days ago I was doing this documentary with George, and that's
what he said. "Be sure to realize, John, that I learned so much from
Nat Cole."

*Let's go back to what we were talking about before. So, Bill Basie
had been around for years, and thousands and maybe millions
had heard him from his radio broadcasts just like you had.*

No, because it was a little experimental radio station, off the regular
part of the dial. It was called W9XBY, and it was 1,550 kilocycles.

And you could get this little station in Chicago?

I did indeed. It was a clear-channel station, and after midnight
all the awful stations thereabouts were off the air. So I was truly
lucky.

*You're not going to give me a chance with this at all. You're not
going to let me say that you hear stuff that other people don't
hear. How about Billie Holiday? She was singing in clubs for
years. . . .*

No, I heard Billie Holiday before anybody else heard her. I heard her just when she had come up from Baltimore. I went to a speak-easy on 133rd Street one night, and I was going there to hear a singer called Monette Moore. But Monette was working with Clifton Webb in a show downtown, and she wasn't there for the set, so she had this seventeen-year-old girl filling in for her. I couldn't believe it. In the first place, you couldn't have a microphone in a speak-easy because the noise might filter out into the street. So Billie was just singing tables, to customers at tables. She was doing a number, and she sang the same song at each table completely differently. I had never heard a really improvising singer until that time. So I knew that she was unique. I can't say that it was any big deal. I just happened to be around at the right time.

Yeah, but you sure are around at the right time a lot of times. How about Aretha Franklin?

Well, I loved gospel music and I loved jazz, and I knew she was the ideal combination of both.

You first heard her . . .

. . . On a demo record. The composer brought in a bunch of his tunes, and Aretha had sung one of them. This was an extraordinary story. There was one tune called "Today I Sing the Blues." I loved it. I knew it sounded vaguely familiar, and I had recorded that tune with Helen Humes fourteen years before for Mercury. I had forgotten the name of it. Then this demo comes in and I hear this girl. Aretha was eighteen. I called up Curtis Lewis, who wrote the tune, and I said, "Where do I find this girl?" He said, "Oh, John, she's in Detroit. Her father is a very famous minister, and she's been in the gospel choir for years. She's a hell of a singer, isn't she?" I said, "She sure is." I sought her out and signed her for Columbia in '61, I think it was.

The demo wasn't even for Aretha.

No, it was for the composer to show off his tunes. We made that tune on our first session with Aretha.

She went on to a rather lackluster deal at Columbia.

Well, I made two albums with Aretha, both of which were wonderful musically but were not particularly commercial. Columbia decided that they might have a hot pop artist. So, they wanted to
record her with strings and big bands and everything.

Was that Mitch Miller's idea?

No, indeed. Somebody named David Kapralik. So, he said, "You
can produce Aretha for albums, but we want to do something
different with her for singles." I said, "Whatever she wants." So
they did it. The relationship deteriorated for about three years
until, finally, thank goodness, Aretha was signed by my friend Jerry
Wexler at Atlantic. I asked, "Jerry, how did the first date go?" and
he said, "John, we put her back in church." And then he found
Otis Redding and other wonderful people to write for her. Columbia would never have thought of that, because Columbia didn't
know what real R&B was. Only the OkeH division put out R&B
records.

How long did OkeH last?

Once in a while they still reissue these. That was one of the original
. . . Otto Heineman left Germany after World War I, and he started
OkeH. It was a hill-and-dale record when they first came out because Victor and Columbia had a cross-patent agreement and they
prevented anybody else from making lateral-cut records until
Brunswick, in 1920, sued them for restraint of trade and opened
up lateral-cut records to everybody. I have a couple of copies of the
original OkeH label, which had a large O, and then a small ke, and
a big H at the end. That was for Otto Heineman; that's why the
label was spelled that strange way. They started making lateral-cut
records, and in 1920 they came out with the first big-selling race
record, which was "Crazy Blues" by Mamie Smith.

*Let's talk about another artist who came to Columbia through your
efforts, Bob Dylan. He had been around the Village for a bit in
the clubs, and he was just one of the crowd. But you saw
something in him that set him apart.*

Well, it was partly that my politics are left, you see, and Bobby was in his protest days when I first heard him. He was not respectful of the Establishment. My two big buddies at CBS were Goddard Lieberson, whom I had brought to CBS in 1939 to work in the Masterworks department, and Mitch Miller, who had been our recording director at Mercury. These were two very progressive guys. I never had any trouble with Mitch on Bob Dylan. Never. But, at the same time I hated the kind of crap that Mitch was putting out on Columbia, *Sing Along with Mitch.* Mitch was one of the greatest oboe players I had ever known, and I had recorded him in the Cimarosa oboe concerto and the Vaughan Williams oboe concerto for Keynote when I was briefly president of Keynote Records back in '46. Mitch's ears were so fantastic I decided that, since we did not have a good pop A&R [Artists and Repertoire] department at Mercury at that time, Mitch ought to have a chance to work doing pop dates. I had a terrible time convincing the people at Mercury that an oboe player could be the head of pop A&R. But I said, "Trust me." And they did.

So Mitch was receptive to Bob Dylan?

Oh, yes. But Goddard was enchanted by Bob. I mean, it was Goddard who was my real backer as far as Dylan was concerned. And Goddard at that time was running Columbia, so he was a very good ally to have. On Bob's second album he did "Blowin' in the Wind," which sort of turned pop music around in the sixties, and turned CBS around. And the only reason Bobby was willing to come to CBS was that I had signed Pete Seeger when he was still black-listed. Columbia Records proved its independence from CBS by signing Seeger. So Bobby figured he couldn't go wrong if he went to CBS, and he didn't go wrong.

Now, you signed him as a minor, and that created some problems almost, didn't it?

It sure did. He got a manager whom I didn't like, Albert Grossman. And Albert Grossman tried to break the contract because he didn't have a piece of the record action. That was why he tried to do that. He wrote a letter to Columbia, and that was my first real acquaintance with Clive Davis because he had just started as an underling in the legal department at Columbia. He asked, "John, what's all this about?" I said, "My God. It's the first artist who ever double-crossed me."

Bob had said that there would be no problem with him signing as a minor?

No, we had discussed it. I told him, "You're only twenty, your mother or father should sign this." He said he didn't have a mother or father but did say, "I have an uncle who is a dealer in Las Vegas." So I said, "I guess that means you don't want me to pursue this any farther." He said, "John, you can trust me." Famous last words. Well, after I was finally able to locate Bobby, I persuaded him to repudiate the letter that had been written by a lawyer named Pete Pryor. It ended up making Bobby rich and making Grossman rich, unfortunately.

You had another, ah, unusual relationship with another manager of another one of your finds, Bruce Springsteen.

Yeah, well, let's not go into that. In the first place it's a well-known story anyway. . . .

That's Mike Appel. Bruce must have been an ear opener when you first heard him.

Oh, exciting, really exciting, still is.

Did he remind you at all of Dylan when you first heard him?

No, no way, Appel tried to sell him as someone better than Dylan. But when I first heard Bruce, I knew there was no relationship at all between the two of them. In the first place, Bruce is a marvelous guitar player and a wonderful harmonica player, which Bobby was not. Though, like Dylan, he was a true poet. The best thing I ever did with Bruce was ask, "Have you ever written anything you wouldn't dare record?" He said, "Yeah, as a matter of fact I have." So he started playing a song called, "If I Was a Priest." He'd never recorded it, except in our demo, the tapes of which I still have.

Suddenly a big bulb lit for me, and I said, "Bruce, were you brought up by nuns?" He said, "Of course." I had assumed that, like Bobby, he was Jewish, and he said he wasn't—that he was a good Catholic boy from New Jersey. And he was a very lapsed Catholic.

You never actually produced any of Bruce's records.

No, I went to his first sessions, and his manager, Mike Appel, didn't want me around. I was too much of an influence, and I hated what Bruce was doing at that Studio 914 in Nyack. He wanted to track everything, so he was working with earphones. I just figured this was no way to record a great artist. That was the first album, *Greetings from Asbury Park*. That was Bruce's title. I said, "Gee, that's a strange title. I don't think that's going to sell many albums." He said. "Yeah, well, that's what I want it to be. That's where I hang out."

What would you have done differently?

If you notice, on that first album we had all the lyrics printed, because you couldn't understand the lyrics from the record alone. So that's one of the things I would have done differently.

Do you think it's important in rock and roll to be able to understand the lyrics?

If you have a poet like Springsteen writing those lyrics, it's all-important.

Sometimes you still can't understand his lyrics.

Oh, yes, you can.

Yeah?

Oh, yeah. You listen to *Born in the U.S.A.* and you can understand everything.

That's a great record.

And how.

Did he change his style?

Oh, yeah, finally, because he had to.

At your request?

Not necessarily at mine; everybody said the same thing.

E-nun-ci-ate?

Communicate, not enunciate. And Bruce is *the* communicator of
this world.

*Did you go out to the Meadowlands to see him perform [in the
summer of 1984]?*

Twice. I was there at his last concert. It was supposed to be family
night, with his mother and sister onstage, but they had already left.
It was still one of the best concerts I've ever heard of Bruce. He
did a twenty-minute acoustic set just of stuff from *Nebraska,* and
it was so great. I got the royal treatment on Monday night because
Jon Landau saw to it that we had a parking pass and an all-access
sticker. Then I had a wonderful talk with Bruce in the intermission.
And he did my television show.

Tell me about your television show.

It's "Fifty Years of Popular Music with John Hammond." I started
making records in 1931, and I've got a lot of the people I've
worked with on the show. In all, about forty-five minutes or one
hour of raps between me and the artists. Alberta Hunter, Pete
Seeger, Bob Dylan, Bruce. George Benson. Gangs of people. It's
my association with various artists whom I have produced on records. Almost all the artists are CBS artists, because I worked with
CBS longer than any other company. And I'm back with them again

now. There's a lot of history that people don't know about. We have
a marvelous sequence with Pete Seeger. We took our equipment up
to the Clearwater sloop, and recorded on the sloop when it was
docked in Hudson, New York. We were able to take on topics such
as his blacklisting, which has never been on television before.

Are you back with CBS now as a consultant?

Mmmhmm. And also as a producer.

What are you going to be doing with them?

A whole lot of things, primarily aimed at the Compact Disc market.

New products?

Uh huh. And, some of the older products that are still in such good
shape that they can be transferred to digital.

What are you going to be doing from the old stuff?

Jazz.

Will we be able to hear some of the great Basie sides, perhaps?

I hope so. And I think we may be able to put out that Basie-
Ellington so-called battle that came out on records.

What's involved in redoing an old session for digital?

Patience and good ears. Since the tapes are still in good shape it's
not as bad as if we were working from old masters, old acetates,
which you would have to de-pop and de-click until the cows come
home. There is also a wonderful machine called a Packburn. I don't
know how it's done, but you put on an old record if you're transfer-
ring a 78. It senses which side of the next groove is better, and
automatically switches from one to the other. I persuaded CBS to
buy one of these machines when we were doing the Bessie Smith

reissues many years ago now. They have two of them. Very few
people even know of its existence. It was developed by two guys
in the GE laboratory, and it's a marvelous machine. Almost all the
Time-Life reissues were made with the Packburn. You don't
smooth out everything, but about 85 percent of the part that is on
the record you can get out.

*Is CBS eager to expand the Compact Disc market? Is that
something that is really going to be taking off?*

Good God, they've opened the first Compact Disc pressing facility
in the country out in Terre Haute. That's where all the Columbia
House Record Club products are packaged. CBS and Sony are
operating this jointly, and Sony knows a lot about pressing decent
Compact Discs. They've not been made in this country before. Only
the Japanese, and Philips does a lot in Holland, and I think they
have a pressing facility in England now, too.

Is the Compact Disc going to be the next wave in audio?

No question. No question at all. It's almost made the cassette
obsolete, and certainly the regular LP. I mean, there are still things
they can do; it's only a one-sided disc, and they can still get an hour
on a side. Do you have a Compact Disc player?

No.

Oh, I have one. A Sony 701, a wonderful machine.

Are you an audiophile? Are you really into your home system?

No, my home system is so antiquated now.

What do you have? Go ahead, tell us.

I have the Fisher 9X speakers, these big huge speakers that Avery
[Fisher] developed many years ago. I have a young cousin now
who's designing for Bose, and Bose is coming out with some wonderful product now; I'll have those soon. I still use my old Dual
player, uh, changer, because it plays 78s, 45s, and 33s, and it's got

a good hysteresis motor. I also have highly developed modern players.

And electronics?

I think Kenwood's. It's not terribly advanced. It was good twenty years ago.

Well, I guess for a man who prefers to record with one mike, there's no reason why the old stuff can't still work at home.

Well, it does. And I have a good little cassette machine next to my bed, and I listen to a whole lot of things. I like to have good metal-based cassettes. But I listen to most things through a good three-speaker Sony cassette player. Three speakers in front and one in the back, and it's pretty good. And of course, I couldn't live without my Aiwa portable machine with the earphones, and Bose has now made new speakers you attach either to the Sony or the Aiwa, or any good taping machine that has its own power supply. They're wonderful.

I was curious whether you had some killer system at home.

No. No killer system. My wife has never really adjusted to the long-playing records. She likes 78s. Because that's how she bought her records, and that's how I bought my records. I had a fabulous collection of records—early chamber music and blues and everything else. I sold my 78s to Bob Altshuler, a record company executive, and he makes them available to schools and colleges and collectors who need copies. Bob is so principled. He's a fanatic. He's got every piece of equipment in the world.

Let's change the subject completely. Your first break as a producer was recording Fletcher Henderson. And you really tried to rebuild his career, but he didn't always cooperate when opportunities were presented.

His personal life was a shambles. He drank and he liked girls. He had a lovely wife who was a friend of mine. Now, I was brought up a Christian Scientist, until I learned better, and we found out we had shared the same practitioner. She was a gung-ho Christian Scientist. Leora and I got along wonderfully, but there was no way of getting Fletcher's personal life together. It was too late. But the great thing I did with Fletcher was to get him together with Benny Goodman. I don't think Benny Goodman's band would have made it without Fletcher's arrangements. The important contribution that I made, I think, was getting black and white musicians together. I did that through the Benny Goodman trio and quartet, and every recording session, really. I had at least a token white. Maybe more than a token white.

What were some of the kinds of resistance you met in those days?

Oh, complete—from the union, among other things.

What kind of excuse did they give, other than we don't want to play with blacks?

That was one of the things, the other was that although New York had a theoretically integrated union, the left wing of the union wasn't interested in integration at all; they were interested in higher scales. When I helped start Cafe Society and we had integrated bands, there were actually union business agents who'd come to us and say, "You don't want to have this going on. That guy there is a communist or thus and so." We asked, "What other class-A jobs are there for black musicians?" We stonewalled them.

You have a crusading history.

I was on the executive board of the NAACP when I was in my early twenties. I was the youngest member of the board by far, and I was one of the more radical members of the board.

Given all that, how do you feel about the position of blacks in the music business today?

It's not good enough. It's a hell of a lot better than it was. But you try and get black artists on MTV and see how far you get.

Is it just racism, or are they worried about racism out in the country?

The music industry is controlled by whites, and they don't know, they really don't know. It's ignorance, really, more than anything. They think the public isn't ready. I think that's mainly it. And yet Michael Jackson's success must give them all pause.

It just blows my mind because over and over again . . . Michael Jackson, Prince, George Benson, Stevie Wonder, Ray Charles . . . is it ever going to change?

Sure. I live in hope. It may not change while I'm still alive, because I'm seventy-three now [in 1984], and it's late. . . . No, I've been through this all for so long. People used to be very bored with me because I was prematurely interested in civil rights.

And they didn't want to hear about it.

They sure didn't.

Have you tried to deal with MTV?

Sure.

And what do they say to you about it?

"We have a policy." I mean, they obviously had to do something about Michael Jackson. It's hard to combat CBS on a thing like this. CBS is pretty good about this, you know. Goddard was wonderful. There was really the great man of the contemporary record business. I'm very thankful to CBS because they gave me lots of opportunities, and I didn't hurt them too much.

I think lots of people have thought that John Hammond is a rich guy. . . .

I'm not. I never made any money off of musicians. It was a policy of mine and it still is. I never participated in any royalties on any of my artists at CBS.

You could have, but you chose not to?

Yeah.

Would a lot of these stars have had careers if you hadn't been willing to put your own money into them?

Quite possibly. I don't want to take too much credit for that. I was getting my kicks too, in developing artists.

How do you stay modern?

Artists like Dylan and Aretha and Benson and Springsteen come along and I guess I was sort of pulled along with them. I did recognize, one of the reasons I'm back at CBS, I know, is because Bruce's new album is so huge that I guess they feel that maybe they owe me something.

Why aren't you a record company president or something now? With all the sessions and people and things you've been involved in?

I'm not a businessman. To be perfectly frank with you, it's one of my lapses. I started out by being agin the Establishment, and I guess I still am.

(August, 1984)

Mitch Miller

Y eah, that's right, Mitch Miller. If you thought
Mitch was just the cornball king of sing-along,
this interview ought to enlighten you, as it did
me. Plainly stated, Mitch Miller is one of the most
important figures in the history of the record industry. He has really done it all. Recognized as one of
the country's top classical oboists, he played for Stokowski and other important maestros. He also made
some of the earliest chamber jazz recordings with
Alec Wilder.

As musical director at Mercury Records in the late
forties, he nurtured the careers of middle-of-the-road
singers such as Vic Damone, Patti Page, and Frankie
Laine, and developed a reputation as a hit-maker
with Laine's "Mule Train." He played on and helped
supervise the famous *Charlie Parker with Strings* sessions at Mercury; in addition, he was a technical
innovator in the studio, and created the first overdubbing.

When Miller switched to Columbia in 1950, he
really took off on a hit-making streak. In two years
he turned Columbia from the fourth-place company
into the first, and throughout the fifties he developed
new singers like Tony Bennett, Rosemary Clooney,
and Johnny Mathis. It is unlikely that anyone will

ever produce as many hit records as did Mitch Miller in his career. Even though he will always be known for his mainstream hits, he was hip enough to sign Mahalia Jackson to her first major-company contract, recognize the genius of Hank Williams, and work with top jazz musicians like Erroll Garner. In the late fifties, Miller took a vocal, controversial (and, he claims, misunderstood) stand against the rise of rock 'n' roll. When he criticized disc jockeys in 1958 for "abandoning adults" and favoring rock, his own records were subsequently banned from airplay.

Despite his track record as a hit A&R man and producer of other people's records, Miller is surely best known for his own hits, like "The Yellow Rose of Texas," and the *Sing Along* records and television show. Still spry, energetic, and outspoken at age seventy-four, [in 1985], he continues to be involved in music as a guest conductor of orchestras around the country.

Why don't we begin by discussing your career as an oboist. You made your professional debut at fifteen, and went on to become one of the finest classical oboists in the country. How did you approach your career when that was your main endeavor?

I never worked with a great oboe teacher. I had some lessons with Marcel Tabuteau, who was a fantastic oboist in the Philadelphia Orchestra. Whenever he fixed a reed, he turned away so I couldn't see what he was doing. So I said that's enough of that. I just went off on my own. I didn't want to model myself after the oboe players that I heard. There were qualities that I liked in many of them, but no one was the guy I tried to emulate.

This was in Rochester, where you grew up?

Yes. Also on records and on radio, and the various orchestras that would come through. I tried to get a sort of vocal sound combined with the seamless playing and phrasing of Pablo Casals. I had his Bach suites, and I would listen to them all the time. I can recommend that any young musician who wants to get the best lessons in phrasing and musicianship listen to these Casals suites, and any Casals recordings. Don't listen to the performances per se, but try to have a microscopic ear and listen to what he does with every note. Pretty soon it becomes a revelation.

How did you happen to choose oboe, or was it chosen for you?

The Rochester public schools had the first public-school music system in America. George Eastman gave them the instruments, provided they would give the instruction. My father bought a grand piano, a square piano, when I was six years of age. He paid fifteen dollars for it, for the moving of it. It was a giant Chickering, took up half the front room. My two older sisters and myself were the only ones old enough to take lessons. He paid a buck a week each on a $42-a-week salary to give us lessons. I was going along pretty well, except I didn't like the teacher. She smelled like she was eating paste. I was playing Bach and Mozart, but I sort of quit. Then when I was eleven, I heard about the instruments in the public schools. So I applied for one. All my friends had shiny brass instruments, and all they had left was the oboe [laughter]. So I said, "I'll take it." I didn't even know you needed a reed for it. Then I found out. As fate would have it, my father was a toolmaker and wrought-iron worker, so he made all the tools for me to make the reeds. You could buy a reed, but that didn't guarantee anything. Everyone has to make a reed that is specially suited for them.

When you were playing classical music, who were some of your favorite orchestras and conductors to work with?

I played with many conductors, and also fine chamber music with the Budapest, Paganini, and Lener quartets. I started with Albert Coates, Eugene Goossens, Fritz Reiner, Molinari, Stokowski, Sir Thomas Beecham, Alexander Smallens, Leon Barzin.

And your favorite?

My favorite—I would have to say there's two, for different reasons. Fritz Reiner and Stokowski. Fritz Reiner, one, because he liked me [laughter]. I didn't realize then that he was a very tough cookie. I found out later that if Fritz Reiner liked your playing at first, you were in forever. When I met him years later, when he was conducting at CBS, he remembered my name and everything. And if he didn't like your playing, even though you were a good musician, you had a tough row to hoe with him.

Where did you play with him?

He was in Rochester. He came from Cincinnati. Eugene Goossens went to Cincinnati and Reiner came to Rochester. Then, of course, the most magical experience I've ever had with a conductor was with Stokowski. I had never met him, and I got a call on a cold Monday morning in 1947. This voice comes over the phone and [with an accent] says, "Michel Millair?" I thought it was one of my friends putting me on. He says, "This is Leopold Stokowski," and I let go with a scatological remark [laughter]. I said, "Seven-thirty in the morning, what are you doing to me?" You know? Without missing a beat he said, "This is Leopold Stokowski and I have been listening to you on the CBS Symphony, and would like for you to record for me." He had a whole bunch of mixed-up accents. He was British, I guess, originally. He was going to record the "Swan of Tuonela" of Sibelius. It's a big English horn solo piece. This was going to be the following Wednesday. So I said, "Fine, I'll be there."

I went to the Manhattan Center on 34th Street, and in walks the cream of New York. I'm talking the cream of the New York Philharmonic. The cream of the NBC Symphony, all the old concertmasters. On the first stand of celli were Leonard Rose and Frank Miller. The first stand of the violas was Carlton Cooley and Bill Linzer. The trumpet section was Harry Glantz, Benny Baker, and Bill Vacchiano. It was amazing. There will never be an orchestra put together like that again. The setup—mind you, this is long before tape; we were doing it on acetate then. The first piece he did was "Swan of Tuonela." He stayed away until he was ready to start.

Then he comes up and says, "Gentlemen, 'Swan of Tuonela.' " He started to conduct, and within two minutes it was like the Philadelphia Orchestra at its best. We just went through the piece twice. I never heard a playback. He didn't allow us in to hear the playback, but he went in and listened. In those two or three days we recorded the "Swan," some Albéniz, the New World Symphony —I played the English horn solo on that—and the "Escales" of Ibert. As it turned out, these are some of the historic recordings of all time. The "Swan" got tremendous reviews. Even when you listen to it now, with all the technique, and all the tape and all the tools we have, here you get perspective, you get the right sound. You may not get the super hi-fi qualities that you do on present-day records, but as a performance it's super, and as for balance it still holds up tremendously. This man had a kind of magic. I can't explain it. It was one of the most exciting experiences, when I look back. It was like meeting a strange, beautiful woman, and you knew all about her and she knew all about you. The phrasing came—I did what he wanted without him saying anything. The orchestra did the same. He also gave you parameters within which you were free; in fact, he encouraged it, to phrase freely within a certain frame. It was one of those experiences that you can never duplicate.

Didn't you turn down a job offer to become first oboist with the New York Philharmonic?

Well, they turned *me* down [laughter]. They asked me to join and I was playing with the CBS Symphony. The Philharmonic was then a thirty-week season, and the manager, Van Prague, said they would like to have me as solo oboe. All I wanted then. . . . See, the CBS Symphony was fifty-two weeks, no vacation, no nothing, but we made about $10,000 or $11,000 a year. This was in 1935, '36. And Labate was retiring from the Philharmonic. So I said, "Just equal my salary." They said no. There were only two people who got $300 a week for the thirty weeks, and that was Harry Glantz and Bruno Jaenicke, a French horn player, a wonderful player, as was Harry Glantz. So they got Harold Gomberg from the Washington National Symphony then, and he's been with them for all these years. He only retired four or five years ago.

Do you regret it at all?

No, I don't regret anything that's happened. Many times I have
missed jobs, and it turned out to be the best thing I could have
done.

*If you had gone to the New York Philharmonic, do you think you
would have gone on to a pop recording career at Mercury and
Columbia as an A&R man and producer?*

That I don't know.

Tell me what the CBS Swing Club was all about.

That was a jazz program every Saturday night [on CBS radio]. They
would have jazz musicians on and play all kinds of jazz.

Wasn't this something you were involved with?

I played in some of them, yes. See, the staff musicians at CBS had
to play everything. I played every Kostelanetz session from 1935
to 1953. André would call up and make sure I was free before
booking the recording session. He did that with two or three other
key players. He, along with Stokowski, knew more about sound and
microphones than anyone. I learned plenty from them. He was very
meticulous in the way he balanced. For a half-hour program, which
is about twenty-two minutes of music when you take the commercials out and everything, we would spend about five or six hours
rehearsing. Not for the playing, but for the balance. So I'd play
Kosty, I'd play the jazz, we had to play everything. Then we'd play
the Symphony, too. We would play Studio One. I played Orson
Welles' "Mercury Theatre." I played in the orchestra that did the
Martian invasion broadcast.

Really?

Yes. We thought it was a dull show [laughter].

He let you in on what was going to happen?

Of course we knew. It never occurred to us that the population, the people in America, were so subliminally upset about what was going on in the world—with Hitler and all that—that they were ready for anything. The reason the panic came on was, Charlie McCarthy was on at the same time—the "Chase & Sanborn Hour" —and we were what's called a sustaining program; the "Mercury Theatre" was noncommercial. So when Charlie McCarthy would go off, people would tend to switch to other channels. We had a simulated news broadcast about this strange ship landing in the swamps of New Jersey—including the "We will take you now for some standby music"—and we did thirty seconds of potted-palm music [laughter]. Then immediately there was a correspondent out there. Now, if people had stopped to think, no correspondent could have gotten there in thirty seconds. But they heard it, and it was done so realistically they began to get in their cars and run out of town. Policemen came up to the studio. But we kept on with the broadcast.

Alec Wilder was a friend of yours whom you worked with. Did you know him in Rochester?

Yes, we were at the Eastman School together. He was a fantastically talented composer, as people are finding out now. His only problem was he would write only for those he liked. That included publishers as well as musicians. I got Alec to come to New York and play some of his songs, some of which are standards now. "While We're Young," "It's So Peaceful in the Country," "Who Can I Turn To?" I was playing with Yella Pessl, the harpsichordist; I was playing Bach concerts and Baroque music in 1937, '38. I said to Alec, "Why don't we use these instruments with the harpsichord, and make a kind of jazz chamber music?" So Alec immediately wrote for us. I got Harold Golzer on bassoon, Toots Mondello on clarinet, Eddie Powell on flute and piccolo, Jimmy Carroll played clarinet. We made these records. They had to be three minutes to three minutes and fifteen seconds long because that was the length of a shellac record. These records are the wellspring that all of the jazz chamber music came from, you know, whether it was Chico Hamilton or Raymond Scott or the Modern Jazz Quartet. You listen to those and you'll hear it. It was the first use of the harpsichord in jazz. Since we were all classical musicians except Toots Mondello and Jimmy Carroll, Alec would write everything out. It's remarkable how it holds up.

Did you produce these sessions?

No. Morty Palitz produced them, I played. Morty Palitz was then head of Brunswick A&R. Brunswick Records was then owned by Republic Pictures. Soon after that Bill Paley bought it. Republic had the old Columbia label, too, long before there was a Columbia Broadcasting. Republic Pictures then sold it to Bill Paley, around '38. It was along then that we did the first octet records—the Alec Wilder chamber jazz. Then we did a whole series of them. There were two or three albums out. We did some later on for Vox.

Let's get into how you went from this high-powered classical career into a career in pop music. You didn't find that an unusual move to make?

No, because while we were at school, along with Alec Wilder and a couple of other chums, we were listening to Louis Armstrong, Duke Ellington, Jimmie Lunceford. When we were students we loved the jazz. I remember the first time I heard the Hot Club of France. These were some classically trained musicians who were playing great jazz. There was Ella Fitzgerald, and Crosby in his relaxed way. The bands came out and we'd buy these three-for-a-dollar Decca Blue Label records. So we were constantly listening to great jazz and popular music.

How did you begin to get a reputation as someone who could be an A&R man or producer of pop recordings?

Well, I played a lot of sessions as a sideman. And in those days, of course, there was no tape; many times, trying to get a balance, they'd say, "Take one to see how it sounds." I would say, "Why not take it for a recording?" Because we had been rehearsing all the time. I'd say, "Why won't you guys listen while we're rehearsing so when we're ready to go, the first take is it." You must remember that if the balance wasn't quite right, or if there was one little wrong note, you had to do the whole side over. It was an exercise in exhaustion as well as frustration. But at the same time the excitement had to be right, and everybody had to do their jobs. That lent a dimension to the record that you don't feel now because everything is safe and cool. If you want to put a note in, you put it in. So I would complain.

As a session man?

As a session man. Because many times you'd have a big solo and it was wasted. You played five, six, seven times, then they'd say, "Now we'll go for a take." I said, "Where were you guys before?" I made a general pest of myself. But on the other hand they wanted me because I played pretty well. That didn't fall on deaf ears, I guess, because when John Hammond went over to Keynote, which later became Mercury, he asked me to come and produce some classical records, remembering when I had bitched as a studio musician. I came and I did. The first thing I did was the Fine Arts Quartet with "Death and the Maiden." He was so delighted with what I did with the musicians. When I'd ask for something they'd look at me quizzically as if to say, "What does this guy know?" I'd say, "Look, do it both ways just for a few bars and come in and listen, and if you don't like what I've told you to do then I'll just take what you're doing." So then they came in and listened and they looked at each other and said, "You can tell us anything you want." [Laughter.] And the record won a prize that year.

When was this?

In '48. So John, after that, said, "Come on and do some popular records." So I went in and did Frankie Laine, Vic Damone, and Patti Page.

Now that was a real switch, to go from classical or even some of the chamber jazz you were doing to Frankie Laine or Vic Damone.

Not really, Ted. I'm always surprised when people say it's a switch. I never compartmentalized it in my own mind. And the same rules apply. You know—taste, musicianship, balance, get the best out of

the artist. Many times the artist doesn't know what his best characteristics are, and you're there to remind them. You can't put in what
isn't there, but you can remind them of what they have and they're
not using.

*But I think the thing that people wonder about is, was this music
you really appreciated yourself?*

Oh yes. Oh gosh, yes. See, there's an art to everything. A great
mystery writer *is* a great writer. It's like saying that Richard
Rodgers is not Beethoven or Bach. And that's right, but there's
room for both. These great popular composers. . . . You know, the
term classical just means something that lasts. So I saw no difference. I used the same approach as I did on classical records and
classical playing. In fact, with some of the artists I would even tell
them how to breathe because many of them did not study technique. If they wanted a long phrase I would show them what to do.
I did this with Johnny Mathis a lot. He was a very fast learner. In
fact, I would stay with Mathis in the studio, and when I wanted that
special choirboy quality I'd have a signal. I'd shake my hand in a
certain way and stay right with him while he was recording, and
he'd soar. You listen to those records and you can hear it.

*You really helped make Frankie Laine, Vic Damone, and Patti
Page stars.*

You have to put down the fact that my father used to have a saying:
You can't make bullets out of shit. These people just had it, and
you'd uncover it. You can't put in what they don't have. So that
was the joy and that was the fun. It's like discovering something.
Then they would come in and hear themselves and they would
know what they did and they would build on that. I would look for
those qualities that made them unique. I would have an image in
my mind. Nobody sees a record. You can hear it for nothing on the
air. What makes you buy a record? It must be something you want
to play over and over again. And remember, in those days every
record shop closed at 6:00. There were no all-night record shops.
There was none of the supermarket feeling. So you looked for
qualities that would make the person buy it. To this day there are

some great records that I would call performance records that you'll
never tune out if they're on the radio, but you'll never buy them,
either. We call those turntable hits.

So were you looking for a vocal quality, or personality?

Vocal quality combined with the song. Oh, the song has to have it.
The song has to be the vehicle for the artist to show this quality.
It also has to have the characteristics so that in four bars you know
who the singer is. If you listen, you know immediately who Mathis
is, who Tony Bennett is, who Vic Damone is, who Frankie Laine
is.

*Mitch, what did you hear in a song like "Mule Train" so that
you said, "This is going to make Frankie Laine a star"?*

Well, remember Frankie Laine had a hit that made everybody
think he was black. It was called "That's My Desire." Some lady
in Cleveland wrote it, I think. He was working in an airplane plant,
in a Lockheed plant out in California. He was on Mercury. When
I came in, I chose "Mule Train" because the image I had of Frankie
Laine was the "blue collar singer." The guy who works for a living,
who understands what it means to sweat and to make a living, and
who pounds his pillow with frustration. That's the image I had of
Frankie and I would look for songs with qualities of that. There
are lots of areas where that could apply, even to this day. [He
sings:] "Up in the morning, out on the job, work like the devil for
my pay . . . but the lucky old. . . ." And you know, the guy worships:
"I Believe." "Jezebel"—anger at this woman who's got him all
turned on, and he can't tie her down. Frustration. Lyrical content
combined with the music.

*Talking about lyrical content, your first disc at Columbia, Arthur
Godfrey and Mary Martin's "Go to Sleep," was banned.*

It was a joke that they should ban it. "Go to Sleep," was brought
to me by Fred Rayfield, who worked for Disney. It's about a salty
couple in their forties, a stream of consciousness, lying down and
asking each other questions. When no one wants to answer the

question, they say, "Oh go to sleep, go to sleep." I got Arthur
Godfrey and Mary Martin, who was in *South Pacific,* and Arthur
was at the top of his popularity. It's a marvelous record.

Why did they ban it?

Because they were in bed! But the funny part is that Larry Parks
and his wife recorded the song, too, and they allowed that one.

*And because Godfrey and Mary Martin were not married, that was
taboo?*

That was taboo. It was banned by my own company, CBS. How
times have changed, huh?

*I want to talk about the Charlie Parker and Strings session you
did at Mercury. Tell me how that came about. I know you played
oboe and English horn on it as well as helping supervise it.*

Norman Granz was releasing his "Jazz at the Philharmonic"'s
through Mercury then. Norman, as you know, did wonders with
recording live jazz concerts. He didn't go into the studio until
much later. He wanted to do Charlie Parker with strings, that was
his idea. But he knew nothing about strings. He said, "Mitch,
will you produce it for me?" I said sure. [Granz claims that
Miller had little to do with actually producing this session—TF.]
We went to the Reeves studio and Bob Fine was the engineer.
We had the best string players. We had Ray Brown on bass,
Buddy Rich on drums, Stan Freeman on the piano, all the concertmasters in New York. Jimmy Carroll did the arrangement. I
had never met Parker. We were going to do the whole album,
three sessions in one day. And that was not unusual. The producers in my day, if we didn't make four sides in three hours we
thought ourselves failures [laughter]. So it was 10:00 to 1:00,
2:00 to 5:00 and 7:00 to 10:00, all the same day. Get the whole
album done. That was three sessions at $38 or $40 apiece. You
know, that was a lot of money. We were rehearsing and Bob Fine
was the engineer. About an hour and a half later, Parker walks in
and looks around and hears this beautiful sound and he turns
around and walks out. Everybody thought he was going to the

bathroom. I was saying, "We're ready, Charlie." And Norman Granz comes around, "Where's Charlie?" He's running up and back, and I could just see, you know, all this money had to be paid to musicians and no Charlie Parker. We kept rehearsing, getting all the sides balanced for the background. Of course, all the arrangements were done. For about four or five hours, Norman was running all over town trying to find Parker. We tried to salvage the session and do "Claire de Lune" or something like that [laughter]. We gave up on it and thought it was over.

A few days later Norman calls me. He found Parker and Parker said he was so overwhelmed by that beautiful sound, he couldn't do it alone. So out of the clear sky Norman says, "Why don't you play with him?" I say, "Are you kidding, Norman? I don't improvise." He says, "But you can play *something*." All desperation. I said, "Look, if Jimmy Carroll will write a sketch for me I'll play around that sketch." Norman told Parker that I would play with him. He came in and we had the musicians there. And, Ted, we made *twelve sides in four hours*. See, the balance was set from before. Everything but one or two tunes was a first take and that was it. I don't think Charlie has ever played better on any record than he did on that. I didn't think we were making history. This record now is legendary.

Of course you knew about Parker and his reputation.

Oh, of course. I listened to him on great nights and on bad nights, too. He was taking another step further in jazz.

And that was all right with you?

Of course! As long as it's related to the subject. See, what drives me mad, especially today, is the pedal point [a bass ostinato] going for two and a half hours and the guy's noodling above it. Improvisation, to me, is to take the tune and do variations on it. And Parker was a master at that. No matter how far out, it had a relation to the tune.

You were known for creating rather unusual pairings, like Burl Ives with a Dixieland band, Dinah Shore with bagpipes. Was this something that became a signature of yours?

That was my job, to think of unusual things that worked. Some didn't. The Dinah Shore with bagpipes, it's funny. You see, since there was no tape we had to get the bagpipes going outside the studio, then open the door while the needle went down to cut the record. And I didn't realize that bagpipes had to be outdoors. They drive a lot of people crazy.

What do you mean, they had to be outdoors?

Bagpipes sound better in the open air. Evidently, on records—a lot of disc jockeys started to play it, then said they couldn't stand this song, and they broke the disc on the air [laughter]. Of course, Dinah soon left Columbia for RCA, I think. No risk, no success, Ted. The whole business of the great jazz players. . . . What makes them great is they risk at the moment of the performance. They try for something. It may not come off, but they're going to try.

There's another element to this, though. You did a number of novelty songs like "Stinky Cheese Polka" by Two Ton Baker, and let's not forget "I Saw Mommy Kissing Santa Claus." Wasn't this another aspect of these unusual pairings?

Not really. You must remember, I was given complete freedom. Goddard Lieberson and Jimmy Conkling both said, "Look, you're running it, you shoot for the moon. We're not going to second-guess you. Just stay within the budget." And what else could you ask for? So I did Rosemary Clooney and Marlene Dietrich with "Too Old to Cut the Mustard." It was a country song and I had the lyrics rewritten to suit them. The idea of these crazy pairings, or unusual pairings, was what I call "sweet surprise." People don't expect it and say, "Hey, what's that?" Then if they like it, they want it. It's as simple as that. It's a hook. You never depend on a novelty record for your basic sales. If a novelty record hits, it's whipped cream on the sundae. If you look at the body of my work, they are all quality songs regardless of what some may say. It's all there for the record; as Casey Stengel said, "You could look it up. . . ." Even Tony Bennett sang "In the Middle of an Island." See, I liked for these artists to be presented in an unpredictable way every once in a while, just to change the menu for them. I did gospel with Johnny

Ray even before gospel was played on white stations. "I'm gonna walk, walk, walk and talk with my Lord," it didn't sell that big, but it stopped the show on the floor. It gave the people another aspect of what he was able to do. Frankie Laine's "This Old House" was gospel written by a country singer that became a number-one hit.

Well, I guess the word novelty itself explains the attraction; it's new.

Yes. And "Mule Train" was a novelty. Believe me, they were standing in line outside the stores on Broadway to buy that record. There must have been twenty covers within one week. I put Mercury into hock because they had to get them pressed, so we went to the MGM plant and they wouldn't press without the money in advance. So Mercury found the money and we were sending the record out with station wagons running up and back like crazy. It was fun! It sold about a million and a half then, which is like seven million today.

In those days a hit was, what, about 200,000?

There were some million-sellers, but yeah, about 200,000 or 250,000. Because there were only about one-fifth as many stereo sets as there are in the country today.

You covered a lot of country music. How did that come about?

You know, when I had a hot record, I'd want to get it to *Billboard* Thursday night so they'd review it in the next issue. I used to go over myself with an acetate. I got to know all the guys—Jerry Wexler, Paul Ackerman, and Bob Rolontz. As I got to know Jerry well, he said to me, "Mitch, why don't you listen to Hank Williams? He's a country singer and he writes great, great songs." I went and listened. The first one I heard was "Cold Cold Heart." I played it for Tony Bennett, Hank with his scratchy fiddle and all that. Tony said, "You want me to do that? Cowboy songs?" I said, "Tony, don't listen to the background, and don't listen to that interpretation, listen to the words. 'Free my doubtful mind, and

melt my cold, cold heart.' " And he said, "Well, all right." Percy
Faith made an arrangement, and whoa, a smash hit. With Tony.
After that I got Fred and Wesley Rose and I said, "Look, I promise
you that if you let me know in advance the Hank Williams songs,
I will give you top artists if I decide to do them, and I will respect
Hank's release in the country field, and not until his song is out
and established will I come." They agreed. So out of that we got
"Your Cheatin' Heart," "Jambalaya," "Setting the Woods on
Fire," "Hey, Good Lookin'," "Kaw-Liga"; we did them all. That
opened up the whole field of country coming to pop. Then I did the
reverse. I had Marty Robbins come up North and we did "A White
Sport Coat and a Pink Carnation." That was my session. In fact,
what happened then—and the Roses told me this—was that suddenly a lot of these country writers started to write with pop stars
in mind, and they lost their touch. This went on for about a year
or two in the fifties. The Roses said these writers had to get back
to the idea of writing the songs that they felt from the gut, and what
crossed over would cross over. But if you start to think in terms
of pop artists, they weren't writing their kinds of songs. But Jerry
Wexler is the one who put me on to this. I did "Singin' the Blues"
with Guy Mitchell. "Just Walking in the Rain" with Johnny Ray,
dozens of them. They all became hits. Hank Williams would come
over to thank me every once in a while. Hank Williams was really
a very taciturn guy. Very few words.

*When you went to Columbia from Mercury—I understand
Goddard Lieberson tried to lure you away from Mercury a number
of times.*

Not really. The first time they lured me away I went [laughter]. The
circumstances were that Manny Saks was the head of Columbia
A&R and had gone over to RCA. The position was open, and
Goddard Lieberson called me up. I had gone to school with him.
He and Alec Wilder and I were in the same class. Then, for the
munificent sum of $25,000 a year. . . . I don't know what I was
getting at Mercury, but it wasn't anything near that. And Mercury
had promised me a piece of the business. When I got to Chicago
and I asked Mercury, "How many hits do I have to have before you

give me a piece?", they said, "Well, we'll give you 5 percent, but you'll have to pay for it." Well, that's all I had to hear. So I was ready to go. I still worked hard, because my ego wouldn't allow me not to, but I wasn't about to buy stock in that company. They worked hard but one thing they did scared the hell out of me. They went into the television business, and made a set that was damn good. They bought Raytheon chassis and had a cabinetmaker make the set. Instead of scratching for the payroll—which they did when I first arrived—here they had a couple million bucks in the bank. I said, "What are you going into the television business for?" You know, sets were in short supply and everybody was selling. But I said, "These giants like RCA and Philco, overnight they'll cut their price in half and they'll destroy you." And it happened six months later. So that also put a sour side on it. But I had a wonderful time working there. They gave me complete freedom. I'd stop in and they'd say, "Kid, you got any hits today?" [Laughter.]

You were at the height of your power as a producer and A&R man when recording tape was introduced. Did you pick up on it right away?

Oh yes. Mind you, it was only monaural, but you could use just part of a record, which was a great advantage in the sense that if the whole record was marvelous except for two edit points, you could do that part over. That was 1951, I would say, a year after I came to Columbia. I used the same technique as before, because with monaural tape you could not remix; even with stereo tape there was no remixing. It wasn't until they had multiple tracks that you could remix.

The technique when tape first came in was that you could use a big chunk of something, and you could save some good performances. Say you had a perfect take, except the ending was no good. You could use the first part and make a new ending, splice on an ending. It was just a tool to save a good performance. It wasn't the tool that became a crutch. By that I mean you can now sit there coolly and say, "Well, if this note isn't right I can always do it on another track and insert it." To me that is. . . . Something happens in the studio, the adrenalin stops pumping. How can an artist work with a background, and the headset in his ear? To me music is interaction. And interaction means it has to happen at the same time.

John Hammond would agree with you, I think.

You can't define it, but you know when it isn't there. It's the extra adrenalin, the urgency, the interaction. Rosemary Clooney put it to me one time: The rhythm track was made and then she put her voice on it. Then they added strings. The record came out and she said it sounded good enough, but "If I had known what the strings were doing, I would have phrased differently." It's the people, too. I was very lucky. I tried to hire the best guys. Percy Faith, there's no better arranger in the world than Percy was, and a wonderful guy. Then I gave Ray Conniff a shot. He had low periods when the booze got to him, and he fought it off and no one would give him a job. He tells this story himself. I gave him a chance to back up Johnny Mathis, and he was marvelous. Then he wanted to do something on his own and I said, "Ray, why don't we take your old Artie Shaw arrangements and just put different colors in them?" He says, "What do you mean?" I said, "We'll use voices as instruments. Double the men's voices with the brass and the women's voices with the reeds." So we did two sides, " 'S Wonderful" and "Begin the Beguine." We put it out as a single and it got tremendous reaction. So we made an album and that's how he got started. And Ray Conniff has sold more records than God!

Getting back to studio technique, you helped pioneer the technique of dubbing, right?

Patti Page, Jack Rail, and I did the first dubbing, before Les Paul and Mary Ford. It was a record called "Money, Marbles and Chalk." [He sings:] "I've got money to spend, marbles to roll, but my chalk won't write anymore." It's a country song where Patti sang with herself. This was before tape. We did it from acetate to acetate. The problem, then, was you'd lose the bass and rhythm sound as you went from one generation to the next. With "Money, Marbles and Chalk" it was easy because there were only two voices. Then we did "With My Eyes Wide Open," which was four voices.

Now, you get to a third and you lose the bass and rhythm completely and we had to throw it all out and start all over again. Then you had the problem of the needle cutting the bass—if you put too much on there would be distortion. We would try to find ways to do it with primitive compression. We managed. It took us a whole morning. The first take we had, and we had to go back and back, and finally it came out. That was the first tremendous hit with multiple recording.

Let's talk about Monday afternoons with Mitch at Columbia. This was the day when any song publisher could come in and audition songs for you. Were you really inundated with song publishers?

Every A&R man was, but I was quite successful so they wanted me. When I came to Columbia we had Dinah Shore and Frank Sinatra. Frank was then at the bottom of his career. Dinah Shore, people don't realize, has had only two hits in her whole life. She's a wonderful performer, but as a record artist she had only "Sweet Violets" and "Dear Hearts and Gentle People." Lieberson and Conkling said, "Go out and recruit. Don't buy artists from another company." So first I listened to artists and that's how I found Rosie Clooney, Tony Bennett, Johnny Ray, Guy Mitchell, The Four Lads, Jerry Vale, Johnny Mathis. They were all unknown. I preferred that because everybody thinks a record producer could force somebody to make a record. You can't. All a singer has to do is do it badly and it won't come out. You cannot take somebody by the ear and tell them to do a three-minute piece against their will. The only weapon I would have if an artist didn't want to do a certain piece would be to give it to somebody else. If that artist made a hit of it, next time they would listen. That worked. I did that a few times. But that didn't make any ill will from the artist. They just, next time around, got their share. You must remember you only have a certain number of bullets a year to shoot. Especially in those days, you couldn't come out with one release on top of another. The pipeline was full, the promotion. If everyone had worked a record and it was a failure, you can't just get them excited immediately, and then three weeks later come out with another record. It's impossible. The pipeline won't take it.

But this stable of talent you built up meant you needed lots of songs, lots of material.

Yes. Also, these Monday sessions were to appease a lot of guys. They wanted to come over and play a song. I couldn't stop what I was doing. Remember, I was working with arrangers, artists, producing all the stuff, flying back and forth to the West Coast. So I set aside this time when anyone could come in with songs. Other people would leave stuff with me and I'd come in at 7:00 or 7:30 in the morning and listen to it. I'd prefer that, because when a song is bad you know it immediately. If a song is good, you want to hear it two or three times to see if it wears well. But if they're there in person, and the writer's there, you can't destroy them. So you have to spend ten or fifteen minutes saying, "Oh, I can't do it." And they ask why. If they left it with me, they would always get an answer. A lot of publishers and writers hated my guts, but they'll agree on one thing and that's that they always got an honest answer. I always kept my word. I'd say, "If you give this to Frankie Laine as an exclusive, I promise it'll be his next release." And I would honor it. See, before, publishers would get all these people to make a record, and they'd say, "The release date is such and such." I'd say, "I don't want that. If I'm going to make a hit for your song, I want to be the first one out." I would never honor a release date. If they brought me a song, they knew that if I liked it and made the record, I'd put it out. In fact, they tried to stop me from releasing a couple of records, but when the records turned out to be hits they ceased trying to stop them from coming out early [laughter].

I must admit that I've never really understood the concept behind music publishing. What is the role of a music publisher?

In those days the role of the publisher was to plug his songs. They would go to the radio remotes, to Abe Lyman and Benny Goodman and Les Brown, and get their songs played on the networks.

Why didn't a record company or an artist just publish the material?

I tried to do that with Columbia. In fact, I set up a publishing company for them, April Music. See, writers would come to me with unpublished songs. I would act as their editor and say, "Do this and this and change the song this way." If I liked it and the artist liked it, I'd say, "Give us an exclusive." Now, the writer would run to a publisher after talking to me and tell the publisher, "I have a Johnny Mathis record on this, give me a good advance." The publisher would call me and I'd say yes, they do. So I thought, if I'm doing this, doing the publisher's job, why doesn't Columbia set up its own publishing firm? I mentioned this. But in the early fifties they were so afraid of antitrust that they were sort of gun-shy. They said no. It started with Frankie Laine's "I Believe." These four guys came in after hours and they played this song. [He sings very slowly:] "I believe for every drop of rain that falls, a flower grows," six, seven, eight. The song was damn good, and it sounded like Frankie Laine. I said, "Why don't you compress it?" They said, "What do you mean?" I said [he sings it faster]. They said, "Yes, but that's a three-bar phrase." I said, "So who's counting?" [Laughter.] It sounded right. We did the song and that is one of the hottest copyrights to this day. I prevailed upon them to put it in April Music. They did, and they gave me a quarter of the mechanicals—a quarter of the record royalties. The publisher got a penny for every record sold, and the writer got a penny. So they gave me a quarter of a penny on record royalties.

What I'm getting at is this: Isn't music publishing a holdover, a vestige from the days when sheet music was an important source of income?

Yes, but publishing songs is still an important source of income. That's why the old catalogs are worth so many millions. Every time a performance is done, that cash register rings. Every time a record is made of a Gershwin song, the income is tremendous. And boy, the writers deserve it. Without the writers there's nobody.

But couldn't the writer just be given an additional cut out of the record, rather than having a separate publishing entity? It seems like a vestige to me.

Well, it is a vestige. That's why most rock musicians have their own
publishing companies, and most artists who write their own songs
have their own publishing companies. But the publishing companies that have large catalogs [of songs they have published over the
years] are worth literally hundreds of millions. Like Frank Loesser
who had his own company. Even when he had stuff published by
somebody else, he had in mind to get it back twenty-eight years
later [upon expiration of the original copyright], and he did. When
the renewal came, he put it in his own publishing company.

*I guess that's the real story behind the rise and fall of Tin Pan
Alley: The rise in the days when artists did not usually write their
own material and sheet music was a big source of income, and the
fall when more artists started to write and publish their own
material.*

That was the decline of the all-powerful publisher. But they're still
powerful because they have all these great old copyrights. They're
all good till fifty years after the death of the writer.

But in terms of new songs, they're not a factor?

Yeah. But on the other hand, that goes back to the record companies. They ask, "Where are the Gershwins, Berlins and Rodgers?"
I know some marvelous writers who go to a record company today
and they say, "You're not for the market," when the whole success
of any artistic enterprise is being *different* from the market.

*We were speaking about picking songs and so forth. Let's talk
about this whole brouhaha with Frank Sinatra. He was at
Columbia from 1950 to 1953. He was under your direction at
Columbia, and he left the company, charging that he was forced
by you to sing what he called "inferior" BMI-published tunes
instead of ASCAP tunes. He felt his career suffered as a result. In
fact, he even sent a telegram to a House antitrust subcommittee
investigating the networks in 1956. How did this all come up?*

There were two reasons, I guess. In the first place, let's start with
the fact that Frank Sinatra had a BMI firm of his own. Also, ASCAP

did not allow country writers in, nor rhythm and blues. It was
shortsighted; they got smart afterward. ASCAP as an organization
was never involved in these charges. It was just certain writers who
felt they were being slighted, writers testifying in front of a Con-
gressional committee. When this came out, the CBS attorneys de-
scended on me and looked at everything I had ever recorded. As
it turned out, 95 percent of the songs I did were ASCAP. Only 5
percent were BMI. And of the BMI songs Sinatra did, two were
published by his own company.

*Where did these charges come from? What would prompt Sinatra
to make charges like that?*

I think he just didn't want to take responsibility for the dip in his
career at that time, which had nothing to do with me. He had lost
his motion picture contract. He had lost his television show. Look,
I have to preface this—the guy's a great artist. I never said that
he couldn't sing. But physically, he couldn't sing well at that time.
     I risked my neck with the union. I can say it now and everyone
will laugh, but I wanted Frank to sing some rhythm songs. He had
done "It All Depends on You"; otherwise, they were all ballads he
had recorded. I had an idea for an album, *Sing and Dance with
Frank Sinatra.* I got George Siravo to do the arrangements. One of
the sessions, Sinatra never even showed up. So under the guise of
balancing, I made a track of the orchestra alone. I just kept the tape
going. Then he came in another time and his voice was off. In other
words, the whole eight sides were tracked. Then weeks later, at
midnight, we snuck into the studio with Frank and finished the
recording. You can hear that album today and it's pretty damn
good. "American Beauty Rose" and all those rhythm songs. If you
ask me, I think he just couldn't face the fact that *he* was responsible
for the drop in his career.

This is when he was involved in an affair with Ava Gardner?

Yes.

But Sinatra did suffer then. You did pick songs for him, right?

Yes! And we had advanced him money to pay his income taxes. So the president of Columbia, Wallerstein, said to me, "You've got to make this money back." Some of the songs we did—"I'm a Fool to Want You," "Why Try to Change Me Now," "Blues Azurte"— we couldn't *give* those records away. But as soon as Frank did the movie *From Here to Eternity* it was his resurrection.

That was right after he left Columbia.

Yes. His being stomped to death in that movie was like he did his public penance. You know, priests were telling kids, "Don't buy his records because he's immoral."

Because he was having an affair with Ava Gardner?

Well, whatever. Don't forget this was in the early fifties. Now, people have babies without getting married and nobody cares. Look what happened to Ingrid Bergman when she had Rossellini's child. She couldn't even get a movie. So that was the morality at the time. They reacted against Frank.

Underlying this whole thing, though, you and Frank obviously had a pretty stormy relationship at Columbia. I believe he said he barred you from the studio at one point.

No. I was never barred from a Sinatra session. Look, he can say what he wants. He still sings good. . . .

But this is your opportunity to say what you want.

All I have to say is, take responsibility for your failures as well as your successes. He said I tried to make him do a song with Dagmar. At the bottom of his career, he was at the Paramount Theater— Jackie Gleason, Dagmar, and Sinatra. They used to do these bits on stage where Dagmar reacted to them in her charming, dumb way. A song came in where a kid's trying to make out with his girl and then the girl says, "Mama will bark." Crazy title. Far out! Since they were together on the stage, I said, "Why don't you try it?" Sinatra's contract said he had approval of everything and it also said nothing could be released without his approval. So how could I hurt him? Imagine *anybody* taking Sinatra and saying, "You do this song." Or what? What could I do to threaten him? Right? Hit him with a pizza? Come on!

The guy had complete control of what he did. He refused to do "My Heart Cries for You" and "The Roving Kind" back to back. I had arrangements made and the session all set. He was flying to Spain to see Ava; he came into the office that Monday morning, listened, looked at Hank Sanicola and Benny Barton, and said, "I won't do that crap." Here I was, stuck with musicians hired and the chorus. There was a kid who I had auditioned on a record. His name was Al Cernick, then Al Grant. I put him in the studio and rehearsed him all day. He had a two-sided number one record with those tunes and became Guy Mitchell. But the point is, if Sinatra did it and did it perfectly . . . I think Mitchell's hit was a stroke of luck for me. At that time people wouldn't have bought it if Frank had done it. He was *persona non grata* with the public and the Church.

Now he leaves Columbia, does *From Here to Eternity*, and starts selling records again at Capitol. Suddenly all his records at Columbia start to sell—all those that I made with him. We repackaged and put them out. Not only did he make back the money that Columbia loaned him, but he got about a quarter to a half million dollars above it in royalties! The records are there for anyone to hear. So if you look at the overall work, don't just take the one song that I tried as a novelty with his permission. After all, he could have walked out of the studio if he didn't like it. He could also have said, "I don't want it released" if he didn't like it. But he had nothing to lose at that time, and we put it out. His friends said, "How could you do a record like that?" But it's very interesting he did one with his daughter, sort of novelty rock 'n' roll, "These Boots Are Made for Walking." Then he went right back to what he does best.

Sinatra has never really been a big record-seller, has he?

Funnily enough, he never has had a million-seller, even at the height of his career. But he sold well. Look, he's the Tommy Dorsey of the voices. He and Jo Stafford. They learned from singing with Tommy Dorsey, the long phrase and the inflection of the notes. If

you listen to Tommy Dorsey play trombone, you can hear Sinatra
singing.

You worked with a number of the masters of the Swing Era in the
fifties at Columbia.

That was one thing Goddard Lieberson was marvelous about. He
said, "We make a lot of money on certain things; we must also have
a history of the great music of our time." Everyone agrees that
Ellington is a fantastic composer and musician. And when he
wasn't selling in the fifties, we kept recording him. It was a joy to
come to work because many times he would put it together in the
studio. I did Sarah Vaughan's "Corner to Corner" and "Perdido,"
I did all those records. She was very easy to work with, she was
a wonderful artist. Except she was married to the wrong guy then.
I forget who her husband was, but he always tried to get the songs
of publisher friends recorded. I had to give in to him a couple of
times. You know you don't have the last word if someone goes to
bed with your artist at night.

   I worked with Benny Goodman once, and it didn't turn out well.
We didn't hit it off. He's a fabulous artist, but this was at a time
when he wasn't selling. The few suggestions I made, he ignored.
So I just asked John Hammond to take over after that. Benny's a
great artist, but there isn't anybody who's been a part of his musical
life who hasn't gone through a time when they couldn't get along.
But that's all right, he has his way! It's what comes out in the end
that counts. If you meet the greatest writers, you may find people
you hate. But if their writing is good, that's all you judge them
by.

You contributed to the folk craze of the early fifties.

I covered The Weavers' "Tzena, Tzena, Tzena" and "Goodnight
Irene." Everybody covered those. I had Terry Gilkyson; he had
"Cry of the Wild Goose" and then he wrote other things that were
ripped off. Dean Martin took a couple of his songs and they became
very big hits. I never tried to follow much. The sales department
would come and say, "So-and-so has this hit. Why don't you make
it with Doris Day?" I'd say, "Wait a minute. Let's make something

with Doris Day where *she'll* have the hit, not be chasing somebody." There again we get back to the bullet theory: If you only
have so many to shoot, you have to husband your munitions. We
covered very few records. You also find, if you look up the statis-
tics, that we had more hits in proportion to releases—way more—
than any other record company. Because we didn't do the border-
line things. Sure, I'd miss out on some things. I'll never forget a
guy who came in with a song called "Till I Waltz Again with You"
in 2/4 time. I said to the kid, "How can you write 'Till I Waltz
Again with You' and it doesn't have waltz time?" He says, "Man,
that's the kicker!" I didn't do it, and he went and gave it to Teresa
Brewer and she had a big hit [laughter]. And that's the only hit he
ever wrote, too.

What I'm driving at is that your strength is going to be your
weakness, too. By that I mean you're looking for a certain quality.
If something comes that doesn't suit your standards, you'll miss out
on it. There was a song, "Let Me Go, Devil," a song written by
Jenny Lou Carson. [He sings:] "Let me go, let me go, let me go,
devil." Then the middle: "The drinking and the gambling, and the
bottles of rye." Hill and Range [music publishers] brought it over.
I said, "The song's marvelous, but who's going to listen to this?
Only recovered alcoholics and down-and-outers. Why don't you
change the lyrics?" They said, "No, this is the story of her life,"
this lady country songwriter. They went to her and she wouldn't
change it. I said I'd give her Johnny Ray. She wouldn't. And Decca
made it, and it was played on every radio station. I never heard so
much play. I thought, "Boy, did I ever blow this." But it was a
turntable hit. Everybody played it and nobody bought it. So I was
right and wrong. It died. Now, a year or two later, "Studio One"
[the television program] is doing a show and they want a song. The
director comes to me and asks, "Have you got a theme song we can
use?" I immediately thought of "Let Me Go, Devil" because it's
got lots of holes in it, lots of long notes, so you can use it in the
background and it won't fight the dialog. The more of that you
have, the more you can use the theme and the more you can sell
it, see? So I called up Hill and Range and said, "Now that the song
has had its chance, will you change it?" In a half hour they had
guys up in the office. They came over with a lyric called "Let Me
Go, Lover." I got this young kid because I didn't want anybody

identifiable recording it. It would have taken away from the dramatic use on the show if they had Rosie Clooney or somebody well known. So there was this gal, Joan Weber, who sounded like she worked in the five-and-dime, like the kid down the block. She did that and boom, that was the first television smash, made by television. The record sold about 2.5 million.

You signed the great gospel star Mahalia Jackson to her first major record-company contract in 1955. How did that come about?

At John Hammond's urging; he knew her well. He wasn't with Columbia then. He said, "Mitch, she likes you." She was being ripped off by the small labels. I just talked to her. I said, "Look, you can do it the way you want it." She was afraid that we'd try to mold her into a pop artist. I wish I could have, sometimes, for certain songs. But she was a true original. I didn't even try, because I knew you couldn't get to step one with that approach. She had to be in the mood, she had to have her grapes and fruit in the studio while she was working. Had to feel right. But we made some wonderful records.

When she made records, did you have everybody in one big room like she did in a church?

The studio on 30th Street *was* an old Greek church, so we *were* in church. That was the best studio. Columbia sold it, and there's an apartment house there now. She was successful, and she got royalties for a change.

When Alvin Barkley died and I was doing the music for the Democratic Convention in 1956, I used her. The place was dark, and on television there was just a pin spot on her. There were twenty-thousand people in that hall and you could hear a pin drop. The place was spellbound by her singing.

Let's talk about another great singer who at least started in gospel music, Aretha Franklin. Everywhere you read about soul music, you hear the story of how Aretha was brought to Columbia by

John Hammond, and Mitch Miller wanted to make her into a pop star. Is that true?

That's baloney! I never had a chance to record her. Never! Look it up.

You never picked songs for her?

Nothing, absolutely nothing. In fact, John put a jazz band behind her. He wanted her to be a jazz singer. I could see why he tried to do that, but it didn't work. So then when she went to Atlantic and Jerry Wexler recorded her with big success, John asked, "What did you do?" Jerry said, "I put her in church." So that explains it. Not only is the story [about my working with Aretha] not true, but I've never *met* Aretha Franklin, to this day! I admire her and I'll go anywhere she's singing, but I've never met her.

Why was she unsuccessful at Columbia? Was it just that John had put her in a jazz vein?

Yeah. Maybe now in a jazz vein she'll sell, too, but to break through to the public. . . . Look, nobody can second-guess John Hammond. If you look at the list of stars, the people that he found, everybody else pales in comparison over the years.

Let's talk about another great black pop star, Johnny Mathis. How did you first hear about him?

He was found by George Avakian, singing in a bar in San Francisco. As is usual when a guy gets a recording contract, who's the manager? The owner of the bar, who turned out to be Helen Noga. George recorded Mathis. See, I had this staff and when they wanted to do something, if it was something original and unique, they had absolute freedom to do it. George came back and said he found this wonderful singer and I said fine, do an album. He produced it, he did everything. Out of that album you could hear Mathis' talent. But as with all young singers, he was influenced. One song was completely influenced by Ella Fitzgerald, another by Lena Horne.

In fact, he even did a Lena Horne song, "Let's Do It," and Lena said, "He stole everything but my gown!" [Laughter.] Each performance on its own, you couldn't find anything wrong with it, but it was all derivative, which is not unusual in a young singer. Then, we were having this convention in Estes Park in Colorado. Everyone at Columbia was high on this album. Everyone was screaming and yelling that he was a new star. I had my reservations, but I kept quiet. Look, I've done things that weren't my taste that I thought people would like, and I thought this could be like that. There was a big hoopla, big promotion and everything, and no sales. As usually happens when everybody is for something and then it doesn't work, nobody really wants to talk about it afterward. Nobody!

So nobody had any plans for Johnny. Only Helen Noga; I've got to give her credit, she was persistent. Avakian couldn't make another album because the first was a failure, so she kept hounding me. Literally, she came in and cried. She said, "You've got to do something with him, you've got to!" I told her, "I'll tell you what, Helen, I'm going to listen to that album and I'm going to find out what he has that is unique, and I'm going to look for songs. If I find songs that are good for him, I'll do a session with him." She kept bugging me. Months went by. I just kept listening for songs. There was a song called "Wonderful Wonderful," these guys rewrote it maybe two dozen times. It sounded like Debussy, that's what attracted me to it at first. Another guy came in with "Scarlet Ribbons." Frank Loesser had a song called "The Twelfth of Never." The fourth one was "It's Not for Me to Say." After about four months I realized I had a session. Mathis came in and I told him what was attractive about his voice. It'd be very interesting for you to hear that first album and then hear these four releases, because it shows what direction I gave him. As I've said, you cannot put in what isn't there, you just have to take the wrapping paper off and show a singer what *is* there. Three out of those four songs became hits. Then Bob Allen wrote "Chances Are" for him, and he was off and running.

Now, get this: The Felds, the guys who own the circus, got to be big rock 'n' roll promoters. They had a touring show and they wanted to give Mathis $5,000 a week to be one of twenty performers. In arenas. That's the complete antithesis of what Johnny Ma-

this is. But he was hot, and Helen Noga had him signed. He was
with General Artists Corporation then, Tom Rockwell's group. I
said, "If you take that, I will not record him."

Why?

Because that would have destroyed him! I didn't want him in
arenas. I didn't want him surrounded by a bunch of groups like
. . . The Four Nosebleeds! The people on that tour, you wouldn't
know who they are today!

You mean you didn't want him stigmatized by rock 'n' roll.

No, I didn't want him. . . . He was a long-term artist. He was in
the category of Nat Cole. If you compare him to anyone, you have
to compare him to Nat. These are the artists that defy him, fashion
—excellence is what accounts for their enduring success. That's
what I'm proudest of about my work at Columbia. Here thirty and
thirty-five years later, Rosemary Clooney, Tony Bennett, Frankie
Laine, Vic Damone, Ray Conniff, Johnny Mathis, and if Percy Faith
were alive, and Erroll Garner were alive, if the original Four Lads
were working—they're all top performers. They may not have big
records, but they sell out everywhere they perform and make big
money. They last. So anyway, I just didn't want Mathis in that
milieu. Helen screamed and yelled and I said, "Well, you take your
choice." She opted not to go [with the Felds]. The funny part was,
three months later he was making $10,000 a week [laughter].

How long did you keep producing his records?

Helen Noga—she said this—she said, "I'm Armenian, and it takes
three Jews to beat an Armenian in any business deal." [Laughter.]
Right away she started a publishing company. So I said, "Fine,
Helen, but the songs have to be good." What would happen is that
writers would come in . . . If I did what she told me to do, I'd go
out with only one side of a record. The writers would come with
a song that suited Johnny and I'd say, "Give it to her publishing
firm." Which they did. Pretty soon she wanted *two* sides of the
record published by her. Of course, I refused that. People don't

realize that whether it's drama, song, or whatever, the writer is first. Without writers we're all dead. Performers come and go. It's true. Imagine no Gershwin, no Berlin.

With Mathis I did all sorts of things. I did an album called *Open Fire, Two Guitars.* We improvised the session. I wanted to get that intimate feeling Johnny has. After that I did *Johnny Mathis' Greatest Hits,* and it was on the chart longer than any other record. That was the first greatest-hits album by anybody. You know, people are always taking bows. In our business what they do is they copy, they imitate and they call it a trend. No one is a pioneer.

How was the greatest-hits idea received within the company?

At that time I could do anything I wanted to. There was no fight. It cost them nothing, just the packaging.

Finally, I had Bob Allen write a song for Mathis, and Bob Allen had his own publishing company. Johnny wanted to do the song and Helen Noga said, "I want to publish it." I didn't care who published it, but Bob Allen said, "No, I'll keep it for myself." She said, "If I can't publish it, we won't do it." So I told her, "If that's the case, I won't record Johnny. You'll have to get another producer. If I'm going to produce him, I have to be the guy who chooses the material. I'm not going to be a yes man for you."

But producers today don't necessarily choose material.

Producers today are carpenters, mostly. With the multi-tracks they come in and they get their name on the album. If I had my name on every hit album that was produced by me, I'd put them all to shame. So what if you've produced even a dozen albums? I've produced a *hundred* best-selling albums [as well as seventy-five Top 10 singles, more than a third of which went all the way to No. 1 —TF.]. But in those days we never put the producer's name on. I wanted to put the engineer's name on just for his glory and ego, but the company said no because it'd set a precedent. Now even the guy who sweeps the floor has his name on the cover.

You feel that what you were doing is what a producer should be doing?

That's right. You have to follow it through. Pick the arranger, go over the music with him. When you came in the studio, the whole thing had to be done, four sides in three hours. Everyone was important. If one of the connecting links broke down, you were up the creek. Sometimes you had to change something. I'll never forget one time with Percy Faith and Vic Damone. People don't realize that "On the Street Where You Live" is just a thing done in *My Fair Lady* while they changed the scenery. The guy's singing to a house. It was just filler. But I saw it as a hit song for Vic Damone. Percy wrote the arrangement and everything, and we came into the studio and suddenly it occurred to me that everything falls on the strong beat. The record didn't seem to get going. It didn't take off until the middle, when Vic sang "Oooh that towering feeling." So I went out to Percy quietly. I never talked through the loudspeaker to give suggestions. I said, "Percy, let's start the record right there, that'll be the introduction. Kill the other introduction." Percy was so fast; he took five minutes. You hear the record now, and the sound goes up and you hear "Oooh that . . ." and everyone's ears perk up. Then you don't mind the strong beat. You need the hook for the listener's ear. It became a big hit. It became a bigger hit than anything else in the show. Everybody began to record it after Vic, including jazz people.

A producer has to have the ability to change and the people talented and flexible enough to do it. I couldn't do it myself. You had to have a wonderful staff. I was lucky that I did.

You were certainly a phenomenal hit-maker, at Columbia especially. In your first year and a half there, sales in pop went up 60 percent.

Yeah, I guess so. Then it went up even more after that. We would sometimes have eight out of the top ten in the country if you look at the charts. Also, this made the success of the Columbia Record Club. Stop to think. If you're going to put out the record of the month, if you have two or three artists, what are you going to do every month? The same two or three artists? We had the classical part, we had the Philadelphia, the New York Philharmonic and the Cleveland—the three top orchestras. In pop we had all these hit artists who could be offered.

How many club members were there?

I don't know; it was all done secretly. They were afraid dealers would complain. It was found money for CBS. There are a lot of people who don't like to go to a record store. *Reader's Digest* sells millions of records so quietly nobody knows. And they do it all by mail order.

Were record-club sales figured in when they computed whether a record was a hit or not?

No. The record became a hit, and then it would become a record-club choice.

Talking about selling records that way, a phenomenal success that I think most kids of my generation grew up with was the Little Golden Records series. I think you sold 33 million of these.

More. Al Massler owes me so much in royalties and I can't even find him [laughter].

How did all this come about? These were little six-inch recordings of classical music, specifically for children.

And we did some popular music. We did "A Child's Introduction to the Instruments of the Orchestra." Alec Wilder wrote it; it's a gem. We took Bach, the Badinerie of his "Suite in B Minor," and called it "The Flute Dance" and put dancing flutes on the cover. We had top musicians play it. It worked. See, Simon & Schuster had Little Golden Books, and they had Pocket Books—the only paperbacks available in 1948. They were in candy stores on the corner, in racks. They were put in on consignment. If you sold them you paid the publisher, if you didn't they took them back. Paperbacks went for a quarter. They were not in bookstores at all. They wanted to put in another rack with Golden Books and Golden Records, which would also be a quarter. So George Duplaix, who was the editor of Golden Books, had this idea. Al Massler used an injection mold with yellow vinyl. Well, it wasn't vinyl, it was dung [laughter]. If the cartridge was heavy, it ground the disc down into yellow powder. But the kids loved them, and they only cost a quarter. We did not play down to the kids. We didn't itsy-poo them at all. Kids keep being born, so they keep buying the records. The Little Golden Records are out on LPs now.

I read that your royalty on that was an eighth of a cent. Let's talk about the changes in royalties and how artists are paid.

Well, the eighth of a cent . . . I'll tell you why I took an eighth of a cent. If it retails for a quarter, it wholesales for eleven cents, twelve cents. If they're going to give you the space in the store, you've got to give them that little profit. So George Duplaix said, "Look, if these sell in the millions, there is no room for a penny royalty. If you sell a million records it'll be $1,250 [at an eighth of a cent each]."

Was that good, $1,250?

It's better than a kick in the ass [laughter]. Don't forget, this was 1948. I was just starting at Mercury at the time. The regular royalty on pop records was 5 percent of 90 percent. I have a suit now at Columbia. They tried to take the cost of the cover off—fifty cents for a cover. All these lawyers are in there; they won't let me in the books. This is an ongoing thing that I started five years ago.

How do you feel about the multimillion-dollar deals recording stars are getting now? Is that out of control?

No. I'll tell you why. Because whatever is coming in, these people are making themselves. Offhand, I can't think of a producer at any record company today who takes the talent, develops it. Today the lawyers and the accountants make deals. They give them so much, and the record is made somewhere else, and they deliver the record. Of course, they spend more on a video than I ever did on a whole record session. So if the artist is bringing it all in, let them get as much as they can. No one forces the record companies. I know that after Simon and Garfunkel left Columbia, to make up for what they called their lost sales, Columbia gave a deal to Wings, to Paul McCartney, where they gave him ownership of the Frank

Loesser music company as an advance. Now Columbia, just by
sitting on its fanny, would take in a million dollars a year just in
performance rights on Frank Loesser's catalog. They were so hot
to show sales, they got McCartney and Wings for two albums and
they gave him the Frank Loesser catalog. Of course, Lee Eastman
is Paul's father-in-law, and he engineered it—he knows the value
of copyrights. If I was a Columbia stockholder, I would sue for
dilution of assets. And those Wings records didn't do well at all,
either.

But to Paul McCartney you would say mazel tov.

Of course. Look, no one held a gun to their heads. But that goes
to show—when the lawyers are making the decision, and a lawyer
is president of the company instead of a musician . . . When I was
at Columbia, we were all musicians. Sure, we had lawyers to tell
us about the contracts, and accountants to watch the budget. But
they weren't making policy. They weren't making the aesthetic
decisions. I'm sure, though the president of Columbia is taking
bows for Michael Jackson, I would bet my bottom dollar that there's
someone on the staff who found Michael Jackson, who nurtured
him or got the idea. Maybe he got a good bonus, but not the credit.

*Let's talk a little about your career as a pop artist. Everyone
remembers your big hit, "Yellow Rose of Texas." How did you
decide to become a pop performer, and how did you choose the
material you did, which certainly wasn't highbrow?*

No, it wasn't, but on the other hand it wasn't lowbrow either.
"Yellow Rose of Texas" was a Civil War song. In the original, like
all soldiers' songs, they were talking about women. They were
comparing the "high yaller" girls of Texas to the black belles of
Tennessee. Of course, that doesn't go now, and they changed two
words and the girls became flowers. But the idea was you certainly
couldn't do that with another artist. I was using choruses with Guy
Mitchell and a lot of people, so I thought, "Why not just use the
chorus itself?" They would be the star. That was a song that got
covered very fast by a lot of companies.

I was called in many times to screenings. *Bridge on the River*

Kwai, I was in the room alone while the picture ran and I'll never forget it. My stomach literally knotted at the opening of that picture. What a masterpiece it was. I'll tell you what happened. The soldiers are whistling "The Colonel Bogie March." Of course, I didn't even know myself then that it was "The Colonel Bogie March." This was their act of defiance. [He sings:] "Hitler, he has no balls at all. Goering has some but very small." They couldn't say the words so they whistled the tune. My stomach knotted at this and I said, "This has to be a record." I went in and I did it with the chorus. It came out and was an immediate hit. In fact, it sold even more in Germany and Japan than it did here. Then they used it to play in the intermission at the picture. David Lean [the director] told me they saved about $2 million in publicity thanks to that record.

Did you make some sort of deal with David Lean?

No, with somebody who wrote the contramelody. They had the copyright.

Nowadays the producers would have that all locked up.

Of course. Another one that I saw the same way was *High Noon.* It was a fantastic picture. I was alone in the Columbia screening room. In the music, the lyrics were telling the story. I called the publisher up and said, "Look, change the lyrics, make it a love song. Because it *is* a love story between Grace Kelly and Gary Cooper." At first they said they wouldn't. But I said, "If you do, I'll give you Frankie Laine." So they couldn't resist. Ned Washington wrote the words over and it became a love song: "Do Not Forsake Me Oh My Darling." It became a big hit and that helped sell *High Noon.*

Probably the biggest controversy in your long career was your stand on rock 'n' roll. You produced some rock precursors— certainly not rock music, but precursors like Johnny Ray's "Cry," which many feel was one of the forerunners of rock, and even Frankie Laine's "Mule Train." Yet you vowed when you were head of A&R that Columbia would never record rock 'n' roll. You

*called rock 'n' roll, among other things, "musical illiteracy" and
just a phase. Now, thirty years later, would you care to eat those
words?*

No, no! Let me tell you. With the artists I had, I couldn't have them
turn around and do rock 'n' roll. Secondly, most of those rock 'n'
roll artists—you can euphemistically call them that; some deserved
the term but others didn't. They needed such nurturing and caring
and rehearsing. I'm sure if you talk to Jerry Wexler, he'll tell you
he would spend days with groups to get the songs right, and *they*
wrote the songs. I didn't have time for that because I was supervising all this other stuff. But also, I saw what was going on in that
deal long before the scandal came out. Payola. Pay to play. I asked
Columbia, "Look, are you ready to pay? Because if you
don't . . . Are you ready to buy time on the stations? I prefer if
you buy time. Buy a spot and they'll play a record for three
minutes." They said no. They couldn't afford to; they owned a
network and had to keep their hands clean. They didn't even want
to go into the publishing business. Now, of course, they're a big
conglomerate, but in those days they were very wary.

*What did you see in payola that was any different from what had
always happened before, when a song publisher would come to an
A&R man and try to romance him into taking a song? How is
payola any different?*

It's different because if a guy took money from a publisher to record
a song and the song was not good, that song would never get
anywhere, no matter what.

*But at least it got a chance to get out there, which it normally
wouldn't have.*

All right, but he's defeating his own purposes. I think any A&R
man who did that was a fool. I know it happened, and there are
all kinds of stories. So that made it easier for *me.* To me, in payola
nothing was being judged on quality. I mean, before payola, you
put a record out and got it started and got reaction and other guys
had to play it, whereas with most rock 'n' roll you couldn't get the

first play without the pay. Payola took all sorts of forms. A payoff in the toilet, for example. Some did it in a corporate way. Some had pressing plants, some had music stores, some had publishing companies. Some had all three.

Who were the big players?

The record will speak for itself. I don't care to start a whole big thing again. There are very respectable people out there today who were big players in it. You must go back further. In those days, certain radio stations like WNEW—you never could have payola there, because they had musicians. They had librarians who listened to songs. Those disc jockeys had taste and they still do. There are other stations, the same. But there were certain stations that didn't pay their guys enough. They were looking for a fast buck themselves, and as long as they had the audience they didn't care what went on.

Are you saying that rock 'n' roll would not have caught on had it not been for payola?

No. I'm saying that I couldn't get into the field because of the payola. I had one experience where I went to a guy who had a big television show. We had a rock-flavored record that we made with The Four Lads using another name, which we put out on the OkeH label. It was a damned good record that was making noise, and we wanted to get it on this program. After keeping us waiting about an hour and a half, the guy suggested that the publishing rights be given to him. I told him we didn't own the rights. So that was that.

So that experience turned you off?

I couldn't operate in that milieu. See, if you were a small company and you had your one or two records, you'd go out and you'd fight and scratch. I had a job to do. I mean, Columbia sales did not go down in that period. Hell, I sold more albums in the midst of all this! Along came the *Sing Along* albums, and they sold 22 million copies. So it goes to prove that there's room for all kinds of music if you don't run and chase after what everybody else is doing at the moment.

But you know, it sounded like sour grapes. It seemed like: Mitch Miller is feeling that this new generation is passing him by, and he does not want them to succeed.

No, quite the contrary. I had no complaints with record companies who made rock 'n' roll records. I had complaints with radio stations. Before FM we had Top 20 and Top 40 and didn't listen to anything else, and played only one kind of thing, and the hippy-dippy disc jockey was king. All I said was . . . program a balanced diet of music—don't abdicate to the very young. I never complained about any of the record companies.

FM didn't come into its own until the early sixties, when the FCC decreed that manufacturers had to put in an FM tuner along with an AM tuner. Now you have every choice of music that you want, from jazz to symphonic to dentist music to rock 'n' roll. In fact, it's very interesting that the best rock 'n' roll stations are on FM, and AM has gone to the news.

You came down very strong in condemnation of disc jockeys in a speech in March of 1958. You said they had abandoned adults in favor of what you called the sub-teen eight-to-fourteen-year-old group. You said these kids had no buying power. First of all, where did you get this eight-to-fourteen-year-old figure as being representatiave of a rock 'n' roll audience? Second, if they had no buying power, then how come rock 'n' roll records took off in such a big way in the late fifties?

I said no buying power for products, Ted, that were advertised. God help them they should buy a bar of soap.

But they buy soda and candy and clothes and complexion cream. What's the difference? The radio stations could sell that junk.

I had no argument with that. My argument was with the lists. If you read the whole speech, I said the stations played the same songs over and over like an automated jukebox.

Which they still do today.

Very few do. Top 20, the stations still have that?

Now you have Contemporary Hit Radio which is probably the most important format in radio. Album Oriented Rock is on its way out. Top 40 is back, Mitch.

Look, my contention was, they were the eight-to-fourteen-year-old group then and they got older as they went along. But I'll just come back with a rhetorical question: Where are the artists of those days now?

You're right that there was a lot of junk, especially in the early days of rock 'n' roll. But there was a lot of junk in the type of pop music you were involved with in the fifties. I mean, "I Saw Mommy Kissing Santa Claus"? Don't you think the percentage of junk was really about the same in all eras of pop music?

Not what was played on the radio. Also, there's the idea of repeating the same four words over and over in the same song.

What about Johnny Ray's "Cry," which you produced?

I'm not talking about rock 'n' roll *treatment* of songs! I'm talking about the songs! Hell, Miles Davis, he did jazz with a rock beat. Fine! I'm not talking about the beat! I'm talking about the content. The literacy and musicality, that's all. How many of those songs can stand that kind of scrutiny?

But frankly, what you were saying came off sounding like censorship. Let's keep the times in perspective. Rock 'n' roll then was coming under vicious attack from all sides—the Church, public authorities, schools. . . .

I never attacked it for those reasons. I attacked it only for its utter lack of literacy. And the thing that bothered me most was the ripping off of the blacks. You take a guy like Little Richard, what a shafting he got. Pat Boone doing white versions, buckskin-shoe versions of his songs, and getting all the airplay. Hell, I recorded Big Bill Broonzy. Don't tell me about blues singers. I recorded Dinah Washington. Hell, Dinah Washington wasn't rock 'n' roll! She was a singer who sang with a rock 'n' roll beat. But she sang great songs and sang them in a wonderful way. Aretha Franklin is not a rock 'n' roll singer. Listen to any one of Aretha's songs and you'll find a literacy and a feeling that you won't find in ninety-nine out of one hundred rock 'n' roll songs that are being played today.

Do you think your protests had any effect? I know one effect it had on you *was that a number of radio stations banned you for a while after that speech.*

Storz stations banned all Columbia records. Sure. I have a feeling some of his guys were the biggest payola-takers of all. I don't think with his knowledge, though. But I wasn't looking for effect.

What I was objecting to was being dismissed from a list, as simple as that. By the way, if you look at what went on, we didn't do badly at Columbia without Storz. We did tremendously. There is also the idea of not running and chasing after something that somebody else is successful at.

But Mitch, wasn't this abrogating your reach to a whole new generation? Didn't you kind of miss the beat? This was not just a new music. This was a generational revolution happening.

Yes, but the generational revolution has suddenly turned around. You have Linda Ronstadt doing standard songs. Same for Carly Simon. That's happening now. Why? Who said there's no future in rock 'n' roll? The Rolling Stones. The politics of rock 'n' roll. Nobody knows it better than they do because they've worked it to the bone.

Perhaps no future for them *after a certain point, but there are new people coming up all the time.*

I'm sick and tired of British-accented youths ripping off black American artists and, because they're white, being accepted by the

American audience. It's as simple as that. Michael Jackson, whatever reservations you might have, I'm delighted to see him making
a pile of money because he's the first black artist who's able to go
out and do the arenas and the stadiums and clean up. The whites
have been doing it on black music for a long, long time.

*In the late fifties, the record business really began to expand and
explode. More people bought hi-fi equipment. Why did records
become so important all of a sudden, especially since TV was
becoming so important at the same time?*

It was the improvement in the reproduction of sound. It's very
interesting because many of the records made years before sounded
sensational on the new equipment. The new equipment is what did
it. So after you had the house and the car, the next thing you took
pride in was the stereo set. The LP—suddenly you were able to
hear performances of Mahler. There isn't anything you can't find
on LP. I think that's the success of the record business. The variety
that you can choose from. Some of the most obscure things are
available. People like to have it at hand to play for themselves. And
not only great reproduction, but reasonable cost. For $200 or $300
you can get a stereo set that's not bad. I think that television had
a tremendous effect, too, by showing the orchestras. I wish they had
more imagination in the way they showed them, and I wish the
sound was better on television, but they're getting there. Stereo is
coming and they are paying more attention to the sound.

*Having your "Sing Along with Mitch" show on television must
have been an incredible boost to sales of those* Sing Along *records.*

No. Quite the contrary, because it confused the public. I had so
many albums out. When I was on the air, the people weren't sure
what records they *didn't* have. They kept selling, but they didn't
sell any *more.*

How did the idea for the Sing Along *records come about?*

It's an old idea. After all, Milton Berle did it on radio with Community Sing. During the thirties and forties, there was a group on CBS

every day called the Landt Trio and White; they'd do a sing-along.
Mine came out of a suggestion from a staff guy named Stan Kavan.
We were sitting around the office and he said, "Why don't we do
some of the songs the guys sang in the service and call it 'Barracks
Ballads'?" So I said, "Hey, it's not a bad idea." I always liked to
play devil's advocate and ask who's going to buy a record, and why.
I reasoned that the guys who'd been in the army wanted to forget
about it, and those who weren't servicemen couldn't care less. But
the idea kept nagging at me. I began to ask Boy Scouts, Girl Scouts,
Kiwanis and Rotary members, "What are the songs you sing when
you get together at a party?" I made columns like a Chinese menu.
All the songs that appeared in everybody's column I put on the first
album. Then I got the idea of making it sound improvised, which
is not easy. Ukulele, guitars, drum, accordion, and harmonica.
Jiggsy Carroll worked out simple but interesting harmonies because
we wanted people to be able to sing in the right key and tempo,
and, if they didn't want to sing, we wanted them to enjoy listening.
The tempo and feeling had to be right. And the records took off
like a rocket in the midst of rock 'n' roll.

Do you think "Sing Along" could come back?

On television? Hell, yes.

*What happened? They cancelled the show abruptly at the height
of its success. Weren't they killing the goose that laid the golden
egg?*

They blamed the demographics; NBC claimed we weren't getting
enough young people. They were looking for the twelve-to-twenty-
year-old group, but they weren't home anyway on Friday nights
[laughter]. Sure, we went out with a thirty-four share. Would you
believe it?

*After the TV show, you went to MCA briefly. You were trying to
develop musicals for Broadway?*

And music for films. A vice president at MCA, Berle Adams, hired
me. He had preceded me at Mercury. He thought MCA could use

the talent that I had shown at the record company. He gave me an office and a good salary, and after the investment of a project was recouped, I would share in half of all the profits. I didn't want to go out to the Coast; I thought I could do it from New York. But I didn't figure that the Coast just wouldn't listen. All the ideas I had just got ignored—they weren't shot down, they just got no reaction. Ideas for musicals, for television shows—I told them about a great young French composer that they should use for films, Michel Legrand. This was 1965. They didn't buy Michel then. I told them about a book—I took the option myself because I thought it was so good—about a black medical student coming home, and there's a murder, and he picks up a hitchhiker. The scene was set in Arizona. They said, "Oh, no." Lew Wasserman [now the chief executive officer of MCA] said, "It's all right, but I know the governor of Arizona, and I don't want any bad reflections. And besides, it's controversial." Two years later *In the Heat of the Night* came out. Without risk there's no success. It's the old story here. Then I urged them to think about making cartoons into movies.

Did you feel there was a place for you in the recording business in the sixties, after the TV show? Everything was quite different then, wasn't it?

Yeah, but during the TV years CBS Records kept an office for me. I didn't get paid, but I had a secretary. They told me, "We just want to be able to pick your brain, that's all." That lasted until the mid-sixties.

Wasn't the direction into rock that Clive Davis took CBS Records in, in the late sixties, a direct repudiation of your philosophy? Or was he, maybe, just changing with the times?

If it was a repudiation, let him repudiate the profits that come from that catalog that still sells like mad, repackaged over and over again. If it's a repudiation, let him say so.

Well, he made a pretty big point, both in his book and when I interviewed him [see the Clive Davis interview in this book—TF], in saying that Columbia was a fuddy-duddy company. That he came along and discovered, after the Monterey Pop Festival, this whole resurgence in rock 'n' roll in the late sixties.

Well, I was out of Columbia from 1961 on. Monterey was six years later. Clive Davis is my candidate for the most self-serving guy you will ever find. Why ask me to answer the comments of a man who has no credentials, as far as I'm concerned? If you ask me, the only credential he has is when people laughingly would say he's trying to make himself another Mitch Miller in the studio.

But didn't he have astounding success with Columbia after he took over, much as you did when you first took over as the head of A&R?

What success?

Commercially, with people like Janis Joplin, Sly and the Family Stone, Chicago, and so on.

Chicago is a good group. If I had heard Chicago I would have signed them. But that was way later, long after I had left.

He never was a studio man, but he did have great success as a record executive, didn't he?

How about some of the performers who weren't successful? Come on! A record executive must be a nurturer, in the mold of Conkling and Lieberson, and not take credit that rightfully belongs to his staff.

There was a great deal of success at Columbia. Wouldn't you have to give him his share of the credit?

No. I wouldn't give him *any* of the credit. There's guys in the field who brought the stuff to him, and the rest were all deals. Where's Laura Nyro today? Ask him. I could take a list of people who were promoted with four-color posters as the second coming of the Lord who couldn't ad lib a burp after a radish dinner. If he's going to talk about, quote, "his" successes, I want him to show you his failures, too. Why, for him to be successful, does he have to put somebody else down? It's very interesting. He always sought me out to sit on the dais when he was given those phony, self-serving honors. You know, the Man of the Year for this and that. You never saw *me* as Man of the Year, and it hasn't been because I haven't been *offered* it. As far as I can see, his ego comes first, his talent comes last. And it is ironic that his two enduring artists are Melissa Manchester and Barry Manilow, both of whom are my kind of artists.

And for you now, you're doing a lot of guest conducting.

I've come full circle—back to symphony orchestras. I conduct all the major orchestras in America, Italy, Canada, some in Mexico. I'll tell you why I'd like to keep doing this. It's live. You strip all the crapola away. No editing, no retakes. People have to pay to hear you. They have to like you or you won't be re-engaged. Sell out the house, great! You come to an orchestra and you have to communicate fast, you have to get the music ready. There's no room for fakery. And I like that kind of atmosphere to work in, with consummate pros. The people are talented and we respond to each other, and we create an emotional experience that takes three or four thousand people out of the here and now, which only symphonic music can do—and I can't ask for more.

(April, 1985)

Milt Gabler

Milt Gabler is one of the true pioneers of the record business. It was way back in the late twenties when Milt convinced his father to stock records in his 42nd Street radio store, the soon-to-be-world-famous Commodore Music Shop. Thanks to Milt's enthusiasm, the store became a mecca for the world's most avid jazz record collectors, critics like Ralph Gleason, Barry Ulanov, Leonard Feather, and Marshall Stearns, musicians, and all sorts of buffs. In 1935, with the ascendency of the big bands, Gabler found it increasingly difficult to find the hot jazz small combo records he and his customers loved. He began leasing masters from the major companies and releasing records on his own Commodore Music Shop label. Thus the first independent jazz record company was born, as were the first jazz reissues. The Commodore reissues became so popular that the majors refused to lease masters to him any longer. Undaunted, Gabler began making his own recordings with top artists like Lester Young, Billie Holiday, and his favorite, Eddie Condon. Gabler also became the first true jazz impressario, organizing legendary Sunday afternoon jam sessions at Jimmy Ryan's on 52nd Street that featured the first (if makeshift) concert seating for jazz music. Gabler continued to be active in his record company and family's store even after he was lured to Decca. At Decca he became a top A&R man producing a variety of top stars such as Ella Fitzgerald, Brenda Lee, The Weavers, Louis Jordan, and Bill Haley and the Comets, with whom he recorded the first rock and roll hit, "Rock Around the Clock." The Commodore Music Shop was closed in 1958, and he abruptly lost his job at Decca in 1971, but Gabler continues to be active in the business through the National Academy of Recording Arts and Sciences— and his classic recordings continue to be discovered by new generations of fans.

I didn't realize that in the early days of the Commodore Music Shop you sold gag items like sneeze powder and whoopie cushions.

Actually, in those days, there was no real record business. It was down on its ass. Radio had come in at the end of the twenties and knocked records for a loop. Originally we were a radio store that took in records. So we took in sporting goods, novelty goods, tricks and jokes for parties—whoopie cushions, sneezing powder, and stink bombs, all that kind of stuff. We'd sell anything to pay the rent. But then I hired a record salesman, Sid Torin, who later became Symphony Sid. He had worked in a store near 14th Street and Second Avenue, and those stores sold sporting goods and cameras, a typical Broadway-type store like Colony Record Shop was originally, and other stores on 23rd and down on Nassau Street. Of course *I* got Sid into jazz when he came to my store in '35 or '36. He was just a pop records salesman. He learned all about jazz at Commodore because that was my main business. He didn't get along with my father, who didn't trust him. One day my father fired him, and he went over to Symphony Music Shop at

Eighth Avenue and 42nd Street. They had a radio program and he became the announcer for them, and that's how he got the name Symphony Sid.

As you said, yours was mainly a radio store. What made you feel that records might make a good business?

I took in records around 1926, '27. We used to play the loud-speaker outside the transom of the store. We played the radio outside to attract customers as they were going by. People began to come in and ask for records. So I told my old man, "We're getting a lot of calls for records; I think you ought to take them in."

Because radio had knocked them out, weren't records almost a novelty then?

Records weren't a novelty. Before radio got big at the end of the twenties, records were the biggest form of home entertainment with the old windup machines before they had electric motors, acoustic machines.

And when radio came in?

What happened when TV came in? They stopped listening to the radio. It just switched over. People were able to get news, sporting events, anything they wanted, plus music on the radio. They didn't have to buy records. Radio had just become electric with speakers in those years, and the sound was much better than the phonograph sound. Even as great as the Victor Orthophonic or the Columbia Grafanola was or the Panatropes were, these loudspeakers in the radios had a much better sound. That's when they invented phono-graph pickups. Playing records through the radio started to bring records back. RCA Victor put out a little record player that you played through your radio. It had a little motor, the same principle as the electric clock, you pushed it to start it. It ran at 78 RPM. It had a little pickup. The whole thing wasn't more than twelve inches square. It had an adapter: You used to pick up a tube and put this wafer through the prongs on the tube, push it back in, and it would play through your radio speaker. Just the same as VHS now playing videos through your TV. What RCA was smart enough to do was they had this special program: They sold you this motor and pickup and I think three free records, I think a classical, a pop, and maybe a country or whatever, for $12.50. Don't forget this was just post-Depression time. Soon they were selling at $9.95. What it did was everyone started to hook them up. Then the companies started making combination radios and phonographs, better models, and people started to like the records again so much that the business built up slowly. Then the war came along and everybody started to buy records.

Is that how records made a comeback? Because they improved the quality of the sound?

That's right. Of course around 1926 or so they started to record records electronically with microphones. What happened was—I have to give him credit—Martin Block came to New York from California and in 1935 started the "Make Believe Ballroom" program on WNEW in New York. He made believe the artist was in the studio, and it became a very popular program. Other stations played records also, but his was the big show. But he started to make records popular again. Then Decca came out with a three-for-a-dollar record with name artists in 1934. Records of top stars had been seventy-five cents apiece before. It all about happened at about the same time.

In your store a customer could swap records with another customer, feel free to play records he already owned, or just listen to records in one of your booths—none of which made you any money.

I'm sure the record swapping went on, but that wasn't the major thing there. The major thing was you met people there that loved music and jazz in particular, and you could always find someone you could talk to about your hobby, including my salesmen, myself, my brothers or brothers-in-law. It became a hangout for the critics, artists, record collectors. We struggled. I wanted to do business. But I never pushed to make a million dollars, or make it the biggest store in New York. I was satisfied with it being the most important jazz store. Don't forget that jazz then, and even now, was a very small percentage of the record industry.

Didn't you used to buy records from the Salvation Army?

Well, that's because the records were discontinued. That's what started me to make my own records. You couldn't get them from the companies.

You bought up all the OkeH stock, no?

When the OkeH company folded up. The record business was bad in the mid-thirties. Columbia and OkeH, which were one company at that time, were doing less and less business. The inventory was just lying there. In those days you had a record return privilege. A record dealer was allowed to return 5 percent of his purchases. My father used to say—he was an old electrical hardware man— he hated the record business, he said "they're like vegetables. The songs get old, and they age, people don't want them." He said, "In my business, the hardware business, a screwdriver or a box of nails always has its value." Now because records would lose their value, you had these record peddlers who would go around buying up bankrupt stock. They'd come around to the store twice a year and sell records to you for a nickel apiece. Charlie Stinson of the Stinson Trading Company got the lead on the old OkeH stock— Columbia was going to change the label, and wanted to get rid of that old merchandise. Stinson said he had the option on the OkeH stock at the warehouse in Bridgeport, Connecticut. I said I'll pay you twice what you ask for if you let me go up there and pick what I want, because OkeH didn't just make jazz records. He said it's a deal. So I went up to Bridgeport and I stayed a whole day, and went through all the cartons. I bought about five or ten thousand records.

You must have ended up with some real collector's items.

Oh, of course. Then I made up a mimeographed list of them. Most I sold for seventy-five cents, the very rare ones I sold for $1.50.

*Why did record stores stop letting people listen to records before
buying them?*

First of all, they had to stop because everything was shrink-
wrapped. I originally had two booths for listening, then when we
moved I had four booths. And people would go in and stay for an
hour or two until they picked out three records and it was a dollar
sale! It was a cheap way to spend a lunch hour and not put nickels
in the jukebox. Jerry Wexler courted his first wife in the booth at
the 52nd Street store. If it wasn't busy I didn't care.

*A lot of great jazz writers and critics used to hang out at the
Commodore. In fact, didn't Ralph Gleason start his* Jazz
Information *periodical in your backroom?*

That's right, along with Eugene Williams and Ralph de Toledano.
They were my customers. I printed the first jazz discography in
America: Charles Delauney's *The Hot Discography* was printed in
America by the Commodore Music Shop. I got the U.S. rights to
it. It was the greatest tool for selling jazz records. The big thing
about the Commodore was to educate people about collecting jazz
records. *Jazz Information* was a periodical where they tried to
correct the information that was in *The Hot Discography* and other
things. It specialized in the ancient New Orleans jazz music and
blues. They were excellent writers. The first edition was run off on
our mimeograph machine, which was very bad. They didn't have
any money. They typed the stencils on our broken-down typewriter.
They improved it in the second edition. It was a marvelous book.
I think it should be reprinted.

*Jack Crystal was your brother-in-law, and came into the store when
you went to Decca. Of course Billy Crystal is his kid. Billy does
his bit "The Face." Any idea who that is based on?*

"Face" was the name for any musician. But it was really a term
used by Zutty Singleton the most. Zutty played at Ryan's a long
while, and he was quite a character. He used to play Jack Crystal's
shows down on Second Avenue, and when Billy was young he got
to know him. You know, when Billy was bar mitzvahed Red Allen

and Zutty and Tyree Glen played the bar mitzvah. Jack and Helen wouldn't have any other kind of band.

Tell me how you made the step from being a store owner to actually leasing masters and releasing your own records.

The record companies would discontinue an item when it stopped selling. I would get calls for it. I found as many copies as I could searching around old dealers' stocks and the Salvation Army or getting it from customers who had duplicates. But I soon realized that I had enough customers of my own to press my own records. I wanted to put out the original Wolverines on the original Commodore Music Shop label. After I put them out I found out they were the wrong Wolverines. They were the ones with Jimmy McPartland. See, in those days you really didn't know who played on the records. You had to ask the musicians or get familiar with their sound and technique and phrasing, and try to pick them out yourself.

You pioneered the listing of recording personnel and dates on the record.

I was the first to ever put that on the label of the record. We had to have dies made because there was so much type on it. I had a special label designed for me by Richard Edes Harrison. Ricky Harrison worked for *Fortune* magazine. He used to do the covers. He had the idea of designing a special label that could fit all of the copy on it.

Oh, yes, you didn't have an album cover then; all the information had to go on the label of the disc.

We had to use the space above the hole as well as below the hole. Also—he was fantastic—what bothered him was that when a record spun at 78 RPM on his phonograph, they always looked lopsided because they had a big logo on the top and on the bottom it would just have the title and record number. The labels were top heavy, and he said "when it revolves, my head goes off center! It's no good." So he designed the Commodore/U.H.C.A. [United Hot

Clubs of America] label so that when it spins it's an even design
and aesthetically it didn't bother him when he looked at it revolving
on a turntable.

*Let's get back to how you began leasing masters from the record
companies.*

I began reissuing records in 1933 or '34. I leased the masters. If
I wanted to put out the Jimmy McPartland record, I had the custom
department of the record company check to see if they still had the
masters to press the record. The used label copy they had in their
file. They researched it and came back and said they did have the
three original Wolverine Vocalion records, which were pretty rare.
It had been out of print for a long time. They said you can't get
them pressed up special unless you buy three hundred of each. I
did a quick mental calculation and figured it would take me about
two years to sell out each one. So I ordered them. They pressed the
records on the Commodore Music Shop label.

Had anybody reissued out-of-print records before?

No. The reason I put it out on my own label was that I had once
ordered "Pinetop's Boogie Woogie" on Vocalion. They told me it
wasn't available. It was still in the catalog, but they couldn't order
less than one hundred records to get the factory to press it up for
them. So I ordered a hundred records. I started to tell customers
that I have "Pinetop's Boogie Woogie" in stock and one of them
said, "I just bought it over at [O. Saporta] on 46th and Broadway."
I burned up! I called Vocalion and said how come [O. Saporta] has
"Pinetop's Boogie Woogie" when I had to order a hundred to get
any! They said when you ordered a hundred we ordered an extra
twenty-five for our own use and he bought ten of them. So I said
to myself that's ridiculous. I had to order a hundred and now
they're taking sales away from me! That's why I started the Commodore Music Shop label. I ordered it from the custom division,
and told them to put my own label on it. This way it was handled
differently. The New York branch wouldn't have it in stock. I'd
have them all.

And this became successful for you?

Oh yeah. First of all it was advertising for the store. I used to give the records to the reviewers to write up so I'd get the publicity, "the Commodore Music Shop just reissued a record." The best thing about it was the publicity. You figure you have to hold records in inventory that long; I had to pay for the records in thirty days, then I'd wait a year and a half or two years to get rid of it. But people would come to the store because I had that kind of merchandise in stock and no one else had it. I once had someone say "who does your PR?" I said "I do it all myself!" All the writers came in there so it was no problem.

Didn't your reissues become so successful that the major record companies stopped leasing masters to you?

I told Jack Kapp to buy back his Brunswick and Vocalion masters from Warner Brothers because John Hammond had gotten a job putting out the reissues for Columbia. I said I would put out Kapp's stuff for him. I always took a little burn because I was the guy that created the reissue market, and started to reissue records, and Columbia hired John. I calmed myself by saying they hired John because he's good, and also because if I went up there to do it, they would lose a good record dealer. John put them out at fifty cents, and mine were seventy-five cents and a dollar, and some, when I had to make masters, were $1.50. So I could see the handwriting on the wall. As soon as Columbia, and then Victor, started reissuing records, Panassié came over and put out a whole series of Bluebird reissues for Victor. As soon as all that happened I couldn't get masters to press: They were in business for themselves. I thought I better start making my own *recordings* because if I paid for a record date and hired a studio and did my own recording, I'd own it forever.

What about United Hot Clubs of America? How did that fit in?

When I got to number fourteen or fifteen on the Commodore reissues, a fellow named Marshall W. Stearns who was a student at Yale came into the store. All the college kids would come into

Grand Central Station and they naturally would come across the street to my store. It was a good place to wait for your next train. So, they had hot clubs in England and France, and the Federation of British Rhythm Clubs. He said, "We ought to form Hot Clubs in the United States." I said, "I'll change my music label to the U.H.C.A. label, and in order to get the record you have to be a member of the club." We charged two dollars a year for membership, which was to cover the cost of postage. Also I said, "I'll run jazz concerts on Sundays to publicize the music and get space in the papers."

Tell me about the first self-produced Commodore session in 1938.

One of my favorite records that got me really interested in free-style jazz was The Chicago Rhythm Kings 1928 record of "There'll Be Some Changes Made" and "I've Found a New Baby," which just happened to have Eddie Condon on it. Various records had Eddie Condon on them, and I realized that this guy must be the sparkplug for the kind of beat and rhythm I like on a record. Unscored music with free-style solos. In fact, when I started doing my own recordings, a ten-inch disc was too small, so I started to make jazz records on [78 RPM] twelve-inch, so the guys could stretch out and take longer solos.

Why didn't twelve-inch 78s become the standard size?

They didn't sell, and don't forget jukeboxes. It was a whole different thing. The greatest record changer was the Capeheart. You could stack up ten records and they would fall, one after the other. And you couldn't mix tens and twelves together. But Blue Note and Commodore continued to make twelve-inch. Everybody started to make twelve-inch 78s for collectors. But, anyway, I felt no record had the excitement of The Chicago Rhythm Kings record. So I thought I would try to get all these guys together, because they were all in New York now, playing in various bands. I had to have all those bands in New York at the same time, when I was able to book a studio. So I couldn't get the band together that I wanted. Benny Goodman was having his concert at Carnegie Hall on January 16, 1938. Finally all the bands happened to be in New York that week.

So I booked a date at Brunswick for Monday the seventeenth. Friday I get a call from Eddie Condon saying that Jess Stacy can't make the Monday session because Benny was going to record. Benny had been an old friend from coming in the store, and he was rehearsing. He was coming out with a record a week on Victor. I said, "Benny, your records are all starting to sound the same. You got too many records out. I need Jess Stacy Monday!" I tell him I've been trying to do this date for six months. I said, "Give Jess a day off and let me do this." He looks at me and he says, "I'll take the day off, you have Jess." So then we were able to do our first Commodore session. But it didn't come out like the 1928 record. It came out fantastic, but I was trying to do a Chicago Rhythm Kings date. This was something I found out later when I became a so-called great record producer: You can get the greatest arranger, and the greatest group of musicians together, and have the charts written on some wonderful tunes, and put it all together in the studio with good engineers and good equipment, and it just won't gel. But here ten years had gone by and the musicians had been exposed to a lot more music and the playing of other musicians. They had become better at their trade, more facile with their own instruments.

Had you done any recording sessions at this point?

I had watched a couple of sessions. The engineers knew how to set the men up in the studio—the way they always set them up. I did my first session at 1776 Broadway, the Brunswick studio. The guys started to run down "Jada" and I said, "That's no good. I don't hear the music the way I'd hear it at a club." I told the engineer, "They sound one way in the studio and another way through your monitor. You don't have the men balanced properly." He said, "Do whatever you want. You set it up." I had hurt his feelings. I took a high guitar stool and I put it by the overhead mike and got up on it with my head near the mike. To me it was just common sense. I told the guys to play and then move around until I could hear all the instruments. Then I balanced the rhythm section because we only used two mikes in those years. Once you balance your rhythm section and you have your guys under the mikes the way you want them, that's all there is.

Tell me about the Kansas City Six sessions with Lester Young.

It was early Lester, when he first came to New York with Basie.
He was great then. The reason I didn't record Lester a lot in those
years was I always thought he was John Hammond's baby. The
same as with Blue Note. I never did their men, hardly. I didn't want
John to be unhappy with Commodore that I had stolen Lester
Young from him, although Lester cut on all the labels.

What was Lester like in those years?

A quiet man. In those years he was sober, straight. As a prelude
to this, John Hammond comes in the store and he had done a date
with Buck Clayton, with Eddie Durham playing electric guitar. It
was the first session with jazz electric guitar on it. Eddie had got
ahold of one of the first instruments. Vocalion wouldn't put it out,
they thought it wasn't commercial enough. I said, "I'll put out
anything you do, John." But he came to me with three sides. I said,
"What am I going to do with a record and a half?" I said I'd record
them again, but I wanted to add Lester Young on clarinet. He said
fine, because he was unloading these three sides on me. They were
very tasty records, but you could see why the sales department
didn't want them. I said I'll make five more sides, so I'd have
enough for four records [eight sides]. I figured if I added Lester's
clarinet to the muted trumpet, with a little quiet guitar in the
background, it would be like a salon recording, like a string quartet. Tasty. So that's what happened. They're classics. Just fabulous.

Tell me about meeting Billie Holiday, and working with her.

She came into the 52nd Street store unhappy one day, too. She was
singing "Strange Fruit" at the Cafe Society downtown. Columbia
was afraid to let her record it, because of the content of the song.
It was an anti-lynching song. Columbia was afraid of the Southern
customers.

*Frank Schiffman apparently was not eager for her to sing the song
at the Apollo Theater because he felt it was too much of a downer.*

It *was* a downer. But it was good for Cafe Society. It stopped the
room. It was fabulous with just a pin spot on her in a darkened
room. You couldn't follow it, even with "The Star-Spangled Banner," when she finished that song. Columbia turned it down. She
came to me and said, "They won't let me record my big number."
I said, "I'll make it in a minute, Billie, all you've got to do is get
permission from Columbia to record for Commodore." So Columbia
got off the hook with Billie that way. I did the date at the Columbia
studio at 711 Fifth Avenue, the World Broadcasting Studio. In
addition to "Strange Fruit" we did "Yesterdays," "Fine and Mellow," and "I Got a Right to Sing the Blues."

Didn't you write "Fine and Mellow" with her?

I wrote one of the verses, but I didn't share a writing credit. In fact,
I copyrighted it for her. It became a hit on the jukeboxes, which
was very unusual because my records were one-dollar records and
the jukebox operators were used to buying thirty-five and fifty-cent
records. It became a smash in Chicago. The guy used to drive in
his car from Chicago and fill up his whole car with cartons of 78
RPM "Fine and Mellow"s. He cornered the market in Chicago on
it. He told me he was getting two dollars a record. "Strange Fruit"
didn't become a hit, it was too special, but it got all the write-ups!
It was such a fabulous thing for a little guy to make "Strange
Fruit." But "Fine and Mellow" was a hit. I got a call from the A&R
guy up at Decca, Bob Stephens, asking for a copy of "Fine and
Mellow." So I immediately knew—by 1939 I was getting more hip
about the record business—I knew that they wanted to copy it for
their blues label. They covered it, I believe, with Alberta Hunter.
So I told him I was out of stock on it. And I had about five hundred
in the back room. I told him I was expecting some in and as soon
as I got them I'd send it over. So I said, "Now what am I going
to do. They'll copy the record and sell it for thirty-five cents. The
first thing I'll have to do is copyright the song." It's just a blues,
but you can copyright the lyrics. So the next musician that walked
in the store, I gave him a record and asked him how much he
wanted to copy this off the record and make a lead sheet for me?
I paid him fifteen bucks, I don't remember his name, and he went
in the booth and copied it off the record. I went over to the 45th

Street and Lexington Avenue post office. I got a registration card
—you could get them from the Library of Congress at the post office
in those years. I said, now Billie's safe, and I took the record up
to Decca. Incidentally, I love Billie, but I have to put her down a
little bit, even though she gets full credit for "Fine and Mellow."
I'm going to digress a minute. All the first black female singers who
weren't trying to do what Bessie Smith or Ma Rainey did got it from
Ethel Waters. She was number one, The Queen—on pop, chan-
teuses. It wasn't until I started to collect her old Black Swans that
I found out that two or three of the verses on "Fine and Mellow"
were from old Ethel Waters blues records! Only two verses were
written by Billie, and one of those I wrote! But it's Billie's. People
have been copying blues from each other for years.

Tell me about how you began working for Jack Kapp and Decca.

The Commodore records were starting to create a lot of attention.
I didn't go to Decca until 1941. By then I had a lot of great reviews
on my recordings. I used to do jazz programs on the radio. My name
was always in the paper. I knew the war was coming, and my lease
was up on 46 West 52nd Street. Now, Jack Kapp used to take
rhumba lessons near there, and he'd come into my store and say
hello. He went by for a lesson and I wasn't there, the store was
closed, the sign said: "Moved Back to 136 East 42nd Street."
Meanwhile, he had gotten the Brunswick-Vocalions from Warner
Bros. So he says, "Oh, Milt doesn't have the store, maybe he'll
come up and put out all those reissues for me." He called the 42nd
Street store, and I was down in the basement looking for a record.
He's holding on the phone, and holding on the phone. Then my
brother-in-law says to me, "Didn't you get that call?" I go to the
phone and he had the switchboard operator still hanging on! So he
asked me. I said, "Well, I have this store, my brother's going into
the service." I said I'd give him half a day, as long as I could leave
Decca by twelve or one o'clock and get to the store for lunchtime
business. He said okay.

*Didn't Kapp have a tough reputation among musicians? John
Hammond talks about how Kapp signed Basie for a contract
without royalties.*

Well, you gotta realize that was the thirties. I'm sticking up for Jack because I liked him. But what Jack did was no different from what Columbia did or Victor. When you recorded a band in those days, you gave them a flat fee, especially on their first session. Until they had a hit. Jack's theory was that they are really unknown until you make the records and the records get played. If he signed a band that was popular on the radio or something, then he would give them a royalty, but when you take an unknown from Kansas City who didn't have the reputation . . .

By the time you began at Decca, you had begun your famous Sunday jam sessions on 52nd Street—Swing Street—and before that, semiprivate sessions around town.

To publicize the music we ran jam sessions, and I would go to a record company around 1935, '36, and ask to use their studios on Sunday when they weren't being used. I didn't have to pay for the studios. We would rent chairs and use the studios as an auditorium. I'd pay the super around twenty-five dollars to run the elevator. I'd buy a case of booze, a couple of cases of club soda, ginger ale, and ice. You couldn't get in. We'd pack them. There was no admission charge, and I didn't pay the musicians, it was just to publicize the music and Commodore.

What made you go public with the jam sessions at Jimmy Ryan's club on 52nd Street?

What happened was there would be a mess, cigarette burns on the studio floor. I ran one at Decca and one at Brunswick-Mills studio where John Hammond had the Basie small band come, Benny Goodman came and Ella and of course the Condon guys, Artie Shaw came and Chick Webb. That, I think, was the greatest free jam ever run. But the record companies wouldn't give me their studios anymore. They said, "I did it last time, go somewhere else." I said the best thing would be to go to 52nd Street because the nightclubs could sell the booze. I wouldn't have to buy the booze. So we went to the Famous Door and I told them I wanted to come in on Sunday afternoon when they weren't open. From five to eight o'clock. I usually had two bands at my sessions. I said, "You just set chairs up and we'll fill this place with people that'll buy booze. It'll be publicity for the Famous Door, and we'll use your house band." John even brought Bessie Smith to the one at the Famous Door. Mildred Bailey was there and said, "I can't sing after Bessie Smith." It was still free admission. Now, because so many people appeared at my jam sessions on 52nd Street, and started feeling good, they stayed for Sunday night, which was usually a dead night in the clubs. The Hickory House's owner, Joe Marsala, was no dummy—he started his own Sunday afternoon jam sessions the next Sunday! WNEW later broadcast them. Mine was free. Next thing you know Ralph Burton started running sessions down in the Village. Pee Wee Russell told me he was charging a dollar admission. I asked if he was paying the musicians, because I wasn't paying them, but I wasn't charging admission either. It didn't seem to bother Pee Wee because he had his booze, and he likes to play. That burned me up. This is now around 1940. I look around 52nd Street and see there's only one club not doing business and it's Jimmy Ryan's. I went in and said, "I'd like to take this place over on Sunday afternoons and run jam sessions here." Jimmy said fine. I got ninety cents there instead of a dollar, because I registered with the IRS and they got a dime.

Was anyone welcome to sit in?

No. Only at the end of the session, the last blues or "bugle call rag" you play. I combined the two bands at the end. I forbid sitting in unless you were a really famous guy. In fact I once wouldn't let Jackie Cooper play drums. He was a student of Zutty Singleton's. I said, "You're not a pro, this is for pros." It was embarrassing.

Were they easygoing or were they really cutting sessions?

No, they all loved each other. When they got up to blow they'd try to outperform the other guy, but it was all very warm. There was no jealousy. In Max Kaminsky's book he says that probably some of the greatest music anywhere, ever, was at the Jimmy Ryan's jam sessions that Milt Gabler ran.

Bebop was coming up at about the same time, and the jam sessions that produced that sound were happening uptown at Minton's and Monroe's Uptown House. Would a bebopper have been welcome at your sessions?

Dizzy [Gillespie] used to come in and wait for the last set, just before bebop really got to be bebop. But it's the same theory I had with my Commodore label. Being the guy that started it all, I could have recorded any jazz musician. In those days nobody was exclusive. But if Al Lion wanted to put you on Blue Note or Dan Qualey wanted to put you on Solo Art, I still sold Blue Note and Solo Art in my store, and it gave me a chance to record somebody else for Commodore.

So you didn't feel compelled to record Charlie Parker, who was playing across the street on 52nd Street?

No. Also, at that time I was really getting busy up at Decca. We got to become known as moldy figs because I stuck to Pee Wee and Eddie [Condon] and Bobby [Hackett], and those guys. I stayed mainstream.

But it wasn't because you didn't dig Charlie Parker or Dizzy.

Oh no. It wasn't because I didn't understand what they were doing. Absolutely not.

You were the first to have regular seats at your sessions for people who didn't want to drink, just listen and watch.

Yeah. What happened was Ryan said to me, "All the kids are coming early and grabbing the seats up front at the tables," even though I put "reserved" on a few. He said the waiters wouldn't work the gig because the kids don't buy any booze and they don't tip good enough. They're college kids. Well, he had a lot of extra straight-backed chairs down in the basement, and I got lattice molding, thin pieces of wood, and I put them through the back of the chairs so they wouldn't move. Ryan's had a dance floor, and I filled it up with chairs. It was the first gallery. I let the nondrink-

ing customers sit there. They were great seats, right in front of the
bandstand! About ten rows. I saved all the good tables for adults.

*Would you say that Norman Granz and George Wein and other
jazz impresarios were inspired by your success?*

Granz used to come to the sessions at Ryan's when he was in New
York. I remember standing on the side, and he says, "Milt, this is
one of the greatest things I ever heard in my life. I'm going back
to California and I'm going to do the same thing in Los Angeles.
And that was the start of Jazz at the Philharmonic. George Wein,
when he had the Riverside Club in Boston . . . Jimmy Ryan's had
two old-time telephone booths up by the checkroom. And invari-
ably at about seven o'clock on a Sunday the phone would ring and
my brother-in-law, who used to collect tickets at the door, would
say, "George Wein's on the phone." Wein would say, "Who's there
this week? Is [Sidney] Bechet there?" and so forth. "I'd like to
book them to play my session in Boston next week." Every week
he'd save time. It started with my free concerts. The only one who
had a concert before me was Joe Helbock, the guy who had the
Onyx Club had that concert with Artie Shaw and strings at the
Imperial Theater, and Hammond had his boogie woogie concerts
at Carnegie Hall. But the commercial weekly things started with my
sessions.

Meanwhile back at Commodore . . .

I couldn't do that many Commodore dates. Then the family built
a [record] factory in Yonkers that was a big white elephant. It
was a bomb. We had to build our own factory in the war because
the major labels wouldn't press records for us, for any independent. So my brother Barney, who was half an engineer, built a
factory in Yonkers, with my approval. It was a scuffle to make the
factory pay. At the end of the forties—we were doing all the
independents, Roost and Atlantic, and we might have done Blue
Note.— As soon as the major companies opened their doors
again with larger facilities they all left us and went to the majors.
In fact, I stopped recording for Commodore because I never got
paid for anything I did for Commodore. In all those years the

family lived off it, because I had my job at Decca. All the profits
from the records went into supporting that plant. I told my brothers, I'm going to stop making Commodores until you make the
plant pay for itself with custom pressing, and pressing the Commodores that you do have. We had to close the plant up in the
early fifties.

You worked with all kinds of artists at Decca.

I did everybody. What Jack Kapp didn't realize when he hired me
was that I was well versed in every kind of music. I wasn't just a
jazz man. I used to sell it all in the store. But Decca didn't know
that I knew all about composers, knew their repertoires. I knew
what sold from waiting on trade near Grand Central. They found
out I knew what the customers in the street were looking for, what
singers they liked. And having sold the other labels, I knew Decca's
competition also. So when I went up to Decca, I was a find, they
didn't want to let me go. The first thing you know, I wasn't leaving
at one P.M. I got so into the recording business, meeting the acts
and the managers and song-pluggers who came up to play the new
songs, that I used to hang around there and I didn't get to my
father's store until five or six o'clock at night, when Decca would
close. And often we would stay behind and just tell stories about
the record business and artists.

*What kinds of things were you doing when you first went to
Decca?*

Well, when I went there I worked for a year or so just transcribing
all the records they had bought from Brunswick and Vocalion, and
starting to put out reissues.

Who were the first artists you worked with there?

I think the first artist they had me work with was Guy Lombardo.
He used to record every week. He was probably one of the most
important pop bands, sweet bands. Then when Jimmy Dorsey
formed his band I did Jimmy. I did Woody Herman. Jimmie Lunceford. Andy Kirk. Bing Crosby. Louis Armstrong. The Ink Spots.

The Mills Brothers, Ella Fitzgerald. Billie Holiday. Carmen McRae. Peggy Lee. Dick Haymes.

Later you were responsible for the first big rock 'n' roll hit, Bill Haley's "Rock Around the Clock."

Bill had had "Crazy, Man, Crazy" on the Essex label in Philadelphia. What Bill was doing was like rockabilly. In fact, he once had a radio show where he was doing country and western. I had been making R&B records with Louis Jordan and Buddy Johnson and those kind of guys. We used to record at Pythian Temple, which was an old ballroom on West 70th Street. We did the Bill Haley date, and I put a lot of tape reverb and reverb from the room on that record.

Didn't you do some early overdubbing on it?

Yeah, for the singing. You play from one mono tape to another. You had to have three machines. It was not hard to do, except you had to mix it right, and put down the proper first track.

Were you a rock 'n' roll fan?

I'd like anything that could swing. I didn't go out and dance to that kind of stuff. But it was music with a good beat. All the tricks I used with Louis Jordan, I used with Bill Haley. I used to have to hum the riffs to him. Haley couldn't read music. It was like recording a barbershop quartet or the Mills Brothers, you have to woodshed it and learn it by rote. They'd work out the harmony among themselves. The only difference between Haley and Louis Jordan was the way we did the rhythm. On Jordan we used a perfectly balanced rhythm section from the swing era—either they played shuffle or they played a good 52nd Street kind of beat. But on rock 'n' roll, what Bill did, he had the heavy back beat, which is what Lionel Hampton's band used to have and I'd have to tone it down. Also Buddy Johnson, the drums would bang so loud he would ruin the take or the wax. But with rock 'n' roll at Pythian, you could blow there because there was this big high ceiling, we had drapes hanging from the balconies, and a live wooden floor. Bill had no cutting edge to his voice, and the guys would play so loud—they weren't studio musicians. When they got it down by rote, that thing rocked! It was different from Jordan. He didn't sing like Jordan. It was an adaptation of an old blues, with the lyrics fixed up. We had the guy slap the bass, and the drummer, Billy Gussak, used a heavy back beat with the rim. I had three mikes on the drums. Then I had Billy Williamson, the steel player, hit what I called lightning flashes, where he'd take the steel bar and hit it across the strings of the steel guitar and make it arc. It'd make POW! POW! I'd say, Give me some of those lightning flashes, Billy!

Were you surprised at how "Rock Around the Clock" took off?

When it first came out, it only sold 75,000 to 100,000. Then Jim Meyers, who published the song, got it in the picture *Blackboard Jungle,* and it opened the film during the credits. You have to realize Hollywood soundtracks in those years pinched the top and bottom of the spectrum of sound. Because in a movie house they had giant loudspeakers and amplifiers behind the screen and the people in the front row would break their eardrums if you had all the high frequencies and the bass in full force. Whenever we used to take soundtracks from the film companies in the old days, we'd bring it into the studio to transfer it to tape to put on a master and the engineers would say, Jesus, what a dead-sounding record. But when *Blackboard Jungle* opened they let it go wide open—when that sound hit the kids in the movie houses, it revolutionized film recording.

You also recorded The Weavers, such a seminally important group to the folk scene.

I liked them. I went down to the [Village] Vanguard where they were working. The one who told me to come down was Gordon Jenkins. I went down with him and we signed them right away. In fact, the first recordings I made with them were without Gordon Jenkins.

Were they considered a politically controversial group in those days?

Not until they got written up in *Red Channels*.

What tunes did you do with The Weavers?

I did them all. "Goodnight Irene" we did with an orchestra. Gordon Jenkins wrote the background for it with other singers, because the idea of "Goodnight Irene" was a singalong. The same thing with "On Top of Old Smokey." Pete Seeger always had hootenannies where everybody joined in. It was a classic group, the blend they had. The four voices were distinctive from each other, and the blend was unique. You can recognize them right away. Mainly because of Pete, who can go up so high. Then you had Lee Hays, the bass. Freddy Hellerman doesn't have the sweetest voice in the world. The only one with a great voice is Ronnie Gilbert. We lost them on account of *Red Channels*. It almost broke my heart when the company wouldn't renew their contract. They didn't want to do them because they were, as you say, controversial. I was going to quit my job. Pete Kameron managed The Weavers, and I asked him if I should quit because I thought the company did wrong. He said, "No, you have a family, stay right where you are. We'll be all right." Pete Seeger wouldn't testify. He said he wouldn't do it even if it cost him his livelihood.

Now, to talk about something completely different, you also did Brenda Lee.

I wasn't the main recorder of Brenda, but I did "Sorry." She recorded mostly in Nashville. I used to go to Nashville. But the first Brenda Lee's were done by Owen Bradley and Paul Cohen. I even fixed "Sorry" up and never got credit for it. It was only like half a song. Ronnie Self brought it in and I went over it. I loved the idea of the song, but it was incomplete. It had no middle, it repeated itself. I told him to fix it up and come back. When I came back to do the session, it still wasn't fixed up. So I said, give it to me, and I wrote the line about love being blind, right there in the studio, then we went back to his opening sixteen bars. It was a smash. When I wanted to get credit for the song, Brenda's manager Dub Albritten had already put his name on the song and they wouldn't give it to me. So I blew another song.

Decca did a lot of show people, didn't they?

There was a point at Decca where they wanted to record a lot of theatrical people. That's how Jack Kapp got *The Al Jolson Story*. He had originally recorded Al Jolson on Brunswick—the "Sonny Boy" session. He wanted to record for posterity, so he did Sophie Tucker, Eddie Cantor, contemporaries of his. Kapp was the forerunner of show albums. He signed Ethel Merman. He signed Danny Kaye. He signed these people just *in case* they made a show. We had a big thing with Ethel Merman where we had her signed as an artist, and sure enough she did a show with an Irving Berlin score. RCA Victor got the rights to the show album. We wouldn't release Ethel Merman. I feel Irving Berlin thought that being Irving Berlin, if he asked Kapp to release Ethel Merman from her contract, she could go to RCA and do the album. It so happens that Decca did its own album with Ethel Merman and Gordon Jenkins. Victor had to put out their album with Dinah Shore doing the Ethel Merman part.

What did you do with Danny Kaye?

We did pop things, and things from his films. "Ballin' the Jack" was one of the biggest things he ever did as a single. Another big one was "Anywhere I Wander." He was unbelievable. And he was always on. He would keep you so amused. One time we were recording at Warner Bros. sound stage with Johnny Green, there was a big studio band. Danny and Johnny were very close. In comes Danny Kaye and he does his conducting bit. He takes the baton away from Johnny Green and he proceeds to conduct that orchestra, killed about thirty minutes of our time clowning around. I did Jerry Lewis also. He did one of Jolson's numbers. "Rockabye My Baby." The record sold a million. He was a pretty fair singer. The trouble was Jerry wouldn't stay with the Al Jolson numbers. If he had stayed with the Jolson instead of trying to do Sinatra material we would have had more million-sellers.

You did Sammy Davis, Jr., too.

Yeah. I signed Sammy. He was working at the Riviera with The
Will Mastin Trio, on the other side of the Hudson River near the
bridge. He used to do all those fabulous imitations. He had done
a record for an independent on the Coast and it didn't sell. I went
backstage and said, "I want to sign you for records." He said, "I
don't have my own voice." In other words, he could do Frankie
Laine, Vaughn Monroe, Sinatra, Nat Cole, he was one of the greatest voice impersonators. I said, "Sammy, if you can do anybody in
the world, you can certainly do yourself. All I have to do is get one
hit song from you, then everybody will know your voice." So I did
"Hey There" and it was a big hit, and Sammy was off to the races.

Let's talk about your work with Ella Fitzgerald.

I loved to do commercial things. Norman Granz always used to put
us down when I did a thing like "Cryin' in the Chapel," and "My
Happiness," which was a half a million seller for her. It sold bigger
than her other records. He was trying to get her away from us,
because he was using her at the J.A.T.P. [Jazz at the Philharmonic]
concerts, and we wouldn't release her from her contract. He wanted
to buy her contract, and I said, "I won't even tell the boss about
your offer because I love her just as much as you do, Norman,
forget it!"

How did he finally get her away from you?

Because of *The Benny Goodman Story.* We had the film's soundtrack album, and it had Lionel Hampton on it, and Teddy Wilson
and one other artist that were Norman Granz Verve exclusive
artists. So he wouldn't allow us to put the soundtrack out. Benny
wouldn't redo it. So we compromised and gave Norman Granz Ella
Fitzgerald a year before her contract was up, but she had to make
the twelve sides due us in that last year before she left. So then
he was able to use all the tapes he had made of her singing at his
concerts. It's a crazy world. As long as you know the guy, you're
still in business and you fight the battles. I hated to lose Ella.

How was the A&R man's job different in those days than now?

There are no more real A&R man jobs. In my day the publisher would come up to your office with a songwriter. They would perform the number for you live. Later on they brought demonstration records. I remember Hoagy Carmichael doing "Oh Buttermilk Sky" for me in the office. He was a great demonstrator and artist. He'd stomp it off, beat on the floor with his foot, just like you saw him in the movies—only without the cigarette in his mouth. I said, "Damn, we gotta make that right away. It's a smash hit song." Nobody could sing it better than Hoagy, and we recorded it with Hoagy.

Who have we missed?

Peggy Lee. I did "Lover" with Peggy Lee at Pythian Temple. There was a great Gordon Jenkins arrangement. It was fast, busy. She wanted the drummer to ride the "buzz" cymbal throughout the whole record. I told her I was rejecting the record. That cymbal was ruining the vocal. She said, "This is the third arrangement of 'Lover' and I gotta have this one." Tears came to her eyes because it was a failure. I said, "Don't worry, we'll come back next week and try it again." I re-recorded it, and I got a hold of Gordon and told him to tell the drummer to leave that cymbal out of his case! We redid it, and it's a classic recording. What a gal she is. I even did poetry with her, and she left me for a no-good reason. She was profitable. Her manager, Tom Rockwell from GAC [General Artists Corporation], called, and I'm waiting for the new contract to come in. He says, "She doesn't want to resign with Decca." I said, "We're giving her a better deal for her renewal." He said, "She wants to record for Frank Sinatra. He promised to record with her if she goes to Reprise." His own label. He had to build a legitimate label because the IRS won't recognize your label if you're the only one on it. He was crazy about Peggy. So she left us, and I waited for the record to come out with Frank. She never made a record with Frank that I know about. Not during that period. All he did was conduct an album for her.

Why were you forced to close the store in 1958?

It was a tough time for the Commodore. We were a tiny library-type store. We were forced to move across the street. There was no display room in the new store. LPs came in and you needed space to display the covers. Then [Sam] Goody opened around the corner. Discount stores came in real big. We just couldn't compete. I was hardly in the store at that point. My father became ill. The rent was going up and up. They just couldn't cut it.

And what happened to the Commodore label?

I was saving them for when I lost my job. I knew eventually I'd lose my job. We had leased the masters when we closed the factory and had to pay the creditors. I leased them to Bobby Shad at Mainstream. He made phony stereos out of those beautiful mono recordings I had. He never even cleaned up the masters to get the clicks out. He didn't put them out chronologically. He'd put out the *The Greatest Clarinet Players, 52nd Street Swing*. After all, it's a collector's label. You have to do it chronologically and have it live as history. Which it is. This must have been the end of the fifties. We never collected proper royalties from him, he never gave statements. He subleased them in foreign countries where he had no permission to do it. He was a fast operator. He's an old friend of mine. The only thing good about it was he gave me a cash advance and we were able to go into a Chapter Eleven and pay off the creditors, and come out clean, and not lose my masters. So I made a three-year deal with him to lease the masters. Then I had to let it lie fallow for two, three, or four years, or maybe longer, because I figured he must have dumped a lot of LPs all over the lot, because that's the way he operated. Then I lost my job with Decca in 1971 and I made a deal with Atlantic to put them out on the Atlantic label. They took it because a film company was making *Lady Sings the Blues* and they wanted my Billie Holiday masters. Then they made token pressings of five other albums. After that I had to let it lie fallow again, and then I took it up to Columbia, and they put it out as Commodore on Columbia Special Products. I had just spent two years touring jazz festivals building up a mailing list, because I firmly believe that collectors' records have to be sold mainly through the mail. It's the only way it can be profitable.

You were the originator of jazz reissues. How do you feel about the current active jazz reissue scene?

I've been away from the scene a little bit, but I realize why they're doing it. Now the Blue Notes are coming out and the Savoys, and Fantasy. They'll find out that it can never be gigantic. It's still collectors' items. It's profitable because they don't have to bring the people in the studio again. They have the masters. What I found out was a vacuum is created when a great old master is unavailable. You put it out and there's a few thousand people looking for it. When you satisfy that market, they stop selling and the dealers don't want to sell them because they're moving too slowly. Then you have to wait another five years for the vacuum to be created again. Then the kids go to college and discover jazz, and they start to collect, they go to clubs and hear the new jazz musicians playing. Then some want to go back to the roots. So they'll go back to Commodore and Blue Note, and all those old catalogs.

Why did you leave Decca?

They fired me. They moved to California and wouldn't take me. I had just come with a whole promotion on *Jesus Christ Superstar.* That was my whole thing, doing it in churches. We had put out a single and it was a hit. They thought it was a rock opera, like *Tommy.* I said, "This is not a rock opera, it's a Broadway show that hasn't played Broadway yet, and it'll take special handling. If you call it a rock opera the *Village Voice* and *Rolling Stone* will kill it." I said, "We could present it to the press in the Lutheran Church on 54th and Lexington Avenue." Pastor Gensel was the jazz pastor and knew me. We had Rice and Webber do it in New York. It broke the front page of *Time* magazine. We took the show on the road. We broke that album in one week. Then they fired me right after that. They moved to California and the president of the record division, Mike Maitland, tells me, "We don't need you in California, we got plenty of young guys out there." There had just been an article in *The Wall Street Journal* saying it takes young ears— the young people are running the picture business, the record companies. He said, "You're sixty years old. You're too old, we can't take you to California." I said, "Someone has to take care of things in New York." He said, "Tom Morgan is going to run things here." After my track record and thirty years of my life that was it. I told you I saved Commodore because I knew one day I'd get fired? With corporations, that's what happens.

(October, 1985)

Alfred Lion

During three decades as the main man behind Blue Note, the greatest jazz label of all time, Alfred Lion produced some nine hundred records. Many producers will say they never made a record they didn't like, but perhaps none can say that with such verity as Lion. Inspired by John Hammond's historic From Spirituals to Swing concert in 1938, Lion made his first recordings with two of the stars of that concert, Albert Ammons and Meade Lux Lewis. He established the reputation of his fledgling company with Sidney Bechet's classic "Summertime" and the Port of Harlem Jazzmen quintet sessions. His friend and partner, Francis Wolff, barely made it out of Nazi Germany in 1941 to join him, and aided by their friend and musical advisor, saxophonist Ike Quebec, they began to document the exciting new bebop scene in the mid-forties. Blue Note was the first to record bebop innovator Thelonius Monk, and at the time many thought they were crazy to do so. Lion also made records with Bud Powell, and young Miles Davis. He recognized the genius of Art Blakey, and made all of the great Jazz Messengers records. In 1953 he hooked up with a young man, Rudy Van Gelder, who became the preeminent jazz engineer, but who at that time was recording sessions in his parent's living room in Hackensack, New Jersey. In the fifties and sixties Lion and Blue Note started or nurtured the recording careers of Horace Silver, Herbie Nichols, Lou Donaldson, Clifford Brown, Jimmy Smith, and Kenny Burrell, then Jackie McLean, Wayne Shorter, Herbie Hancock, Freddie Hubbard, Donald Byrd, and Andrew Hill, among many others. He also explored the avant-garde with Ornette Coleman, Eric Dolphy, and Cecil Taylor. Health problems forced Lion to sell out to Liberty in 1966, and Francis Wolff stayed on until his death in 1971. But it was no longer the same great company after Lion left. From the mid-seventies until the early eighties there was sporadic reissue activity. Lion and all jazz fans were cheered in 1985 as Capitol/EMI backed former CBS Records chief Bruce Lundvall, and producer Michael Cuscuna, in an ambitious revitalization of Blue Note— complete with original covers. Here Alfred Lion talks about the past, present, and future of his superb record company.

I know you were first turned on to jazz in Berlin in the twenties, but it was really John Hammond's Spirituals to Swing concert in 1938 that led you to do your first recording.

John Hammond is really responsible for me getting started, without him even knowing it. I want to give him a lot of credit. He's a fabulous man. I met John Hammond in a post office and we started to talk. He told me that he was going to give a big concert at Carnegie Hall, and gave me two tickets. I was very much surprised. I was going to go with my girlfriend, but she couldn't get out of the house. So I went by myself and gave the other ticket to a fellow outside. I listened to the concert and was flabbergasted. John was so far advanced at the time. Albert Ammons. Meade Lux Lewis. Everybody else. I was absolutely gassed. I made up my mind— having been with jazz for years and years, and always having my own ideas of how I would do it—I decided to record Albert Ammons and Meade Lux Lewis.

You'd never recorded before, had you?

No. I just made the decision after I got out of the concert.

Were there already good records on Ammons and Lewis?

There were records, but they were ten-inch records. 78s. They were so short. People could do maybe two or three choruses and the record was over. I always figured, "My gosh, those guys need more room to stretch out!" To come to a climax.

Where did you do the recording?

You know, I can't remember. It was a little studio somewhere on the West Side. One of those little studios where a man was running it by himself. It had a big nice Steinway, though.

How did you approach Ammons and Lewis?

I went to the Cafe Society, where they were playing, and told them I'd like to make some records with them. They were kind of astonished. They said, "Are you going to pay us?" I said, of course. I told them, "You've got time with me, because I really want you to stretch out on those records."

Your intention was just to make private recordings, no?

Yeah. I had no ideas of going into the business yet. I just wanted to make those records.

But you had no studio experience.

Absolutely none. It wasn't a hard session, though. We came in and they tried out the piano, which was nicely in tune. They decided who would be first and who second, when they would play together. I already had the selection in my mind: "The Boogie Woogie Stomp" and "Honky Tonk Train Blues" by Meade. Then we just made the records. It was late afternoon, and the sun was kind of mellow. I remember how it came through the windows. Ammons said to me, "You got a little taste for me?" I said, "Sure, for you I got bourbon and for Meade I got Scotch." Ammons was a rugged personality. He drank bourbon, no water, nothing. They started to play. There was one suggestion I made very early. I told them, "When you play 'The Boogie Woogie Stomp' at Cafe Society you come up to a nice climax, then change to a waltz. That doesn't go together with that hot stuff. No, Albert. Let's leave the waltz out and keep on building to the end." He said, "I dig you, I dig you!" Everything went quietly and nicely. They had their drinks. I loved what I was hearing. When it was finished I paid them right there. Then I was supposed to pay the guy with the studio, and I said, "I may not have enough money." He says, "That's all right. I'll hold the plates for you." I wasn't very flush then. So I kept on with my job for the next two weeks, then I bought my plates back. I listened to the safety plate back home and realized that it should really be heard by the public. So I decided to make some pressings and go into the record business. But I had no idea about how it was done. And what was the competition? Victor. Columbia. Decca. That was all. The three big companies.

What about Commodore.

Yes, Milt Gabler was recording. But at that time it was strictly for their own store. But I had no store. Anyway, I knew I needed a label. So I had a good friend, Martin Craig, who was an artist and sculptor. He lived in Greenwich Village in a real bohemian loft. I asked him to make me a nice label, something modern. And Martin designed the Blue Note label. We started pressing twenty-five or thirty of each of those things the guys made—six twelve-inch records. Now we had to figure out how to get the records out. Milt had his store, and he was an outlet. I went to Milt at his store on 52nd Street, and he was nice and everything. But I'll tell you the

truth, he didn't really want anybody to be competition. You know
what I mean? But they took them because we all were friends. But
with them it was business. They didn't want Blue Notes, they had
the Commodore label. Somehow my records weren't displayed very
prominently. (Laughter.) But my first customer was a music store
in Philadelphia [H. Royer Smith], it was like John Wannamaker,
a classical old store with everything. He said send me three or four
of each.

Did you do mail order also?

Yeah. We tried to make up a little pamphlet. I didn't know about
stores and distributors. There were no distributors except the big
three companies. There was nothing in '39. No books where you
could check out things. Nothing. You had to go by your wits. Slowly
I sold maybe one hundred copies of each. Then I started to send
out review copies to all kinds of papers. I remember I sent it out
to the *Times* at the same time I sent it out to the *Daily Worker,* the
communist paper. There was a fellow on *The New York Times* by
the name of Harold Taubman, a famous classical critic, and he
wrote up some of the records, and so did the *Daily Worker.* People
read it and it got around. Interest started and slowly, slowly it got
a little bit better. I sold a little from my very moderate apartment,
a cold-water flat on the East Side. That's where Blue Note started.
Slowly.

*Among the first really important Blue Note sessions were the Port
of Harlem jazzmen sessions. How did that come about?*

I met Sidney Bechet and made some records with him, like "Summertime." He was on this session, with Frankie Newton, J. C.
Higginbottom, Teddy Bunn, Albert Ammons, Sidney Catlett, and
Johnny Williams. That was my first band session, in 1939. My
feeling for jazz is strongly based on the blues. I loved Ma Rainey,
and Bessie Smith as a kid. I came up with a blues tradition. I think
it's very basic and important in jazz. It's there all the time, I don't
care if they play "out" or "in," you hear the blues. You can hear
it on the Blue Notes especially. I was very much in favor of getting
music that had this kind of feeling. That was in the back of my

mind with the Port of Harlem session. If you listen to it, what it really is is a blues. They're not playing popular songs. It wasn't a traditional New Orleans blues, it was a '39-type New York City blues.

To stimulate this feeling, you scheduled the session for late at night or very early in the morning. Right?

I always liked to record late at night. I never liked to record during the day because I feel better at night, and I know the musicians are more with it at night. They play at night. You get a guy up at eleven in the morning, and rush him to the recording studio at twelve or one o'clock, he isn't quite together yet. His time is night, and not too early, either. These sessions took place after they closed Cafe Society, about two o'clock, two-thirty. When we got to the studio the engineer wasn't there and we were waiting around, and it was a hot night. We started to drink a little bit, and everybody took his shirt off, and we opened the windows. Then the guys started to noodle around and play. Before we knew it we heard some noises outside and the cops came up. We told them we were doing a recording session. They look around and all the guys have their shirts off, and [Big Sid] Catlett was sitting at a typewriter. They were wondering what's going on with all these colored guys. They told us to close the windows. We're finally almost ready to start, and in came a big party, banging on the door. It was a party from Cafe Society. All kinds of people. Swanky. They were out balling, and heard about the session. And who was with them? Billie Holiday. They all came storming in. I got more upset all the time. "Hey, I want to make some records here." We hadn't cut anything. I told them and they all left, and we finally got it going. Billie was kind of surprised that I asked her to leave, too.

I guess that was the session that put Blue Note on the map.

Yes. That was the first band session. It came so beautifully. You can hear it today. I felt it, and I got what I was driving at. There was a man by the name of Max Margolis, and he named some of those records for me. The title "Port of Harlem" was his idea. It was a nice handle.

Let's talk about Bechet. How did your relationship with him begin.

We were living in Berlin. My mother was in the theater set, the movie set. She was like a jet-setter in a way, and she was very good looking. One day she told me she met a very strange man. A gorgeous-looking man with a turban and two big white dogs with him. She said, "We stopped and talked, and he told me he was a musician, and invited me to come see him play." She took me to where Bechet was playing; this was very early, it must have been 1922. I was a kid. It was called the International House or something. On different floors were different types of music. There was an American bar with pictures of cowboys and such. And there was Sidney with his soprano sax, dressed up like a cowboy. So years passed and I went to New York. One day I heard something about Sidney. Somebody tipped me off he was living somewhere uptown around 125th Street. I met him, and he was very nice. I mentioned my mother, but he didn't remember, he'd known so many women in his life. He wasn't doing too much. He'd had a tailor shop. I said let's get something to eat. So we went to an Italian grocery store for some sandwiches. There was a little room behind a display with a couple of tables. So we sit down to eat the sandwiches. We looked around and one of the walls had toilet paper stacked up to the ceiling. He said, "Now we're really in the shithouse." I asked him why he didn't make records. He said he wanted to make "Summertime" for RCA Victor and they told him no. They said, "That's not something for someone of your color." Sidney was a little bit pissed off. I said, "Make it for me, make it for Blue Note."

Was that record recognized right away as the classic that it was?

Yeah. That set off Blue Note in a way, too, because it was so outstanding for that time. It was soprano sax, and had different intonation, everything was classic. He made the soprano sax popular like Jimmy Smith made organ popular. On that cut, Frankie Newton was out in the toilet. Sidney said, "It's okay, I'll make it all by myself." Later on I read that someone had said he must have done that deliberately, he didn't want Newton on that song. No. That was not the case. Sidney was not that kind of person.

Tell me how your friend Francis Wolff came over to join forces with you.

Frank came over in 1941. He lived on the same street in Berlin. A very nice, swanky section. We met on the street and got acquainted. He was always nicely dressed, but not Germanic, he dressed like the Americans, or English. He was also a jazz fan. That was very early. You know you have friends in your life, but maybe only one *friend* really. Frank was that person for me. We were together day and night for almost thirty years. We were friends for fifty years. I left Europe fast when I noticed things were not going the right way. Frank was there until he got caught in this Hitler thing. The Gestapo came to his apartment. I was working feverishly to get Frank out. His brother and sister got out to England. I got him out on the last boat. The Gestapo came to the boat shed as it was leaving and examined everybody again. He thought it was all over, but somehow he was passed and he got to New York.

He had no recording experience either, did he?

No, he was just a record collector. Like me. I had the company started, and had done a few records. We got together right away as partners. He stayed in my place. I was working for an import firm and Frank had no job. He met a woman photographer with a little studio. She shot bar mitzvahs and weddings, and occasionally she sent Frank out to take some pictures. Between the two of us we made a living.

How did you two work together and divide responsibilities?

It came very naturally. I'm the kind of person who likes to run out and do things. I was the horse and he was the cart. All those things that I didn't want to be bothered with, Frank picked up. The business end of it. He did a lot of the detail things like the books, and taxes, and royalty statements. I saw the musicians and tried to get the sessions together. But he wasn't just sitting with the books. Frank was a jazz man. We always discussed things together. And he knew all the musicians, and the musicians all liked him because he was a very soft, nice person. You know how when two people

are together all the time they start to look alike? People used to
ask me about my brother Francis.

*Didn't he work for Milt Gabler for a while when you got drafted
during the war?*

Yes. Gabler wanted to distribute the records and sell them to the
army. When I got out of the army we got together again and started
Blue Note again on a larger, but still small, scale.

*You always seemed to encourage especially free sessions. Do you
think that helped lead to the bebop revolution of the forties?*

The music we recorded in the beginning was a little different
already from the usual. It had a certain flavor that stuck out from
the other things that were more set already. This was in the Swing
Era. That's when I met Ike Quebec. He was playing for Cab
Calloway. It was a popular band with some fabulous musicians. Ike
took Ben Webster's place after he left. I heard him play some solos
and I said, My gosh, the man plays so beautifully, but he gets two
choruses all through the evening, and he's finished. I said to myself
let him stretch out, let him play. I brought him in to Blue Note and
we became very good friends. We had girlfriends together, and
went out to make the scene together. I felt more comfortable
uptown. Anyway, when bebop came along Ike was just as confused
about it, in a way, as lots of other guys. When bebop came along
a lot of famous players stopped and said I can't play like that, I
can't think like that. Ike had open ears and everything, though he
was a member of the old school. But the both of us went to different
sessions. We went often to 52nd Street to see Dizzy, Milt Jackson,
Max Roach, and others, and they were improvising and playing the
new way. It was so free, almost like Dixieland in spontaneity. Of
course they weren't playing Dixieland, but it was a free music. Ike
realized it was a new way of thinking.

*So although you did not immediately understand bebop, because of
your instincts you were receptive to it.*

Yes. Receptive, of course. But I didn't dig it all the way. I'm sorry.
I didn't, and I'm not the only one who didn't. Then I started to

hear. I was always interested in drummers. I love drummers. So when I heard Max Roach I said, "Yeah it's different." But I didn't know what it all was because I'm not a musician, and I could never read a note. All those years I had Blue Note I went by my ears and by my feeling. So I didn't know what they were doing with different timing and so forth, I just heard the *difference.* But it started to click for me. I could hear it better. Ike came to me and said, "There are some good pianists around. Why don't you listen to them?" One was Thelonious Monk, and the other Bud Powell. So Ike and I went to see Monk, and when I heard him I keeled over. I said, "That guy's so different—the compositions, the beat." I loved him, and that's how we started with Monk and bop. Then Bud came up the same way. He was fantastic, and I went for that.

You recorded Monk in the forties before anybody had.

Nobody else had! It was such a struggle because people thought we were nuts. Nobody wanted to buy the records. Except for a few like Ira Gitler. There were other big critics who didn't want to hear about Monk. We couldn't give Monk away. But we made some records. And we made some records again! And I liked it so much we made some records again! The hell with it. I thought, "I've got to get this all down on records." I went uptown to Harlem with the records. All those people who are supposed to be simple, no culture, they said, "Hey, this guy's good." Then he made " 'Round Midnight" and oh boy! They put that on the jukebox. What a personality he was. He played the same way in the forties as he did later on. He never became a big technician on the piano. But he had his own thing. He had twenty-seven compositions, and I wanted to get it all down. We recorded everything he had. He didn't compose very much more after those.

Let's talk about the Blue Note studio sound. How did you come to work with the great engineer, Rudy Van Gelder?

I was introduced to Rudy Van Gelder by a very fine musician named Gil Mellé, who was a baritone horn player. He told me about this man who had a very small studio, but he was a jazz fan and had good ears. Rudy's father and mother had a little house in Hackensack [New Jersey], and he had his studio in the front room.

He was maybe twenty-five. I started to record there. I told him what
I liked to hear in a recording, which was a different sense somehow.
When I listened to some of those commercial records that the big
companies did, the drummer was always put in the back somewhere
and you could hardly hear him. I could never hear the sock cymbal.
Rudy suggested I put a microphone down there. So Rudy was
always working to get what I wanted. He was very good, very
sympathetic, and we worked together constantly. People say the
records made at Van Gelder's have the Blue Note sound.

*He has said that the Rudy Van Gelder sound is really the Alfred
Lion sound.*

He's very modest. It wasn't just the Alfred Lion sound. It was the
combination of the two of us.

Tell me what the studio was like, and how you worked there.

It was small. His equipment was limited, naturally. I don't know
all the technical things. He had a nice, modest console. But he got
good sound out of it. He had a separate booth where he sat behind
the glass, and the musicians played out in the living room. We
moved all the furniture out, of course. I never changed engineers
after that. You know I only had two engineers in the history of Blue
Note. One was at WOR studios on Broadway, where I recorded for
two or three years. There was one engineer there I waited for all
the time, named Doc Hawkins. Then came Rudy after him. After
we recorded in the living room for a little while, he built the big
studio. He built it himself, and it took about a year. Oh my gosh,
did he spend time! But it's a fabulous studio. He had fabulous
equipment that was way out—better than what anyone else had.

How would he work the sessions?

Rudy set up the mikes. He knew what we wanted, with all the
experience we had together. He always improved on it, too. I didn't
interfere with what he was doing. He has a good feeling for jazz,
and when the guys played out there, he knew what to do with them.
Sometimes he'd make the guy sound better than he actually did in

person. He gave them a little extra, which you can do in the studio. The musicians learned from him, too. There's a mike technique. Like you know how a singer holds the mike different ways? So musicians learned that, too, after a while. Rudy's a very knowledge-able and soulful person. He's not like some—you know they call them "needle noses"—they just look at that needle on the meter.

You used him so often, why didn't he become part of Blue Note?

Oh no. He didn't want that. He had his own business there. He didn't want any part of Blue Note in that way. He never wanted to go into the record business. And Rudy made records for all kinds of people: Prestige, Riverside. But somehow that Blue Note sound differed from the Weinstock's (at Prestige). You notice? We had something going between us.

What was the difference between yours and the Prestige stuff?

Maybe Rudy felt that those people were not as interested in what he was doing. They just came in there and said, "Make me a record session." The way they recorded was completely different from the way I did. They'd make a session in three hours, six tunes, let's go, boom boom. Then the next one, next one. Three hours. "We used two rolls of tape? That's fine." They never did playbacks. It takes time. Who's going to waste ten minutes listening back? They didn't want to hear about sitting there for four or six hours, and having a pause and eating a sandwich, and then starting again. I didn't care about overtime. I didn't care about how much money it cost me. I wanted to get the thing right. So I never rushed musicians into the studio and rushed them out. When we went into overtime, which was double for everybody and triple for the leader —forget all this, let's make the records, right? The musicians didn't do it just for the money. They wanted to do it right, too. They listened to the playbacks, and they'd say if something wasn't quite right and go back and do it again. If I wanted to use Herbie Hancock or Monk or whoever, and they weren't available, I'd wait for them. I wouldn't just use someone else. Other people didn't do that.

*That's leads to another question. You developed a sort of company
of players at Blue Note. Did you intentionally try to create a
group of people who would be associated with Blue Note?*

No, I didn't have that thought at all. It came very naturally. I used
the men on the dates that sounded good to me. If the record came
out really well, I'd say, let's make him a leader next time. I'd ask
him if he had any good material. That's how all those guys developed at Blue Note. Herbie Hancock. Wayne Shorter. Lee Morgan.
Now they say I was developing a repertory company, but I didn't
dream this up.

Were they signed to you?

Some were. I couldn't sign them all up because I didn't have
enough money for that. When you have a star like Lee Morgan or
Stanley Turrentine you have to concentrate on them. I could only
have so many people under contract because each one had to be
catered to and developed. I wasn't RCA Victor. But I was all right.
I had enough people, and they were all good ones.

*How important were records as a source of income for jazz
musicians, or did they make most of their money on club dates?*

The records were a nice sideline. Sure, if they play a week in a place
they'd get so much, but by the time they got out most of the money
was already spent. Record dates paid much better than a gig. There
were union minimums, so much for the sidemen and double for the
leader. But we didn't go by that. At times the leader got four times
minimum, and some of the sidemen got more. Still, it wasn't anything like it could cost today. But in those days an LP was $3.75
and today it's $8.50.

What was a good sale for a Blue Note record in the fifties?

If it initially sold 5,000, and then took off to 15,000 or 20,000 or
up to 50,000 or 60,000. Average was maybe 25,000 or 30,000.
But it didn't make any difference to me. I didn't say, "Oh, this guy
sold only so much, and that guy sold better, so let's drop this guy

because he doesn't sell enough." The whole income picture for the company made it good for those who didn't sell so good. I'd stay with them if they were good: Hank Mobley. Jackie McLean—twenty-five years with Blue Note, Horace Silver—thirty years with Blue Note, Lou Donaldson. They stayed with us.

Did you always keep the records in the catalog?

I never cut one out. I kept them going because people always came back to them again. Maybe the big companies can't do that anymore.

Well, you had a core audience of people who would always buy the Blue Notes.

That's interesting. Bruce Lundvall [head of the rejuvenated Blue Note] said when he was a young guy he used to run to New York, whenever they came out, to buy Blue Notes. A woman at the concert [the One Night with Blue Note concert held at Town Hall in New York on February 22, 1985] came up to me. She looked like an old housewife from Connecticut. She said, "Mr. Lion, I want to shake your hand. I bought all your records. I couldn't get them where I was living and I used to come to New York especially to get them."

There was a feel to them. The covers were gorgeous. The pressings were great.

Everything was always quality with Blue Note. I saw to it myself. I got into it so heavily that I had to look at the label copy, the print, how the photos came out, the cover—it had to be right from A to Z. Frank was the same way. There are no mistakes in the liner notes. We read them over three times.

You made nine hundred records, but you never took a producer's credit.

I'll tell you. Whenever you have a Blue Note in your hand, I don't care what it is, and you don't see my name on it, that's the one I made. [Laughter.] Not with the ones I had in the can that were only recently issued, though. Michael Cuscuna put my name on those. I just didn't feel that I should put my name on it. I did my part, but the most important part was the musicians. They're the ones who came and gave their best. Yeah, I was the producer, so what? I always put Frank's name on them for the photos, Reid Miles who was the cover design artist, and Rudy Van Gelder, the recording engineer.

Reid Miles developed the Bauhaus look of the album covers.

Right. I liked that modern look. You can even see it on the very early Blue Notes. Always modern. Reid made most of the Blue Note covers. Reid was also working at CBS. In fact, Bruce Lundvall was president of CBS Records at the time and knew Reid. But Reid told them at CBS that he would continue making covers for us because we gave him that freedom that he couldn't get there. He was not a jazz fan, though. That's funny. He likes classical music and popular singers. But it didn't matter. We'd sit down and I'd tell him, "This is what the music stands for. This is rock house. This is a little softer. This is lyrical." He'd come back with a cover.

Let's talk about some of the artists you've worked with over the years. How about Miles Davis?

He was a teenager when I first met him, and I was very young. I always admired the way he looked. He was always dressed sharp. He was a swinger. And of course I loved his playing. We were friendly right away. In the beginning we made the two records with J. J. Johnson, Art Blakey, and Jackie McLean. By the way, Miles was the one who brought Jackie to the date. The first date Jackie ever made was the Miles date for me. Jackie was just a nice young kid, but Miles knew he had something. Jackie also wrote a tune for the date, "Donna." Miles was still finding his way then, but he always knew what he was doing. There was no wishy-washy stuff with Miles. He was not hard to work with. Later on people say he was very temperamental, but not with me. I remember on that first date, we were talking afterward and Miles said, "You know that Art Blakey, he really kicked everybody's ass."

Let's talk about Art Blakey.

I brought Art Blakey to that date. I first heard Art with Billy
Eckstine's band. There was a disc jockey by the name of Freddie
Robbins who was a good friend of mine. He had an idea that he
wanted to put some jazz on the air, but he didn't know anything
about jazz. So he says "Alfred and Frank, why don't you write a
show for me with your old collector's items." That's how he started
as a jazz disc jockey. Later on he picked up on things very fast and
he had Monk on there and Dizzy Gillespie. He did such a bad job
with Monk, he asked him such a foolish question that Monk got
disgusted and told him off on the air. Freddie was so disturbed he
told me to never bring this guy to the show again! Monk figured
what kind of turkey is this? Anyway, Freddie took me up to some
club in Harlem with his wife to hear Eckstine's band. It was an
afternoon thing. He had some very good soloists, and I heard his
drummer. But I couldn't see him behind the band, and it was dark.
Art was playing this jungle stuff. I asked Billy who he was. He said,
"That's Art Blakey." I said, "I'll remember that name." He hadn't
made any records or anything yet. He had an enormous drive. It
was African! Fire! Daring!

You first brought Art in as a sideman . . .

. . . on the Horace Silver trio date. Horace had four or five numbers.
On the last number I told Horace, "How about a solo for Art
Blakey, and Sabu on the congas?" We put it on that record.
"Message from Kenya" it was called. I think it was 1954. The Jazz
Messengers came together then with Horace and Art.

Horace Silver is great.

Can you imagine an artist staying with one company for thirty
years? All his work is on Blue Note. The saddest thing for me was
when the lights went out for Blue Note, after we sold it. The
company we sold it to didn't know what to do with this stuff. It all
ended up in a warehouse.

How did you get involved with Horace?

He came into the office with a test pressing. We had a little, very unimpressive office with boxes all over the floor. Two rooms on Lexington Avenue. He couldn't have been impressed with the setup. He played it and it sounded good. Here was another original, funky guy. We set up a date that was supposed to be Lou Donaldson's date. For some reason we couldn't make the date with Lou, so we made Horace's trio session. I always appreciated deeply what he did, and I gave him all the freedom he wanted. But we always discussed things together. We listened to all the takes and decided which to put out. Horace became very well known. "Song for My Father" was a big hit. When he played it for me, right away I knew that song should be number one on the LP. There were two takes. I liked the first, but he said he played more piano on the second. I said the first fits the tune better. That's the way we worked together. We listened to each other.

That kind of funky sound was really a precursor of soul music.

Yes. That became soul music. They had something the others did not. I don't want to say the whites are not as good, but I didn't go to the West Coast (style of jazz) music. I stayed with them.

In fact, I think you were one of the first to use the term soul *in an album title.*

Yes, we did. We didn't mince words with our titles. When we brought out Monk, it was "Genius of Modern Music." I didn't give a damn what anybody thought. *I* thought he was the genius of modern music. "The Incredible Jimmy Smith," "The Amazing Bud Powell," "The Eminent Jay Jay Johnson," "The Fabulous Sidney Bechet," and so on.

Let's talk about Herbie Nichols. He was so wonderful, but he died in obscurity. What happened?

It's true. I don't remember how I met him, but he played me what he had in some studio. He asked me which tunes I liked, and I told him I liked them all. It was like Monk. They were colorful, you could draw pictures.

Why did he never record with a full band?

It never got to that. He made one LP for me, and of course it didn't
sell at all. On the second one he did just about all of the rest of
the tunes he had. And he was sick, so he passed away before
anything really happened. It was only a trio. On one record we used
Art and on the other Max Roach. Actually I think Herbie liked
Roach better. Roach was better suited to him. Herbie could have
been one of the great ones. There was another one like that who
was my last protégé—Andrew Hill. Very original. I think he was
right up there with Monk, Bud Powell, Herbie Hancock, anybody.
He made some very good records for me, but then the lights went
out when we sold Blue Note. Andrew Hill didn't come in until the
sixties, and I wasn't able to get all his recordings out before that
like I should. But now I'm doing everything I possibly can to bring
him back with the new Blue Note. I told Bruce Lundvall, that's my
last project.

Staying with the keyboards, let's talk about Jimmy Smith.

He was a completely different thing, but unbelievable. He gassed
me from the minute he sat at that organ. The first thing he played
me was a number called "The Champ." It was a fast blues written
by Dizzy Gillespie, but he played one chorus after another, and the
tempo and the feel—my gosh, who ever heard of an organ like that!
Soul. I remember I got him a job at some little club in the Village.
There was an audition and Miles was there, too. Afterward he said
to me, "Alfred, he's going to make you a lot of money!" Jimmy did
make some money. They played his records on jukeboxes. I tell
you, though, I didn't think in those terms. I didn't care about the
money, I just liked him. I must be a real turkey. [Laughter.]

No. That's how you end up with nine hundred great records.
But when you had a big hit like Jimmy or Lee Morgan's
"Sidewinder," didn't that almost force a change of direction
in the company?

It didn't really change our direction. But the distributors were
leaning heavily on me. "Hey Alfred, get me something like that

again." I thought, ah, those guys are in business. What I would do is maybe try to put something a little more funky into some different sessions and put the funky takes at the beginning of the LPs. But they just came out good like "Sidewinder," and other things. I put a little thought into that. I thought if they like it they'll buy it, and it's good. Maybe it's not the most advanced jazz, but it's good funky music. I thought it would open the door for some artists and bring the buyer in a little faster to dig some more musically advanced takes on the LPs that followed.

Later you got into some pretty far-out stuff. I guess it started with Jackie McLean.

Jackie McLean. Then Cecil Taylor. Andrew Hill. Eric Dolphy. I was never stuck in one groove. I loved it when Michael Jackson came out, and I'm crazy about Prince. They knocked me out.

I see you have two pictures of Michael Jackson on your wall.

I like the way he looks. On one he is all blazing full of life, and on the other he looks like a royal Prince Charming.

Let's talk about McLean's "Destination Out."

He had played a little more "in" before and was always good. Then one day he came in with this, with Grachan Moncur. The sound was Jackie, you couldn't miss him, but he had changed his sound. We just shifted over to it. He had some other older things that hadn't been released yet. But he said, "You know, Alfred, this is a little more up to date, why don't you bring this out first?"

Did you then go out to recruit people playing the new music, like Sam Rivers?

Well, yes. My taste also got modernized. But I still also liked James P. Johnson, or Art Hodes. There was room for everything. It's like Picasso. Is his blue period something you don't want to look at anymore?

Blue Note launched a lot of great musicians in the sixties. Herbie Hancock. Wayne Shorter. Freddie Hubbard. Joe Henderson. Tony Williams. Lee Morgan. Bobby Hutcherson. Grant Green.

That was all the kind of thing where they started as sidemen on some of our sessions and then became leaders. It was a natural evolution.

Many of those people became the vanguard of the fusion movement after they left Blue Note. How do you feel about what they're doing now? What about Hancock's "Rocket?"

To me it's a very inventive little thing. It has a lot of humor and rhythm in it. It's very catchy. There's nothing wrong with it, and it made a lot of money. I don't believe in that selling-out business. An artist doesn't have to constantly be sweating and starving for his art. If he hits on something a little tight and catchy that makes a little money, that doesn't mean he sold out. The tune probably came to him very naturally. It's him. To make a little dough is very important. Herbie will always be a musician of invention and dimension. He never gets boxed up and becomes stale. He is full of life and surprises.

Why did you decide to sell the company in 1966?

My wife saw me getting worse physically. At one point I had a little heart attack, but I didn't pay too much attention. But she was worried. She said, "You've been doing it thirty years, why don't you sell the company?" I didn't want to do it. Another thing was that the company [Liberty Records] came to me and wanted to buy me. I didn't have to go out and look for a buyer. I thought it was the right time to do it. So I did it, and I think my wife was perfectly right. I never really regretted it because when we moved to Mexico I had another heart attack, and I had another one here [in San Diego] late in '85 which was quite bad. I had my time. I did it for thirty years, and I did everything I could and I loved it. Francis stayed on for another two years after I left. Then he dropped out because he had cancer.

How did you feel about the Blue Note material after you and he left?

To tell you the honest truth, it wasn't really Blue Note anymore. They tried to go into big band setups, and big productions. They put huge bands behind Jimmy Smith. You can't do that successfully to jazz so easily.

After that they became more fusion-oriented with Ronnie Laws and Earl Klugh.

It didn't sound anymore like Blue Note. They didn't get very far. Then Bruce Lundvall and Michael Cuscuna, a full jazz-oriented A&R man, saw that Blue Note was really worth bringing back to life, and they got big backing from EMI of England and Capitol in Los Angeles. They decided to really go to town. All right, they bring out reissues because it doesn't cost them as much as producing new things. But I don't think that's a problem. They want to reissue those records because they're really worth bringing out. They're bringing them out with the original covers and liner notes, and it's beautiful. I'm really happy. It's better pressed and the sound's better. The new processing sounds fresher and cleaner.

How do you feel about the new artists they've signed, like Stanley Jordan?

I was the happiest person when they signed up Stanley Jordan. I have never heard a guy on guitar like him. I was fascinated the minute I heard him. I heard him for the first time in a private recital at Capitol in Los Angeles. I couldn't believe my ears. A genius. I was happy that his LP was such a hit. It's already sold 300,000. The first new Blue Note artist, and a hit! Blue Note was always a lucky label for so many. Artists used to say, "When you get to Blue Note they make it happen, they work with you and for you."

Some people don't like the record, though. Some have said that now that Blue Note is back with a splash, instead of Stanley Jordan, there are young, inventive people with new sounds that are still unrecorded or underrecorded.

They did that with Stanley Jordan. He was an unknown playing on the streets. Then they have the "Out of the Blue" guys. That's six young guys who play well, and have a good feeling for jazz. But I feel that I've recorded so many geniuses that it's hard for me to say, "Oh, those guys are the greatest." They're very good, and they will get better and better.

But aren't there Mileses and Coltranes out there who are still unrecorded?

Definitely. Those people are out there.

Is Blue Note still the kind of company that will go out and find them?

I know that they are trying to do that. I think they're looking for people with talent who they can bring out and make stars and leaders—knowing that they're not going to bring the walls down all at once. They are trying it, and they will try more. I think Lundvall is a very honest person. As long as it's possible, he'll try and do that. You know, you can't tell because they're a big company, and you don't know exactly what will happen. But they have good intentions, which they are showing all the time. They want to keep up the quality and artistry of Blue Note. And maybe it doesn't even sell that well, but they want to do it. Now how long they can do it, or will do it, I can't tell. But I think they are doing it. A good example is this new guy Benny Wallace.

But that's a good example of the critics' complaint. It's got Dr. John and Stevie Ray Vaughan on it. They're not really jazz, but they'll sell some records. That's not taking too much of a risk.

But you should hear the record. It's a new way of doing the old stuff. It fits into Blue Note somehow, perfectly. It's like they went through the feeling of older Blue Note material, and then made this up. He is a very intelligent, soulful musician. It's a new interpretation.

To sum up, what is your response to those who say the new Blue Note has not reached out for exciting new things the way you did with Monk in the forties or Cecil Taylor in the sixties?

Well, I'm not so sure about that. They might not want to go out as far as we did fifteen years ago with Cecil Taylor or Ornette Coleman—which was so absolutely radical. I don't know if they want to do this today. I don't know how far they would go out. But they'll go "out" all right. They'll find daring people. I know I went way far out with Coleman and Taylor! I'll tell you the truth, it took me a long time, even after I made those records, to hear what they were doing, and I still need more time today! But I heard it was something different. Some people today can't even tell you what was going on. Now how far Blue Note will go I don't know, but I really feel that they will be advanced. I hope so. I want to say that Bruce and Michael are not just ordinary executives looking to make a fast buck. Bruce is a real musician himself. He goes out at night and listens to all kinds of stuff. They've both got that Blue Note spirit.

(December, 1985)

John Hammond with Bob Dylan, 1962. I said, "I guess you don't want me to pursue this any farther." He said, "John, you can trust me." Famous last words. (Courtesy CBS Records)

With Aretha Franklin, early 1960s. I loved gospel music and I loved jazz, and I knew she was the ideal combination of both. (Courtesy CBS Records)

With Stevie Ray Vaughan, 1984. I like natural sound. I hate overdubbing. Fortunately, in Stevie I have a guy who agrees with me. (Courtesy CBS Records)

In 1985. I started out by being agin the Establishment, and I guess I still am. (Courtesy CBS Records)

Mitch Miller at the controls. You can't define it, but you know when it isn't there. It's the extra adrenalin, the urgency, the interaction. (Courtesy Mitch Miller)

With Tony Bennett, mid-1950s. Tony said, "You want me to do that? Cowboy songs?" (Courtesy Mitch Miller)

With his public, and a rack of Columbia hits, early 1960s. These are the artists that defy whim, fashion —excellence is what accounts for their enduring success. That's what I'm proudest of about my work at Columbia. (Courtesy Mitch Miller)

They gave me complete freedom. I'd stop in and they'd say, "Kid, you got any hits today?" (Courtesy Mitch Miller)

Milt Gabler (kneeling) with Chick Webb on drums, Artie Shaw on clarinet, and Duke Ellington on piano at one of Gabler's free jam sessions at 1780 Broadway, about 1937. You couldn't get in. We'd pack them. (Courtesy Milt Gabler)

**Outside the Commodore Music Shop on 42nd Street, November 1950.
From left to right: father Julius, brother Barney, brother-in-law Jack
Crystal, brother Danny, and Milt.** I told my old man, "We're getting a lot of calls
for records; I think you ought to take them in." We took in records around 1926,
'27. (Courtesy Milt Gabler)

**With Louis Jordan in the
Decca Studio, 1944.** I'd like
anything that could swing. All
the tricks I used with Louis
Jordan, I used with Bill Haley.
(Courtesy Milt Gabler)

Emceeing a jam session at Jimmy Ryan's, 1941. They fired me. They moved to California and the president of the record division tells me, "We don't need you in California, we got plenty of young guys out there." (Courtesy Milt Gabler)

Alfred Lion, 1944. Whenever you have a Blue Note in your hand, I don't care what it is, and you don't see my name on it, that's the one I made. (Courtesy Alfred Lion)

With Sonny Rollins, 1957. The most important part was the musicians. They're the ones who came and gave their best. (Photo by Francis Wolff, courtesy Alfred Lion)

With Stanley Jordan, 1985. The first new Blue Note artist, and a hit! Blue Note was always a lucky label for so many. (Courtesy Alfred Lion)

Jerry Wexler

I n rhythm and blues and soul music, one record
company set the pace and dominated the scene
throughout the fifties and sixties. Atlantic. Jerry
Wexler, record collector, jazz buff, former *Billboard*
magazine writer, was brought into the company by
founder Ahmet Ertegun in the early fifties. At that
time, Wexler had practically no experience making
records, and Ertegun was still wet behind the ears.
But oh, did they learn fast! Wexler and Ertegun
produced some of the greatest stars of the fifties,
including The Drifters, The Coasters, LaVern Baker,
and a host of others. As Ertegun moved more to the
business side, Wexler emerged as the premier producer of black talent in the sixties, especially with
the classic sessions he produced for Ray Charles and
Aretha Franklin. He put the obscure hamlet of Muscle Shoals, Alabama, on the map, and developed the
Memphis-Stax sound through his work with artists
such as Wilson Pickett, Sam and Dave, Solomon
Burke, and Otis Redding. He was responsible for
The Allman Brothers, signed Willie Nelson when
nobody else wanted him, brought Bob Dylan to record in Muscle Shoals, and, after he moved to
Warner Bros. Records in the mid-seventies, signed
such seminal New Wave bands as The B-52's and

The Gang of Four. He is an old-style Jewish hipster who owes his fabulously successful career to his virtually unfailing sense of taste, dedication to quality, and openness to new sounds. Jerry Wexler respects the artists he works with, and most important, he *listens* to them—not just what they sing or play, but what they think. Perhaps that is the key to soul.

As a person who's been involved in making records most of your life, how do you deal with your personal taste versus what you're making?

That's an interesting question. As a fan, you know, when I was a record collector in the thirties, we all ran together. We all knew each other. Of course, John Hammond was the *doyen,* the guy we all looked up to, and he already was making records, and Milt Gabler was making records at Commodore, and Alfred Lion and Frank Wolff at Blue Note, and then a wonderful guy named Dan Qualey who had a label called Solo Art. We all wound up in the record business, and we now had to deal with this question of what I call Column A and Column B. We always imagined that what we recorded would all be from Column A. We'd find something we liked, we would bring it in, we'd record it, then we would promulgate it and offer it to the public, and they would buy it. That was true, up until a certain point. It was true until rock 'n' roll. In the beginning, we loved what we did in the studio. I must say, to this day I've never personally produced anything that I didn't personally like. Never. I've *signed* a lot of acts to Atlantic, and some of them were hugely successful, but not only could I not see myself going into the studio with them, I would never even play their music at home. There came a point, around 1960, '61 or '62, when the crossover happened, when Ahmet Ertegun and I had to stop staying with Column A; we had then to deal with Column A *and* Column B. And then Column A became an indulgence.

Who was in Column A after those years?

After those years? My God. You're talking about all my flops [laughter].

You don't have to say who was in Column B, just some of the people who were in Column A. . . .

Well, Ray Charles and Aretha Franklin, there was no problem about empathizing with them, and loving to work with them, and loving their music. There was no problem with my working with Muscle Shoals or Memphis musicians on anything I ever did in the South. It was always a joy, Muscle Shoals or anything I did in Memphis with Stax or Chips Moman and the American [Studio] band. Whatever we did with King Curtis, or The Sweet Inspirations, or taking Wilson Pickett down to Memphis, or Ronnie Hawkins to Muscle Shoals. Because it was all unadulterated music. The commercial compromise was never programmed into those records. That may sound mealy-mouthed for a producer to say. But I never did it, with Dusty Springfield or whomever I worked with. That doesn't mean I just went careening down the road doing what I wanted. My job was to serve the project.

Was soul music something you consciously sought to develop? Or did it just happen after artists like Ray Charles, Aretha Franklin, Otis Redding, Wilson Pickett, Sam and Dave, and so forth came under the Atlantic umbrella? Certainly the Atlantic artists appeared to be a movement.

This is, like, evolution. It works day to day, and it's not apparent as you're doing it. The categories only emerge in retrospect; you just go along. It's survival from day to day, and survival means growth. Grow or die. Small record companies either grow or they die. You're going with a pulse, a feeling. There are very deep socioeconomic roots and conditioners that have to do with this music, and you don't apprehend them consciously. You react to them. You go into the studio with someone and say, "Play me a song," and say, "Yeah, that feels like something we should do next week." You can't articulate it.

When soul music was at its absolute height, we had this absolutely incredible roster. We had all the Stax people and all the people from the South—Joe Tex and Percy Sledge, and on and on and on—and then the Capricorn operation. It was just like a pantheon of soul artists. And I said to Ahmet one day, "It's going to be over in about a year, all at once, with this whole roster." And you look back and, suddenly, they were obliterated. It all went. Otis Redding died. The other people stopped selling. It just all changed overnight. The Stax operation ground to a shuddering halt, and Rick Hall's Fame Records . . . suddenly it went away, just like that.

When you started as a writer at Billboard, *is it true that you were the one who got them to change the title of the "race" charts to "rhythm and blues" charts?*

Yeah, it was a staff project. I don't know whose idea it was, maybe it was mine, that we needed to upgrade this term that was starting to sound a little perjorative to us. We all chipped in with ideas, and I said, "rhythm and blues," and they said that's it. And as I've said before, it probably should have been rhythm and gospel because rhythm and blues is based far more on gospel changes than on blues changes.

But you still couldn't make that jump from "let's call this rhythm and blues" to "why don't we just put all this together into one big chart."

Oh, we thought about it all the time. But, I am for separate charts. Absolutely. Just as I'm for separate radio stations. There should be specialties, and there should be categories. The idea that there are perjorative racial implications here is utterly silly because it gives you the opportunity to start something. Specialization is marvelous. I'm a great admirer of what we call the ethnic labels today—for want of a better term—of people like Chris Strachwitz at Arhoolie, the Rounder people, and Bruce Iglauer at Alligator Records. What would happen if that was blotted out? Because once this becomes one big gray blob, then you lose it all. So you need the labels that are specialists. Columbia's not going to send teams of people down to Lafayette, Louisiana, to keep up with the latest zydeco trends.

*But at Atlantic didn't you sometimes feel limited when, for
instance, the Chords' "Sh-Boom" or Big Joe Turner's "Shake,
Rattle and Roll" was a rhythm and blues hit, but never had the
chance to cross over and become a nationwide pop hit? They
should have been because they were better songs.*

That's right. But the world was not ready.

*But don't you think having those separate charts kind of aided
that?*

Not at all. The charts only reflected the situation. The records were
exposed. We were making black records, with black musicians and
black singers for black buyers. It never occurred to us in the
beginning that there were crossover possibilities. Because if there
were we probably would not have gone into that business. The only
reason we could survive was because we were specialists. Because
we could do it better than Columbia records or Victor, because we
paid attention to it. Decca did a terrific job because Milt Gabler was
there and he knew what to do with Louis Jordan. They opened the
door for us, but we had to specialize. Once you specialize, those
records have to be made that way. They have to be merchandised
to people who will buy them. The salesman had to carry them in
a briefcase down to a shoeshine parlor someplace in Biloxi that also
had some records in it. That's how it was done. You had to stigmatize the music, and call it what it was, otherwise it would never have
seen the daylight. It would have been lost—blotted out by the
Ames Brothers and Patti Page. So it's fine to specialize. Our records
could not be played on the white radio, not because of charts or
anything, or because of terminology, but white radio—which
means the whole big panorama, the whole big scene—programs for
results. It programs for advertising. They had to watch their customers, the advertising agencies, or the client. They could not put
this music on their radio at this time. But it *could* go on another
kind of radio, that which was rhythm and blues. Separateness. You
have to have it. Otherwise you lose the wellsprings of this music.

   Let me say one more thing about this. When we saw that there
were possibilities of crossover, we were damn mad when we
couldn't get our records on white radio, once we became aware of

that. Once we found out from our distributors in the late fifties
. . . It started in the South, everything starts in the South—white
Southern people started buying our records, the beach records in
the Carolinas, all of those crazed young men studying drinking at
the University of Virginia who were listening to Gene Nobles on
WLAC, that's what's broke it open—Southern people. And when
our distributors in Charlotte would call us and say "Hey, I'm
getting calls from white one-stops in white locations for this new
LaVern Baker record," this was purely amazing to us. But we very
soon accommodated to the notion. Then we wanted it all, and we
couldn't have it. It took a long, long time dealing with black music.
We never really made it in England, and Motown did. And that was
another thing, that was always a source of discomfort and annoy-
ance. Otis Redding broke through. Aretha Franklin never really
made it in England. Ray Charles never made it in England. Wilson
Pickett never made it in England.

Why not?

Because of the sensibility of the music. The Motown music, just as
it went directly to white American teenagers, Motown was not
beamed to black people.

Do you consider Motown soul music?

Some of it was. Some of it wasn't. Marvin Gaye. The sax player,
Junior Walker. Martha Reeves. The Temptations. And a lot of it
was just teenage romance magazine lyrics, but done with very
wonderful music production. And of course it had that 4/4 beat.
It always had four beats to the measure. We only had two beats
to the measure. We had the backbeat. It was a whole different
music.

*Did that bother you that Motown's people could cross over and
your people couldn't?*

It didn't bother me that *they* could cross over. I was glad to see that
they could cross over. It bothered me that *we* couldn't.

How did you get together with Ahmet and Herb Abramson at Atlantic?

Ahmet and Herb started the company in about 1949. Max Silverman, of Waxy Maxy's in Washington, D.C., was in on the formation of the company, and so was a man named Jerry Blaine, a record distributor who owned Jubilee Records. But as it turned out only Ahmet and Herb were really involved in the original formulation of the company. Most of the money was put up by a Turkish dentist in Washington whom Ahmet knew. The father of Ahmet and his brother Nesuhi was the Turkish ambassador to the United States. They lived in the embassy and had a good time. Herb Abramson was sending jazz groups down, people like Ben Webster and I don't know who all. They had jam sessions at the embassy. So, in 1952, we were friends, we all knew each other, all people who collected. I was working for a music publisher at the time and they asked me to come over and go to work.

As a producer?

Not as a producer, as an anything. Run the music-publishing company, do administrative work in the office. It wasn't specified as to whether I'd be producing records or not. I said, "No, I've got a job." I said, "If you want me to come over, I want to be a partner." I had the effrontery, and they thought that was hilarious, but a year later, after they'd picked themselves up from rolling on the floor, they said, "Come over and you can buy a piece of the pie." I said, "That's fine." So I came in and I became a stockholder in Atlantic Records. I became a partner.

What was the state of the company at that point?

Herb Abramson was leaving. He owed the army reserve some time. He had gotten some education on army time and so on, and he had to go to Europe for eighteen months or something. They thought I'd be a good stabilizing, balancing influence there. I started making records immediately, with Ahmet; Nesuhi wasn't there yet.

Had you ever made a record before?

Yeah, I'd made one or two records. I'd made some demos, working
for a publisher. I'd produced a session with Woody Herman, oddly
enough. A friend of mine named Howie Richmond was a music
publisher. At that time bands like Woody Herman's were not
getting contracts with record labels. So Howie financed a date with
Woody Herman to plug a couple of his tunes. I don't even have a
copy of that record today. I wish I knew how it sounds. That was
my first actual recording session of a commercial record, although
it was not a very commercial venture.

Was Ahmet, by this point, a pretty seasoned producer?

There were no seasoned producers at this time. Nobody really knew
how to make records. What you'd do is you'd express your taste,
and it worked pretty well. We kept making records until we learned
how. I don't know exactly how many years it took, but it took a
long time.

*How did you and Ahmet divide the responsibilities and duties and
so forth?*

We didn't. We each did everything. If there was a point of difference, we'd proceed sort of Socratically. We'd always reach some
conclusion. We weren't always 100 percent in agreement, but we
were amazingly accommodating to each other, and it worked. And
we had a very good team. We had Tom Dowd as our engineer, and
Tom was so outstanding that I'm a technological cripple to this day.
I never had to bother to learn anything about the board or microphones.

What would you tell Dowd?

Everything that needed to be elucidated about a record. Such as:
"Watch it, in three bars we've got a sax solo coming up, so watch
the pot and be ready to bring it up." Such as: "Brighten the
cymbals, because we're losing them in the bridge." Everything that
had to do with sound and feeling. That was working with Tom on

the board. Then there was what needed doing out in the studio, when it came to microphone placements and things like that. I'd know what I wanted to hear. I just didn't know how to get it. I just said, "Tom, do that," and he did it. I didn't *always* say, "Tommy, do that." I'd say, "Tommy, what's good here?" Tom was also a producer masquerading as an engineer for many years. Then there was the matter of directing the music, aside from the sound. Remember, there are people playing music out in the room, and it's coming over wires and onto a piece of tape.

Who picked the songs?

Ahmet and I did, of course with the approval, input, and cooperation of the artist. Now, some artists picked more songs than others, some artists didn't pick any. Aretha Franklin picked most of her songs, maybe as much as 60 percent to 75 percent. Ray Charles wound up picking 100 percent of his songs, and wrote them all after a certain period. Later on, when rock 'n' roll became very crystallized, a great deal was attached to the idea of people who could write their own songs. I don't think that is as important as it was made out to be, as it came to be in the rock 'n' roll era. Of course, it's great when you get a superb artist like Ray Charles who wrote all of his own songs while he was at Atlantic. The minute he left us, I don't think he ever wrote another song again, but his career went on and up, without him writing his own songs. If you think of the really high points in American music, you want to talk about Bing Crosby, Al Jolson, and Sophie Tucker, and on the stage, Ethel Merman. There were songwriters like Johnny Mercer and Harold Arlen writing songs for singers like Bing Crosby and Al Jolson and Lena Horne. What's wrong with that? I see nothing wrong with that, providing you're using great entertainers.

You also had a house arranger working at Atlantic.

We had Jesse Stone, who is an incredible man. He also wrote great songs. He wrote "Shake, Rattle and Roll" and "Smack Dab in the Middle." He wrote under two names: Charles Calhoun and Jesse Stone. He had a BMI name and an ASCAP name.

Is that why they did that?

Sure. Jesse was one of the great figures of American music. He came out of the Kansas City area, the Southwest, Oklahoma or Kansas. He was very close to the era of Jelly Roll Morton. Jelly Roll was one of the first people to begin arranging music, and Jesse was right there, very close in time to Jelly Roll. Jesse was one of the people who developed the arranging of the jazz orchestra. He brought that over into rhythm and blues; it was just a natural.

There was also Arif Mardin.

Well, Arif came later. That was in the sixties. He was a "hey, you" in the studio. He started doing little horn sketches and one thing led to another. He's developed into one of the greats in the industry.

I want to get a little deeper into this working relationship between you and Ahmet and Tom Dowd and Jesse and, later, Arif. Can you explain how a session would come together?

Let's take a Drifters' date, for example. The Drifters' first date is a good example because it was very early. When Clyde McPhatter came in, he assembled a group around him. "Money Honey" was one of the songs on that first date, and it was written by Jesse Stone. Some of the other songs on that date came in from other people, and maybe Clyde McPhatter brought in a song or two. We rehearsed. That was unheard of; nobody else was doing that. We would rehearse for weeks. We would line out the arrangements with Clyde and Jesse Stone there. We'd work out the routine, and actually pick the key, get the layout. We'd rehearse the song with the group and the piano player, maybe it'd be Jesse or somebody in the group. We'd all sit around chipping in with ideas and notions for songs, arrangements, tempos, the whole thing. Then we'd bring the group back again and drill it and drill it. Then we'd go into the studio to record it. That's why Atlantic Records sound so good today. They're in tune and they're in time. I know it sounds like braggadocio, but you check them out. Compare them with some of the records from the golden age of a cappella that were being made at the same time.

And they sounded so good because you rehearsed?

Yeah. Either it's because we rehearsed or because once we got in
the studio, we wouldn't let anything get by, because we *heard* it
when it was wrong. A lot of records were being made at that time,
but though the people sitting in the booth didn't hear what the hell
was going on, they were hits anyhow.

Is that still happening?

Not so much anymore. Today the state of the art is such, both
technically and production-wise, that a lot of people now know what
goes into a phonograph record.

*I've also heard you say your philosophy of making records is
"miss 'em quick."*

Oh yeah. That means you don't spend endless time agonizing, and
hundreds of thousands of dollars, taking a year to make a record.
Like The Rolling Stones said, "It's only rock 'n' roll."

*Let's expand on your philosophy. How could you, in the fifties and
sixties, make those classic records in a day or two, when now
you've got people spending a year on a record?*

I can't understand people spending a year on a record. I take three
to four days, that's it, to do the tracks for an album. A lot of agony
can start after the basic tracks if you have problems with the singer,
if you don't know what sweetening you want, if there's a lot of
"Hamlet" over the backing and filling of these horns. Within this
simplistic restriction, there's room for fine-tuning a lot of individual
variations. Some artists have to work slowly and more molecularly.
Some, at times, have to go through the whole exercise, and you
have to respect that.

Who worked that way?

Well, I'll tell you who didn't work that way. Aretha Franklin, Ray
Charles, Bob Dylan, Wilson Pickett. I did a nice record with a
group called The Sanford-Townsend Band, *Smoke from a Distant*

Fire. I put a lot of time in. It took a month to make that record, and that's a lot for me. But I don't think there was a lot of wasted time, any indulgence. See, when you're dealing with a rock 'n' roll group, it's a different story. Think about it. When you're dealing with a singer like an Aretha Franklin, with a backup band of the best studio musicians, you get right down to it pretty quick. You grab it while the bloom is on. It's not a question of people who are rudimentary players hoping to play into a groove, and hoping to learn their instruments while they're taping. In a lot of rock 'n' roll groups, people are still trying to master their instruments. And I'm no good with groups like that because I'm not a musician. I can't tell a guitarist what he's doing wrong. I can't put my fingers on the frets and say, "Do this." But if I've got Cornell Dupree or Hugh McCracken or, God bless him, Duane Allman, I just say what I want to hear and that's it. So it's much quicker when you work with studio musicians and a singer.

You don't have to deal with four or five different egos, either.

You don't have to deal with four or five different egos, and you don't have to deal with people who always feel, you know, "Learn while you earn." That's not to say that there aren't many rock 'n' roll groups composed of master musicians. It took a long time for rock 'n' roll to evolve into a situation like that.

What are the limitations of a record producer?

Ahmet Ertegun has a great expression about that, about record producers. He's very blasé about record producers, and I think it's really fantastic. He said, "Show me a great artist in the studio, and I'll show you a great record producer in the booth." There's a whole lot to that.

Thinking about the great sessions you've been involved with, what was your input as a producer? What did you do for these people?

I got excited. I went out there and I did The Jerk and The Monkey and The Boogaloo, and I danced the groove for the drummer. And I told the artist a story to create the attitude. Then I would sing the song to the artist and say, "Phrase it like this, the accent goes here." I've read a lot of interviews with a lot of producers, and there's a lot of talk about who programs the Linn drum machine, and a lot about the proper use of synthesizers, but I haven't seen a whole lot about singing in many of these pieces. And finally what this is all about is a person and a song. A singer and a song, that never changes. In my opinion, not enough attention is paid in a lot of records to what the singer is doing out there. To help the singer to find . . . to take her best shot. I say "her" because I love to work with females.

I would talk the lyrics, because good music phrasing is conversational. Just by talking and singing to them I could say, "This is the way you should go." Attitude—singing has to do with who maintains their attitudes and phrasing. And attitude can be any one of a million things; it depends what the song calls for. It depends what the music is saying at the time. For instance, if I was working with The Staple Singers I might go to Mavis Staples and put one hand on my hip and twitch my butt and say, "Get sassy now, sweetie, like this." Or, "This is dejection." Or, "This is triumph. This is misery: You just cooked a dinner and now it's four o'clock in the morning and the beans and ham hocks are cold on the stove. Your man hasn't come home. And you've called seven bars, and he ain't there. And now you're ready to go out to an after-hours joint, and fuck him. That's what I want to hear in this song." You have to run librettos and stories. The singer may have an idea that's good, but you may have an idea that better amplifies and expands on what the singer says.

So in addition to being the central reference point, you have to be the artists' inspiration.

Yeah. The players have to feel good, they have to be fired up, and you have to grab it at the earliest possible take. Sometimes maybe the sixty-seventh take becomes a hit, but it's much better if it's the fourth take—for all concerned, including the finances. It's better for the singer. It's better for the record if you get it early.

What you say is so simple, so basic. Sure, there ought to be somebody there inspiring the artists, but that's not what most

people think about, and I'll bet you that's not even what most
record producers think about when they think of their role.

The producers that I respect the most are producers who think
about that, like Jerry Leiber and Mike Stoller, Bob Crewe, Phil
Ramone. Of course, Ahmet Ertegun thinks the same way. Tom
Dowd thinks that way, and so does Richard Perry. They know
there's a breathing body in the booth, and they know how to
communicate to get the best out of the singer. And you also have
to have the brass balls and the effrontery to go up to the singer and
sing the song and say, "Sing it like this, the line starts with this
accent, the 'and' beat after 'one.' "

I suppose that could be abused and has been abused. I think about
that scene in the Buddy Holly movie where Buddy's in Nashville,
and he's trying to do his thing, and there's some asshole in the
booth who's telling him, "No, man, that's not the way to do it,
this is the way to do it." I suppose that's the bad side of that
philosophy of producing. No?

Well, the Buddy Holly thing is very complicated. Norman Petty was
left out of that movie. Norman Petty had so much more to do with
Buddy Holly than people imagine. In the long run, it's like the
question of who does what to whom in bed. Nobody knows. You've
got to be under the bed with a tape machine. Nobody knows what
goes on at a record session unless you're sitting there. And the fact
is that most record producers don't have any idea how other record
producers work because they're not there when it happens. In the
long run, what emerges is that the credit accrues to the whole team.
The question is always going on among the people who have nothing else to do, because basically they're not employed or they don't
have any projects; they sit around and say, "Now over at this
company, who's the man? Who really is making this record?" All
this speculation, "Well, shit, man, the engineer, he's the one who
gets it done. Those schmucks, those ones with the vests and the
briefcases don't. . . ." Nobody knows.

Certainly, I would assume, you decry the tendency to elevate star
record producers?

I do. The final litmus test is durability. How long have they run
with their thing? Five years is a long time, ten years is incredible,
and beyond that is unbelievable.

*Another aspect of the producer's function is to decide where to
record. What went into your decision to do it in New York or
Muscle Shoals or Miami or Los Angeles?*

It's a combination of . . . You computerize it, you put all the factors
together and ask, "What's the best place?" It depends on the
singer, the background musicians, the songs, what sound you're
trying to get. It usually runs in cycles. People get addicted; they
get comfortable recording in certain places and then move on to
other places. People criticized me for staying at Muscle Shoals for
too long. Maybe they're right, maybe they're wrong. I don't know.
But I got very comfortable there. It's what's coming through to you
in the control room. Where you start feeling it the best is where
you want to go. In the case of Muscle Shoals, it was not the studio,
it was the players. They did many, many different things for me
and for themselves and for other people that were exceptional. We
did Willie Nelson there. Aretha Franklin, Bob Dylan, Wilson Pickett. And the same four people played all that music with different
lead guitarists, sometimes somebody from Muscle Shoals, or maybe
I'd bring a guitarist.
    Also, there's the fact that I like to be away. I don't like to be
home when I'm recording. The funny thing is, I heard Manfred
Eicher say the same thing about ECM, which is a whole different
thing. He recorded in Norway, in Sweden, someplace very close to
the Arctic Circle, where it's very cold. He does all his recording far
from his home in Munich. I don't like to come back to my home
environment when I'm making a record. I want to be, like, in
retreat—in the Catholic sense, in the James Joyce sense. I want to
be away from everything that I know. Because you're concentrated
and relaxed at the same time. I don't want any interference,
whether social or domestic, I just want to be making a record. And
I'd rather be away from any regular place, and Muscle Shoals had
all of these charms for me. After you make the record, you go to
wherever you're staying—I stayed with Barry Beckett, one of the
musicians—and you play the tapes that you'd made all day, and

you analyze them, and you get ready for the next day, and that's really fine. I don't need to boogie down, you know, to get rid of my tensions when I'm making a record. I don't want to go out. I don't want to go to a movie afterward.

How long would you usually stay in Muscle Shoals?

Two to three weeks. Then, maybe I'd come back one or two times to sweeten it and mix it.

Did you mix all the Muscle Shoals stuff in Muscle Shoals?

No. It's very interesting. I lost interest in mixing records way, way back. I used to let Arif Mardin and Tommy Dowd mix the records that I made. They would present them to me for comments, and I would comment, and they would make some small change that I asked for. I pretty much knew what sound I wanted. I knew what was right. But when computerized mixing came in, I got very excited, and now I mix records again. I love it. Mixing used to bore me.

What's the difference?

The way I work, and the way a lot of producers do, I imagine, is when it's time to mix the record, you let the engineer make the basic setup. That takes anywhere from three to five hours. Then you get a phone call: "I've got something for you to listen to." From there you take it, and adjust it, and fine-tune it to what you want. The basic setup is always something good enough to begin on. It's never horrendously off the mark. Maybe sometimes you say, "I can't deal with this." But ninety-nine out of one hundred times, it's your starting point, and it's a good one. But then it becomes a matter of your discretion, and your taste, where you want to take it from there. Now, you've always got it, because it's computerized, and there it is. It's in the tape, and you can go back to it, and back to it. If you want to redo background vocals or a guitar lead or a synthesizer part, the keyboard, anything, you've got it without disturbing the whole record. In retrospect, there are some records I'd like to remix.

Which ones would you like to go back to and improve?

Some Aretha Franklin records. I would love to have more voice and less strings.

On some of the later ones?

I don't even talk about some of the later ones [laughter]. I think that I was a little lax with Aretha Franklin.

You think her recordings could have been better?

Better mixed, with more voice and less background.

You're talking about the classic Aretha Franklin sides?

Well, no, not the *classic* Aretha Franklin sides [laughter]. But there are a lot of good ones that aren't classics, a lot of great ones.

You know, some people say she peaked too early.

Oh, that's wonderful! Saying that is like saying . . .

They say that she couldn't live up to those early ones. That those early ones were so great . . .

That's almost like a computerized prizefight between Jack Johnson and Marciano. You're playing with immutable facts—there it is, that's what it is. Peaking too early . . . It's never too soon to get great [laughter].

You said Ray Charles taught you a lot. In what way, and what was it like working with him?

It took a while for Ray Charles to crystalize, to become Ray Charles —until about 1954, '55, when he had his own band. It was a seven-piece band, four horns and three rhythm, no guitar. We did "I Got a Woman" and other incredible records. Before that, he worked the way our other singers did. He had an arranger, and he had sidemen. He did very good records. Songs like "Sinner's Prayer," "Losing Hand," "It Should Have Been Me," those were arranged records, studio records. Before he came to us, his big influences were Charles Brown, Nat Cole, Guitar Slim. Then he found his own voice, in the sense of his own persona. When he put this band together, he did it all himself. It used all his own ideas, and they started playing his arrangements. He would dictate them to someone like Hank Crawford, who would write them out. They are marvelous.

How did you work with Ray? Obviously, this was a unique individual who knew exactly what he wanted.

He sure did. With Ray, what would happen is he would call the office. He might get a hold of me or Ahmet and say, "Well, I'll be in on such-and-such a day." It would be like twenty-five days from that date, and he'd say, "I got some tunes and I'd like to cut them. Could you get me some background singers? Get me three girls." Or, "Get me a good, authentic Latin conga player." Once he even asked for a pedal steel guitar, when he was recording "I'm Movin' On," that Hank Snow thing. Ray would come in and he'd have the songs and the arrangements. We'd just open up the mikes, and there was very little for us to do except pay attention. The records were mixed on the fly, all mono. No remixing to do, no sweetening, because there it was. It was done. He did the whole thing.

Did you have to do for him what you described earlier, get him in the right mood?

Absolutely not. Ray Charles and Aretha Franklin are two people who I could never speak to about singing. With Aretha I probably had more of an input on the arrangements and the music part of it, but very little on the vocalizing. And with Ray, nothing. Maybe "faster" or "slower, Ray." [Laughter.]

What were your favorite sessions with Ray Charles?

Oh God, there were so many. "What'd I Say" was tremendous, it was one of the last ones. I loved the out-of-town sessions, the one

at WGST, the Georgia Tech radio station in Atlanta, where we cut
"I Got a Woman." They didn't know how to cut records there, and
there was no control room. We were in the news room, and we had
to stop the session every half hour while they gave the news
[laughter].

Why did you cut it there?

Because that's where Ray was at the time, with his band.

There weren't any better recording facilities available?

No. There were no recording studios around the country in those
days. You went to a radio station. We went to a radio station in
Miami with Ray to cut "This Little Girl of Mine" the next year.
Then we went to WDSU in New Orleans, which I think was Loyola
University's radio station. And we cut a big one, "Don't You
Know." There was another session that I enjoyed with Ray called
"Ain't That Love," which started with a tambourine lick. He
brought these church ladies up there to play tambourine, and he
kept firing one tambourine player after another. So I grabbed a
tambourine. He says, "Who's doin' that?" I said, "Me." He says,
"Do it." [Laughter.] So I actually had the strain of starting the
record, initiating the groove by playing four bars of tambourine
unaccompanied.

A little Jewish soul.

Yeah.

Was he being advised to leave Atlantic for another label?

He was, and maybe his advisers had something to gain by the move.
Who knows? ABC looked like a more eclectic record company. We
were just a funky little R&B company. ABC was connected to a
television network, presumably to Hollywood and pop radio. All
the goodies that a rhythm and blues singer . . . He thought he was
expanding his horizons.

Did that really hurt, when artists left you after you had worked so hard to nurture their careers?

Well . . . Bobby Darin and Ray Charles left us the same year. You can imagine, I had a lot of white nights, you know, looking at the ceiling.

Did you think that was going to seriously affect your company?

Seriously? I almost went crazy. I mean, I figured there was very little chance to survive after that. How do you lose Bobby Darin and Ray Charles in one year? And go on?

Did you consciously think about having to do something pretty soon to shore yourselves up?

We thought about that every day, no matter what. We *always* ran scared. We *always* ran worried about what's going to happen tomorrow. And we always wanted to get the best singers we could.

How did a performer like Bobby Darin end up on Atlantic, an almost all-black record company?

He was our first white artist. He was a singer looking for a gig, and he played the piano like Ray Charles and he was very soulful.

Was he unknown at the time?

Oh yeah. He had made some records for Decca, five or six records that flopped. Herb Abramson brought him in to Atlantic. (Herb had come back from the army.) We started the Atco label for Herb to administer. So he signed Bobby Darin to Atco. And nothing happened, but we liked Bobby a lot. All of us did. His manager at the time was Donny Kirshner, who was also managing Connie Francis. His first hit was "Splish Splash," which Ahmet produced. Ahmet had a lot of belief in the song. I thought it was an unspeakable piece of doggerel [laughter]. Ahmet said, "This is going to make it. This is going to go." And it did.

Did you work on "Mack the Knife"?

No, Ahmet worked on that. We all did some sessions with Bobby, but mainly it was Ahmet. "Mack the Knife" was a big break-through, and won the first Grammy for best pop record of the year. So Ahmet Ertegun's is the first producer's Grammy. Darin was wonderful. On a nightclub floor he was unbelievable, the best. I mean, even Frank Sinatra would have to worry about Bobby Darin when he was out there on the nightclub floor.

Let's go on to another favorite of yours, Clyde McPhatter and The Drifters.

Ahmet always loved The Dominoes. "Have Mercy Baby" with Clyde McPhatter, he loved that voice. And Billy Ward used to run The Dominoes like a paramilitary organization. Like James Brown. Fines for unshined shoes, missing a beat or dropping a note, or whatever. So Ahmet went to Birdland one night to see The Dominoes, and he saw that Clyde McPhatter wasn't with the group. So he went backstage to see Billy Ward, and he said, "Where's Clyde?" Billy said, "I fired his ass." Ahmet went up-town like a shot, found Clyde McPhatter and signed him up. The first problem was the name: Clyde McPhatter and The Drifters. It sounds like a cowboy group. But Clyde wouldn't let us change his name. He was right; names don't matter. Then, as I mentioned before, to do "Money, Honey" we got this gospel group. We did the session with a lot of rehearsal, and after we heard it we didn't like it. So we called Clyde in and we canned the record. Clyde went and got a new group. This is when he got the good group that had the Thrasher brothers and Bill Pinkney. We redid the whole session, because we didn't like the groove. That first thing stayed in the can, and the record that came out of "Money, Honey" was a hit for Clyde. Not a crossover hit, but a rhythm-and-blues hit.

I remember reading that you thought you and Phil Spector blew the original version of "Twist and Shout," that The Isley Brothers' version done with Bert Berns was much better.

That's right. Oh boy, where do we start with this one? Phil came to New York, and Leiber and Stoller were told to kind of watch out for him. He came to us and went on Atlantic's payroll, working for me and Ahmet in the studio. He never made a hit. One of the projects was to record "Twist and Shout," which Bert Berns had brought to me with a duo called Derek and Howard. They were otherwise known as The Pearls. And we just butchered it. Bert Berns was sitting in the booth and he wasn't allowed to say anything.

What was Bert's position at the time?

He was a songwriter. I had not yet realized his production ability. (Shortly thereafter, I took him in with me to coproduce Solomon Burke. One thing led to another and Bert stepped out; though later he did very well as the producer for Van Morrison, Neil Diamond, The McCoys, and others.) I want to tell you that Phil Spector has all my respect and admiration. He is really one of the great people in the business, but this particular time there was nothing coming.

What other artists was Spector working with at Atlantic?

Gee, I can't even remember. It was a string of flops. As soon as he left us he went to work for Big Top records, which was owned by Hill and Range, and he did nothing but cut hits—Ray Peterson, Don & Juan, "Lavender Blue." Then he was home free. At Atlantic, it was just one of those things.

What happened to "Twist and Shout"? It's such a great tune.

You mean, how did we make a bad record out of it? Easy. There's a million ways to make a bad record, but only one way to make a good one, and we didn't find the one way.

Can you describe the old Atlantic studio at 234 West 56th Street?

Over Patsy's restaurant. It had the slowest elevator in the East; people used to be scared to get on that thing. The room was about the size of this living room, about twenty by fifteen feet, maybe

twenty by eighteen or twenty-five by twenty. It was our office.
Ahmet and I had two desks that were sort of catty-corner to each
other. We used to do three to four sessions a week, because, when
you come to think of it, there were no albums in those days. We
had a big roster, and what we'd do is record three or four sides by
a singer, then put it away, and that would be two singles. We used
to put out four records every three weeks. There was a constant
demand. We didn't have any producers or anything. We had to
make all the records ourselves, three or four nights a week. The
idea was, you had to get four sides done in three hours because of
union regulations, and we did. Mono. No remixing. When we had
a session we'd push one desk against the wall, and we'd lift the
other desk and put it on top. Then Tom Dowd would come out and
put out the camp chairs—the folding chairs—for the musicians,
and set up the mikes. We had a tiny control room, which was also
the place where we used to store our reference records. It couldn't
have been more than three feet wide. We had a little mono, four-
channel mixer. Two people could sit and one could stand. Tommy
would sit and either Ahmet or I would sit next to him. The other
person would stand behind him. We cut some good records there,
"What'd I Say," "Shake, Rattle and Roll." By 1958 we had the
first eight-track Ampex that was used commercially by a record
company. It was the third one that Ampex put out. The first one
Les Paul had, and he took it to his house in Bucks County [Pennsyl-
vania], and that's where he made all his terrific records with his
wife—"How High the Moon" and all those things. Number two
was owned by a man named Jiggs Carroll, who was Mitch Miller's
contractor and concertmaster. Jiggs used to live in the Hotel Wood-
ward, a funky hotel on 54th and Broadway. He kept this eight-
track in his room, and he played with it. The third one we had,
which was bought at the instigation of Tom Dowd. As a con-
sequence, everything in the Atlantic catalog from 1958 on is in
true stereo.

Why didn't everybody go out and buy an Ampex?

I don't know. Why didn't everybody record Ray Charles [laugh-
ter]?

Wasn't this a revolutionary new technology? I mean, the possibilities . . .

Multitrack recording, we were three to four years ahead of the pack. Even before we had eight-track, when we were back with mono in that little place, Tommy did revolutionary things with how he would mike the bass and drums. Nobody used to mike drums in those days, but he would place the mike somewhere at an optimum place between the bass and the drums to get them both. Of course, later on he started using multiple miking. We learned all the advantages of remixing and sweetening. We also learned the value of eight-track, and as people became associated with us, we drew them into this eight-track orbit. There was a typical reaction to eight-track. Leiber and Stoller said, "My God, we're going to lose our soul." Bob Crewe said, "I can't deal with this." Sooner or later, everybody fell into it.

What was the difference between Atlantic's production techniques, aside from the eight-track, and other record companies in the fifties who were doing rhythm and blues?

Back in those days we had a thing called the Atlantic sound. Nobody has a "sound" anymore, because everybody knows how to do it. I would describe our sound best as clean funk. We had a very stong bass line, a lot of bottom, a lot of bass drum. We had a very good midrange, and I always fought for treble in the remix. It's amazing how, to this day, people are careless about getting the top end in the proper perspective. I don't know why there are so many records where you don't hear the articulation of the high hat or the ride cymbal crisply. And if there are acoustic guitars, why you don't hear the top end, the ring of the guitar. It's a very simple little thing. You put a record on, or a tape, and everything's straight up —no EQ. If you run up the treble, let's say to three o'clock or six o'clock or all the way, suddenly you start hearing the high hat when you don't hear it straight up. Somebody has fucked up. Because when you add EQ into your home system, all you should be getting is *more* of something; nothing new should appear. If a new sound jumps in, a new frequency, somebody has failed to mix that record properly. I've been hearing a lot of that all my life, especially with respect to that business of cymbals. If the man's playing cymbals, why don't you have it on your record, mister?

Let's talk a little more about some of the many artists you've worked with over the years. Let's start with Solomon Burke, who many feel was the first soul star.

I could go on and on about him. There was a disc jockey in Philadelphia named Jimmy Bishop who was a friend of mine. We were sitting around in my backyard one day. He and his wife were there. We were having a barbecue and playing some music. It was in the middle of the Soul Era, and I think I had just gotten the record of Otis Redding's "Satisfaction." Somebody asked, "Who's the best soul artist?" People came up with different names: Sam Cooke, Willie John, Clyde McPhatter. Jimmy Bishop said, "The best soul artist is Solomon Burke with a borrowed band." You have to understand Solomon Burke. He'd make a deal, he'd make a contract with a promoter to work someplace in Louisiana or West Texas or whatever, and show up without a band because he knew that Joe Tex would be there with his band, or Joe Simon would be there with his band, and he would persuade the other guys to lend him their band for his gig. Solomon has always been a guy who knows how to fend for himself.

Do you consider him to have been a great recording artist?

Oh, fabulous. See now, Solomon would do whatever I asked him to do. Any song that I gave him, no problem. After he made it, after he got big, he got a little careless about learning the material. He'd come in, I'd give him a demo, and he wouldn't have learned it, and sometimes he'd fake it. He'd try to get by, by doing a lot of note bending and what I call oversouling. I'd say, "Solomon, that ain't the song. Sing the song. Sing the music."

Let's talk about your first Muscle Shoals session with Aretha Franklin. I know there were some problems down there with her husband Ted White and some of the white musicians.

It was just one trumpet player. To this day I can't remember who the guy is; he was not important. I had asked Rick Hall to hire a certain horn section out of Memphis which was mostly black. And I wanted that section, because my whole rhythm section was white. Not that that's the main point; I just wanted to get a certain balance of feeling and sensibility in there. And Rick Hall just plain forgot to hire these horn players. So we had to get whomever we could. What happened was that this one trumpet player got loaded, and he and Ted started "doing the dozens" [a verbal game in which insults are traded] with each other, and one thing led to another. I was hoping to cut two sides the first night, and we only got one side done, but we got it complete, "I Never Loved a Man." We did it live, the horns and everything. Then we cut a track on "Do Right Woman." All we had was bass, drums, and rhythm guitar. But the session was over. So we knocked off. The party went on for some —not for me; I went to bed. Things got a little rough out there. Next thing I know, Aretha Franklin has packed and gone back without finishing, and Ted White is packed, and they're going back to Detroit. That was the end of it. Now I have this finished record, "I Never Loved a Man," and a three-piece track on "Do Right Woman." I get back to New York and I start sending out dubs on "I Never Loved a Man" to the R&B jockeys, and I get a fabulous reaction. The distributors start calling for the record, and I don't have a B side. I can't find Aretha Franklin, because she's having a domestic problem. I finally get her into New York with her two sisters. So Aretha puts two keyboards on, organ and acoustic piano, does the lead vocal, and then she and her two sisters do the backgrounds. And that's all "Do Right Woman" is. I had a record, and we put it out.

Did you find her to be responsible and on-the-money and all that?

Pretty much, for me. After all, I was not booking her or managing her. I would have some problems getting her into the studio sometimes. She would be depressed or maybe a little moody. But once we got her into the studio, it was pure joy.

What would you do to get her out of a mood and into the studio?

Hold her hand and beg. I'd go wherever she was and beg her, and hold her hand and talk to her, and try to convince her.

Was she insecure about her abilities?

Oh, no. She knew who she was. Her problems all stemmed from her personal life, nothing from her assessment of herself as an artist.

You know, I've always been a big Otis Redding fan, but I don't think there's any doubt that she cut him on her recording of "Respect."

When I played him the tape of her record, he said, "Hey, that little girl done took my song away." [Laughter.] She did a better job than he did, using the arrangement she came up with, the "sock it to me's." We did a little arranging work on it. For example, there is no bridge on Otis' version. There's no instrumental bridge, no musical bridge, it's all one strain. So when we did Aretha's record we built in a four-bar bridge and took the chords from the bridge of Sam and Dave's "When Something Is Wrong with My Baby" and used that for the chords of the instrumental break on "Respect." To me it sounded like too much of one strain. I needed to get some harmonic relief in there. See, Aretha worked out the vocal arrangement by herself with her girls, her sisters. When she came in, it was all done. We put the instrumentals in together, the underpinnings, but it all came from her playing and singing. She would go home and she had a little electric piano—I don't know if it was a Wurlitzer or a Fender Rhodes or what—and she would work with her own vocal group or her sisters, and work out the whole arrangement. So she'd come into the studio, sit at the piano and start playing the song and singing it with her girls until the whole layout would emerge. Sometimes we might change the key, persuade her to raise it one tone, or whatever. But then we would fill it in, like brush strokes. She'd be saying, "Okay, let's have a bass part here, now guitar, drums, second keyboard." And there was your record. Putting horns in, or whatever, was an incidental thing. When we added horns or strings, usually Arif Mardin would write those charts, sometimes Tom Dowd would write or sketch a horn part.

Otis Redding, he never recorded a bad record.

Oh, he was marvelous, he was really an artist. He had a great sense
of himself, and a sense of music. But the best voice of the sixties,
the best pure voice, would have to be Solomon Burke. Think of that
voice. And remember who we had. There was Joe Tex, Ben E. King,
Otis, Sam and Dave, Percy Sledge, we had a bunch of people going.
But the voice is not everything. It's the music that's charging
it. It comes in three parts: It's the head, that's the musicality; it's
the mouth, that's the voice, and then there's the heart, that's the
emotion. The ideal is the optimum combination, and Aretha is the
one who combined those better than anybody.

*How did the Stax-Volt Memphis connection come about? And how
did Atlantic Records begin to distribute the Stax-Volt product?*

I got a call from Buster Williams, who worked in our pressing plant
in Memphis. In fact, he owned the pressing plant. He said,
"There's a pretty good record we're pressing a lot of down here;
maybe you can get it to distribute." So he sent me the record. It
was called "Because I Love You" with Rufus and Carla Thomas.
I liked it and I went after it. I went down to Memphis and I saw
Jim Stewart, and I made the deal for that record with an option on
anything else that might come out of there within a certain period.
One thing led to another. The record didn't make it, though it was
a local hit. But a year later out comes "Gee Whiz" by Carla Thomas
and we had the rights to it, and that's how the thing with Stax was
formulated. The next big hit we had was "Green Onions," and then
it all started to roll. The next real move came when I brought
Wilson Pickett down there, and we cut "In the Midnight Hour" and
all those other things we did in Memphis.

*You've been credited with almost creating the Stax-Volt rhythm
sound in that "Midnight Hour" session. Changing it around.*

Well, I think there's a lot of romance there. I just wanted to show
them a certain groove. So I went out and danced a little beat for
them that I thought would work better than the one they were
working on.

This was for Steve Cropper and Duck Dunn and all those guys?

Yeah, I'm very uninhibited [laughter]. I'll tell you, in the beginning, when I first started recording, the idea of dancing in front of veteran session players would have been appalling. I mean, I was very timid about even asking to do anything. But after a while I figured what the hell, I'm signing the checks around here [laughter].

Did the Stax-Volt musicians play differently after that?

Yeah, well, that's what they say. We just pushed two and four a little bit. Instead of leaving it back in the slot, we just advanced it. [He hums, accenting the second and fourth beats.] It gave it kind of a snap, a punch which was new, which was coming off The Jerk. I was just doing The Jerk with them.

Tell me about American Recording Studios, Chips Moman's place. I hear they had two two-track machines that were somehow patched together, and some funky, three-track board.

It was pretty much like that. Tom Dowd came up and helped them with the engineering. Chips used to play guitar in the Muscle Shoals band, and then he stepped out on his own. I guess I helped him get the American studios started. I financed it for no interest, for no involvement. I just liked him, and I figured it would be another good place to record. I did that in Muscle Shoals, and I did that in Miami, both to a greater extent. In other words, I enabled Muscle Shoals to buy a new board and a tape machine, and the same thing with Criteria in Miami, another place where I used to like to record.

You didn't have any problem working with such a makeshift technical setup at American?

I tell you, I never cared about that. I let Tom Dowd worry about that stuff.

Let's talk about Duane Allman and Capricorn.

I had this association with Phil Walden. He was Otis Redding's manager. With all of Otis' success, we spent a lot of time together, and Phil and I hit it off pretty well. Phil expanded with a booking agency and management company. Then he came to me in my capacity as one of the principals at Atlantic and said, "Could you front me a setup in Macon so I could have my own studio?" I said, "It sounds okay to me, but let's go it one better. I'll finance you in a label." I wanted to motivate him because I was hungry for product from the South, and he was right there in position. We decided to call it Capricorn, because we both come under the sign of Capricorn—not that I believe in any of that nonsense. We decided to try to put The Allman Brothers together. They'd been together before, but not successfully—The Allman Joys, and something else. Henry Stone had some sides on them out of Miami. Now, Duane was under contract to Rick Hall at Muscle Shoals as a sideman. Rick never signed anyone as a sideman. Musicians to him were interchangeable. But somehow he had the instinct, the smarts, to sign Duane Allman. So I bought Duane Allman's contract from Rick Hall, and Rick Hall thought that the heavens had opened up because I gave him $15,000 for a guitar player who couldn't sing and didn't write songs. I freed him up and turned him over to Phil, and Phil put The Allman Brothers together. Our interest was that we distributed the label. It is still some of the best music that I know out of the South.

You brought J. Geils in, also?

That was through Jon Landau. Jon knew the Boston area; he was living up in Boston. He bedeviled me until I signed The J. Geils Band. I gave Geils a $30,000 advance, which was a fortune, unheard of, with the condition that Landau would produce them. He hadn't produced anything then that I know of. We caught The MC5 on their second bounce, and I know he worked with them, but I don't remember the chronology. But I thought enough of Landau to entrust the session to him, my investment. I was under some heavy scrutiny from my associates to make good on this $30,000 investment. So Landau goes into the studio with them somewhere up in Massachusetts, I guess, and two weeks later he calls me and says, "I want out of this. . . ." He couldn't or wouldn't, or what

have you. I've been faced with this before, where you sign somebody on the strength of the producer connection and then the
producer takes a cab. So, the first producers for The J. Geils Band,
if I remember, were Brad Shapiro and Dave Crawford, two guys I
had put together. Dave Crawford was a disc jockey out of Atlanta,
and Brad Shapiro was a Henry Stone pupil. Of course, J. Geils
flourished but never realized their potential on Atlantic, as you
know.

Let's talk about Dylan. How did you and he come together for
Saved *and* Slow Train Coming, *both of which were done in*
Muscle Shoals?

He asked me to do it. At that time I guess I'd known him ten years.
That was about '77 or '78. Let's see, in '77 I did the score for *Pretty*
Baby for Louis Malle, so I guess that was '78. I met Dylan through
Doug Sahm, Sir Douglas, who is one of my greatest friends in the
business and a person I have the greatest affection for, and admiration and respect. If you asked me who's the best rock musician of
all time, and I had to pick one person, I'd say Doug Sahm has about
the best ability. Unbelievable man.

Did Bob say, "Jerry, take me to Muscle Shoals and do it the way
you did it with Aretha and Wilson Pickett," and so forth?

That's right. He wanted to get that sound. What he wanted was
more of a tailored, big funk sound, which he didn't have on his
records. He wanted a little more precision, a little more musical
input. It was something he felt was time. That was the general idea.
When I said Muscle Shoals, no problem. But even more interesting
to me, and what I'm pleased about, the innovative part of it, was
bringing in Mark Knopfler of Dire Straits as the lead guitar. Instead
of going with the regular Muscle Shoals section, I changed it a little
bit. And of course, Barry Beckett was coproducer on that, and a
lot of him is on that record.

How did you work with Beckett as coproducer? Was it similar to
the way you worked with Ahmet?

Very much the same, yeah. There's got to be a lot of respect, and a lot of listening to the other person's ideas. Barry does more on the arranging side and leading the band through the studio, and I'm more in the directorial position in the booth. But in the preparation we just worked the same way together, equally. Before I invited Barry to be coproducer, he, in fact, was coproducing. It always works like that. He had come out at the keyboard, he was putting a lot of things together that I'd just jump on instantly and say, "That's it, let's go with it." At some point it would have been indecent if I didn't invite him to become a participant. The same thing with Tom Dowd.

How about Willie Nelson? You opened Atlantic's Nashville office. Was Willie the first country artist signed?

No, because we had people running the office, and they were signing people down in Nashville. But Willie I signed. I signed two people, Willie Nelson and James Talley.

Willie was without a label at the time, wasn't he?

That's right. It was no problem signing Willie. It was not a heavy deal. Nobody wanted him. He was over forty years old, and he had the pigtails and earrings. He was like *persona non grata* in Nashville. The outlaw. What a bunch of bullshit that "outlaw" stuff was. But Willie played it for all it was worth, and God bless him, he should have. The way I met Willie: There was a songwriter named Harlan Howard, who wrote some great songs. He used to have an open house every year in Nashville. I think that house burned down since then. But everybody would be there playing and picking. It was a party. There would be Conway Twitty and Waylon Jennings, a whole panoply would be there. I had never met Willie Nelson until that afternoon, but I loved him to death. Everything about him—the voice, the music, his guitar playing, his concept, the total picture, his songwriting. I had recorded his "Night Life" with Aretha Franklin long before I met him at Harlan's. He's got to be something if B. B. King and Aretha Franklin recorded a song by this country boy from Texas. But I believed very much in the affinity of certain country players for the blues.

What did you finally end up cutting with Willie?

The first thing that I cut with him was *Shotgun Willie* but Arif Mardin did most of that, as line producer. I turned the project over to him. I was sort of executive producer, although I don't take executive producer credits. I don't like that title. Then I line-produced a couple of his songs, and that got him off to the races. Then the next one I produced, I took him to Muscle Shoals, and we used the Muscle Shoals rhythm section amplified by Fred Carter on lead guitar. Up in Nashville they were saying that it couldn't be done, that Willie Nelson cannot cut country music in Muscle Shoals because it's too funky, it's too black.

What came out of Muscle Shoals?

Phases and Stages. A lot of people still think this is Willie's masterpiece.

Now, more recently, you signed The Gang of Four and The B-52's. I think The Gang of Four was one of the best bands to come out of that whole era.

Yeah. They were kind of like white boys playing James Brown with polemical lyrics. And I signed The B-52's because I heard this amusing quality in their record, but most of all, I knew they had a following. That's the best way to sign somebody, when they've got a built-in following. You very rarely have that opportunity. By the time you know that you can get a group, they've got followings in six cities, and CBS already has them signed.

(November, 1984)

Leiber & Stoller

"**K**ansas City" is one of the classic rhythm and blues songs. To this day many people assume it's a traditional blues presumably passed on among itinerant black singers who emerged from the South to sing in the honky-tonks, turpentine camps, and shantytowns of the American heartland. In fact it was written by two young Jewish fellows, lyricist Jerry Leiber and composer Mike Stoller, who had absorbed the black culture they loved so well that they both were able to add to that culture, and help it merge and meld with white culture to produce a new sound—rock and roll. The first record they produced, with Big Mama Thornton in 1952, "Hound Dog," epitomized rock's genealogy from black R&B to mainstream rock via the cover of a white performer—in this case, Elvis Presley. They went on to write many other songs directly for Elvis, including "Jailhouse Rock." After tiring of seeing their songs incorrectly produced by others, and after getting burned with their own short-lived company in the early fifties, Leiber & Stoller joined Atlantic Records as the first-ever "independent producers." Indeed, the term was coined for them. There they wrote and produced some of the best and funniest rock 'n' roll records for The Coasters, and produced some of the most advanced and beautiful pop records to date for The Drifters. Their mentor Lester Sill discovered a teenage whiz-kid named Phil Spector and convinced the duo to take young Phil on as their apprentice. At United Artists in the early sixties they produced pop classics such as The Exciters' "Tell Him" and Jay and the Americans' "Only in America." They worked with the best of the Brill Building songwriters: Doc Pomus and Mort Shuman, Ellie Greenwich and Jeff Barry, Carole King and Gerry Goffin, Cynthia Weill and Barry Mann. When they started their own record company, Red Bird, in 1964 they had great success with classic girl groups like The Shangri-Las and The Dixie Cups. As they tired of this sound they moved on, creating Peggy Lee's mid-life crisis epic, "Is That All There Is?" Just middle-aged themselves, they already have more than two lifetimes of accomplishment behind them. They are now writing for Broadway, in what may be the second golden age of Leiber & Stoller. But this interview begins with two hip kids, back at Fairfax High School in Los Angeles.

Let's talk about how you got together.

Leiber: I was writing songs with a drummer, and going to Fairfax High School in Los Angeles. The drummer lost interest in writing songs and suggested I call Mike Stoller, whom he had worked with in a pickup dance band. I called Mike. He said he was not interested in writing songs. I said I thought it would be a good idea if we met anyway.

Mike, you were really into jazz and modern classical at that time, no?

Stoller: I was a very big modern jazz fan really. At the time Jerry called me, 1950, I was very into Charlie Parker and Thelonious Monk and Dizzy. And through modern jazz I got interested in Stravinský and Bartók. When I lived in New York—before I moved to California when I was sixteen—I used to hang out on 52nd Street.

Didn't you take piano lessons with James P. Johnson?

Stoller: I did when I was ten or eleven. Four or five lessons. That was my earliest love, boogie-woogie and blues piano. But the thing that cemented our relationship was when Jerry showed me his lyrics and I saw that they were blues in structure. Most of them had a twelve-bar structure—a line, then ditto marks, then the rhyming line. So it wasn't difficult for me to relate to it and go back to my first love, which was Pine Top Smith and Meade Lux Lewis, and Albert Ammons.

Jerry, were you more rhythm and blues oriented?

Leiber: Boogie-woogie, rhythm and blues. I was working in a record shop on Fairfax Avenue after school. But actually I was exposed to boogie-woogie when I was a little kid in Baltimore. My mother had a grocery store just on the border of the black ghetto. She had many black customers.

It seems like an almost fateful encounter. You were both so heavily into black culture.

Stoller: We were, but my background was a bit different. I went to an interracial summer camp, which was very unusual in those days. Starting in 1940, I went there every summer for eight years. I heard the older black kids playing the upright piano in the barn. A couple of them played very good boogie-woogie. I tried to emulate what I'd heard.

When you first started, were there songwriters you tried to emulate or whom you admired?

Leiber: I was trying to imitate certain styles—sounds that I heard on records. Some of the writers I was imitating, I found out later were actually the performers.

You both were totally into the black scene in L.A. at that time. You had black girlfriends, and would go to the black clubs.

Leiber: Oh yeah. We lived a kind of black existence. I'd say eighty percent of our lives were lived that way. It's an interesting thing. I sometimes look back on it and I think, why did I do that? I think that somehow or other I was alienated from my own culture and searching for something else. My father died when I was five. My mother was a refugee from Poland. I don't know what fragments of tradition there were left in my family, but they were so slight, there was little to go on.

Did you feel that way, too, Mike?

Stoller: No, not exactly. My family life was very warm, very emotionally comfortable. My mother and father were very supportive. My mother in particular was very supportive of me, and later of Jerry as well. But I must have felt somewhat alienated from my white peers. I felt there was something more special about not only the music I heard, that came from black people, but the black people themselves who made the music. I belonged to a social club in Harlem when I was about thirteen or fourteen.
Leiber: The black neighborhood was groovy, and I was accepted there right away. Part of it was my mother's doing. Her store was the only store within ten blocks of the ghetto that extended credit to black families. So I was a welcome person in the black neighborhood.

This translated itself immediately and automatically into the stuff you were writing, didn't it? Your songs became authentic black songs of the period.

Leiber: Leroi Jones, writing about us in the sixties, said that we were the only authentic black voices in pop music. [Laughs.] He changed his tune a few years later when he became [Amiri] Baraka.

We were flattered. Actually I think we wanted to be black. Being black was being great. The best musicians in the world were black. The greatest athletes in the world were black, and black people had a better time. As far as we were concerned the worlds that we came from were drab by comparison.

Jerry Wexler said in his interview with me that he supported the separation of black and white music into the pop and rhythm and blues charts because he felt that created more opportunity for black artists. How do you feel about that?

Stoller: I never thought about it that way. I always felt that it was sad, in the early days especially, that artists like Ray Charles and Lloyd Price and Big Mama Thornton weren't exposed to a wider audience.
Leiber: If they had had exposure on the major stations, then Georgia Gibbs wouldn't have been able to make all those covers of all those great records by Ruth Brown and LaVern Baker.
Stoller: And Pat Boone, who was covering Fats Domino records and Little Richard records . . .
Leiber: . . . wouldn't have happened. If Richard was played on all the Top 40 stations, nobody could have sold another record of anything he made. Could anybody cover Elvis Presley?
Stoller: The point is that today people are still buying and listening to Little Richard, Fats Domino, and Laverne Baker. Nobody is buying their songs in a cover version by Pat Boone. Nobody wants to hear a Georgia Gibbs' record or The Crew Cuts' record [of The Chords' original "Sh-Boom"]. What I imagine Jerry Wexler meant was that within a smaller and separate pool you could support more new fish. But I think the black fish in that smaller pool were being denied an ocean in which they could have very well survived.

Let's talk about how you two worked together as songwriters.

Leiber: Often, in the early days, I'd stalk around Mike's room. There'd be an upright piano against one of the walls. I'd just walk around and smoke and mumble, and he would jam until I would just get struck by some notion. Then I'd start yelling some kind of

line. If Mike dug it, he would pick it up somewhere. Sometimes
Mike would yell out some lines, too.
Stoller: It was like spontaneous combustion, like Jackson Pollock.
You threw a lot of paint at the canvas. I would just play riffs and
Jerry would shout lines, almost like automatic writing.

*Mike, it's been said you had an almost encyclopedic grasp of
musical styles, and you could throw out ideas from everything
you'd digested over the years.*

Stoller: I think that's somebody else's description.
Leiber: I think it is true, although I don't think he was conscious
of it. We used to just use shorthand after a while, sort of make
signs. I'd say, "More Fats" [Domino] or "More Richard" [Little
Richard] or "More Amos" [Milburn], "More Charles" [Ray
Charles]. All these were signals for different styles pianistically. If
I was talking about Toussaint [Allen Toussaint], it meant New
Orleans.
Stoller: If he said Fats, it generally meant triplets.
Leiber: Hard triplets, at a certain tempo.
Stoller: But we're talking about the way we *used* to work. Our mode
of working has changed through the years, and also the type of
work that we do has changed.
Leiber: The songs for the Peggy Lee album were written in a
different way. A number of songs were written where the lyrics
came first, and Mike set them to music.
Stoller: On others I wrote the music first and then Jerry wrote the
words.
Leiber: So it wasn't the same kind of spontaneous combustion that
occurred with the early writing. This [later] stuff was much more
complex. Much more deliberately worked out, structurally.
Stoller: The early things were almost written as if it were an
improvisation.

*It sounds like a maturation to a more traditional method of
writing.*

Stoller: We've talked about the kind of music which brought us
together, the thing that really got us going, the propelling force—

different styles of black music. But at the same time, we were not
unfamiliar with . . .

Leiber: . . . many other forms. . . .

Stoller: George Gershwin's music, and Rodgers and Hart and so on.
There's a thing we used to say to each other, we said that what we
wrote were records and that these records were like newspapers or
magazines in that they'd last for a month and then they'd be gone.

Leiber: We didn't think we were writing songs that would last.

Stoller: All the standards had already been written, *we* thought. We
were writing songs that we loved and that we were *compelled* to
write. But we didn't think they had any lasting value.

*You didn't think you were in the league of someone like Cole
Porter?*

Leiber: Absolutely not. We never thought so.

Stoller: The type of music that we write now is different.

Leiber: It requires different working habits.

Is it not as much fun now?

Leiber: No. It's not as much fun. And yet, it is sometimes, finally,
more gratifying.

Better product?

Leiber: Different. I hope it's better. We play what we feel are some
of the finest songs that we have ever written and some people say,
"You know what? You'll never write a better song than 'Hound
Dog.'" The people we admire most and the people we want to be
most admired by are our fellow songwriters. I remember Johnny
Mercer coming up to me one day and saying, "Kid, you finally
wrote a good song." It was "Is That All There Is?" [for Peggy Lee].
I think that was the greatest compliment I've ever received.

Stoller: That's out of a different tradition than our earlier work. It
no longer holds my attention to work in the format of the traditional
three- or four-chord blues that we used to work in. So I choose to
write something other. At *that* time I was absolutely happy with
the basic colors in my paint box.

Let's pick up now with the chronology. Lester Sill was the guy who . . .

Leiber: . . . introduced us to everybody—the Bihari Brothers of Modern Records, the Mesner brothers who owned Aladdin, and Ralph Bass. . . .

Stoller: Lester took us to New York and introduced us to Ralph Bass, who was with King and Federal Records. Ralph then moved to California and we started to work with him out there.

Leiber: Ralph was a friend of Lester's. Lester was the national sales promotion man for Modern Records.

How did you meet Lester?

Stoller: Jerry was selling records in Norty's Record Shop after school. . . .

Leiber: He came in one afternoon to check the sales on certain records. We got to talking. He asked me what I was going to do with my life. I told him I was interested in becoming a songwriter. I sang him some lyrics. He was very encouraging.

Stoller: He introduced us to a disc jockey named Gene Norman. Gene Norman ran a series of concerts called Just Jazz, like Norman Granz' Jazz at the Philharmonic. But he also had an annual blues jamboree at the Shrine Auditorium. He gave us the names of the artists who were going to appear on his 1950 blues jamboree and he told us where they were staying. Jerry and I went down to the Dunbar Hotel to see artists like Wynonie Harris, Percy Mayfield, Helen Humes, and so on. We had one song performed at that concert—"Real Ugly Woman"—and Jimmy Witherspoon sang it. It was our first public performance. What a thrill!

When you went around to the record companies with Lester Sill, would you play piano and sing to demonstrate the songs?

Leiber: We would play and sing our songs to the record company owners, and if they were accepted, we'd teach them to the artist.

Let's talk about "Kansas City." Wasn't it first titled "K.C. Loving?"

Stoller: It was written for Little Willie Littlefield. We called it "Kansas City," but Ralph Bass came to us and said, "You know, 'K.C.' is the hip thing, so I'm going to change the title of your song to 'K.C. Loving.' " We said "Okay. Just put it out!"

It's so authentic sounding, but different, it's not just a twelve-bar blues.

Stoller: Actually it *is* a twelve-bar blues, but it's a *melodic* one, as opposed to a traditional blues melody, which is basically just a series of inflections. I wanted to write something that, if it was played on a trumpet or a trombone, people could say it was a particular song, instead of that's a blues in E flat or F. I wanted something you could listen to instrumentally, and say, "I know that song."

Most people then, and probably to this day, think the song is traditional. How do you feel about that?

Stoller: At first when that happened we felt we had achieved something, that we had written something good enough to be thought of as traditional.
Leiber: At the time we were writing it, Mike and I had a little bit of an argument, and Mike turned out to be right. I didn't want it to have a melody. I wanted it to have a traditional straight blues contour, that any blues singer would sing in his own style with just the changes and the words. Mike said, "I don't want to do that, I want to write a melody. I want this to have a real identity." I said, "The other way it's much more flexible." He said, "Well, man, you're writing the words and I'm writing the music, and I'm going to write the music the way I hear it." [Laughter.]

At this point, and until the "Hound Dog" session with Big Mama Thornton in 1952, your records were being produced by other people. . . .

Stoller: Yeah. In the case of "Kansas City" we went out to Maxwell Davis' house. He was an A&R man, producer, arranger, songwriter, horn player. And he was the house musical director for Aladdin

Records. He also made records for Modern, Specialty, and other labels, including Mercury.

Leiber: If he were alive today, he'd be making a million dollars a second. He was wonderful. There were four or five guys around the country at this time who had this ability.

Stoller: Like Jesse Stone, who worked for Atlantic, or Bumps Blackwell, who worked for Specialty. But up until that time, after we performed a song for an artist, we frequently went to the studio. At first it was like, "You guys can stay here, but be quiet." Later we began to express some ideas to whomever was running the session. Sometimes they'd use some of the ideas. After all, when you're working with the blues, which is pretty repetitive, you need as many ideas as you can get to make it a little different. We would be invited to the studio with songs after a while. Ralph would call us to bring songs to the studio. We would run them down with artists like Little Esther or Bobby Nunn or Little Willie Littlefield with Johnny Otis' band, and discuss how they ought to go. They would be worked out on the session. Sometimes we'd bring three songs with us and write a fourth during the session. When we did "Kansas City," it was the first time we had the opportunity to really spend time before the session laying out the ideas with an arranger who actually wrote down the ideas, as opposed to the way we had worked with Johnny Otis, where the charts were head arrangements done on the spot.

During this time when your material was being produced by others, were you happy with the way it was coming out?

Leiber: A lot of the stuff was misinterpreted. So we started to involve ourselves more and more in the making of arrangements and the running of sessions until we got to a point where we could run our own sessions. After a while they were calling us to produce records.

Stoller: "Hound Dog" was the first record we produced, although unofficially. Johnny Otis had played drums at the rehearsal. He had the snares turned off and was playing some old Southern, Latin-sounding kind of beat. On the actual recording date, he had his road drummer playing because Johnny was supposed to be running the session for Don Robey of Peacock Records. It wasn't happening. So Jerry said, "Johnny, get on the drums the way you were." Johnny said, "Who's gonna run the session?" and we said, "We will." Jerry went into the booth and directed from there. I stayed on the floor and worked with the musicians. There were only two takes, and both of them were good, but the second was better than the first.

You were known, along with Jerry Wexler and Ahmet Ertegun at Atlantic, for doing as many takes as necessary to get the song right, and for rehearsing your artists before entering the studio with them. That was pretty unusual in rhythm and blues at that time, wasn't it?

Stoller: I think so.
Leiber: We took a lot more time than the Biharis and the Mesners did. They'd do two, three, four, five takes and good-bye. We'd lay in there for two hours on a side if we had to. But we almost always got four sides in the allotted three hours—two A sides and two B sides. In fact, "Searchin'," which we did in the last six minutes of a session as a B side, was the fourth song of the session and we just *had* to get it. I mean if we had come out of a session with only three sides, we'd have felt like failures. We were very thorough. We would rehearse for three weeks before a session, eight hours a day. Every lick was planned. The only thing we would leave to chance on the session was the feel, and the tempo. Sometimes Mike would take a note or two out of a bass pattern because it was too cluttered, or add a note or two. We knew what kind of a beat the drummer was going to lay down because we knew the drummer. We knew more or less how the piano player was going to play because Mike was playing piano. So we knew pretty much what to expect. The only thing we were looking for was that magic, that thing that comes together when everything is cooking.
Stoller: I used to write out some kind of road map for all the musicians. When it came to The Coasters, it took lots of preparation. Harmony was not their forte, and I used to rehearse them for weeks till they could remember who had which note.

Were the musicians available for this kind of extended rehearsal?

Stoller: No, no. We never rehearsed the musicians, only the vocal group. The musicians came to the studio where we had these little charts written out for them so that they wouldn't have to start learning from scratch what the bass pattern was, whether we had a four- or eight-bar intro, or where the break chorus came.

You had been working for a number of record companies, then you and Lester decided to start Spark Records late in 1953.

Stoller: It lasted about a year and a half.
Leiber: We didn't know what to do in terms of promotion. Well, we knew in a sense. Lester [Sill] knew that we couldn't get past the Rockies.
Stoller: We were underfinanced. We couldn't afford to send Lester on a trip. We were selling 100,000 singles in Los Angeles and nothing in the rest of the country.

And Lester was quite a promotion guy, quite a character, wasn't he?

Leiber: Fantastic. He'd do a sand dance—take some sand out of his pocket, throw it on the floor and dance to a record . . .
Stoller: . . . in the record store, to show the store owner what a great danceable record it was. Anyway, Atlantic liked our records very much. They convinced us, which wasn't very hard to do, that they were better in selling product, or records, I should say. I hate that word, product. They took our last release, the Robins' "Smokey Joe's Cafe," and put it on one of their labels, Atco. They sold a quarter of a million after we'd sold 100,000 in L.A.

What was the deal that Ahmet and Jerry made you at Atlantic?

Leiber: Two cents a record. And we arm-wrestled over getting our names on the records as producers. Jerry Wexler said, "What do you mean? You're getting the money. What do you need? We don't put our names on the records." I said, "Yeah, but you own the label."
Stoller: He said, "Well, you have your names on as writers." And he said, "Man, we tell everybody that *you* made the record!"

Leiber: He said, "We told [Waxy] Maxy, and Henry Stone knows, man. Who else do you want to know about it?" [Laughter.]

Stoller: Actually, although we kept this argument up for a number of years, it only began to make sense to them when we started producing songs that we hadn't written.

Leiber: We got good at producing, and we started doing other people's songs. We would give assignments to Doc Pomus and Mort Shuman, Bacharach and David, Mann and Weill, Goffen and King. Sometimes we wouldn't write for the sessions, we just wouldn't feel it. If we were doing a Drifters' date, we'd write a song, but we weren't going to write *four* songs. We would try to get the best song from each team.

Stoller: Then we would concentrate on ideas for orchestral coloration.

Leiber: It actually varied the work. We didn't feel like writing all the time. So we'd devote some weeks to writing, and sometimes just devote time to producing or producing in another style other than that which we were writing.

Until you came along, records were generally made by staff producers. You were really the first independent producers, weren't you?

Stoller: Jerry Wexler told me that we were, so I assume we were.

Leiber: There were people doing independent record dates with their own money, like Buck Ramm. But we were the first independent producers ever, as I understand it, formally contracted by a label to make records.

Stoller: [Laughs.] We were record company owners who were persuaded to give up their company and become producers on a royalty basis.

It was a new job title.

Stoller: And a misnomer which we didn't invent ourselves—producer.

Leiber: It should have been director. The producer has always been the money raiser and the manufacturer.

Stoller: Like the producer of a film or a show. We were the supervisors, the directors.

At Atlantic, how would it be decided whether you guys or Wexler or Ertegun would be the producers?

Stoller: In the very beginning we brought in our own artists.
Leiber: We brought The Coasters in and produced them. Later they would say, "You want to do Ruth Brown this week? She's coming in and we need some new ideas." Or LaVern Baker. Or: "Hey, we need a hit for The Drifters. We went cold on The Drifters."

Stoller: In '59, after being a hit group for years, The Drifters got cold and finally broke up. Atlantic still owned the name, and felt it was a hot name—so the managers hired some new group to be The Drifters, and Ahmet and Jerry asked us to take over the production.

These lush productions you did with The Drifters were really ground-breaking.

Leiber: That's one of the reasons we did them. We wanted to have some fun with the arrangements. We didn't feel we could do these arrangements with The Coasters because The Coasters were, for us, a vaudeville act.

Let's talk about both The Coasters, whom you were obviously very simpatico with, and also The Drifters, which was a much more sophisticated sound. Why did you and The Coasters work together so well for so long? They almost seemed like alter-egos.

Leiber: They were an extension of us.
Stoller: They thought our songs were funny and they were able to perform them funny.
Leiber: Stoller and I were essentially, I feel in retrospect, comedians and social satirists as writers. It was only many years later that we wrote some romantic songs and some love songs, some complica-

ted songs. We were doing either some kind of really truckin' blues number that you could dance to or the songs were jokes.

Of course, you wrote a lot of funny songs, probably the funniest rock 'n' roll songs ever written—"Charlie Brown" and "Poison Ivy."

Leiber: See, what they are are tall tales. They come out of folk culture. Like "John Henry." They're Paul Bunyan stories. This is all braggadocio. It always comes out of cultures . . .
Stoller: . . . that are suppressed. Out of those cultures you get heroes that are strong men, and the guys who, against all odds, end up winning—by either outpunching or outsmarting somebody. But the hero in our songs didn't always have to be triumphant. Some of our heroes were the guys who always got knocked around or framed . . .
Leiber: . . . or the mark in "Little Egypt" who gets taken at the strip joint. They're like three-minute radio plays. I think I was very much influenced by listening to shows like "The Shadow" and "Bulldog Drummond" as a kid.

The Coasters were the ideal group for the funny songs.

Leiber: They were a bunch of comedians. We put them together for that reason. We selected those guys. When The Robins broke up, we took Billy Guy and Carl Gardner. We saw comic qualities in Carl that Carl didn't see in himself and still doesn't. Carl considered himself a romantic ballad singer, and he is very well equipped to do that. But we also heard in his voice a kind of a pompous, authoritarian sound that used to knock us out. We used to use him in that way. He was the barker at a carnival.
Stoller: "Step right up, folks."
Leiber: Billy Guy was always like the fool.
Stoller: Billy was actually discovered later. Carl and Bobby Nunn came out of The Robins.
Leiber: The Coasters were a vaudeville comedy act that gave me the opportunity to employ every gag and routine I'd ever seen or heard in the movies or on television, from the Marx Brothers to Amos 'n' Andy.

Did the humor help get the songs across to a broader audience?

Leiber: I think what really got the stuff across more than anything was the rhythm section. If it didn't have that swing, then it didn't mean a thing . . . [laughs] . . . and then the joke wasn't funny and the song didn't matter.

Stoller: I mean, we could have done those same songs with The Modernaires! That's not what they were about. We cast the songs, and then when we had the cast for the songs, we wrote the songs for the cast. It was organic.

Leiber: We had our characters. Like Ralph Cramden, Gleason on "The Honeymooners." The stories changed. One was about cowboys. I mean what could be funnier than a bunch of black cats doing a send-up of a bunch of white cowboys? What could be sillier?

Stoller: I think the most fun we ever had working with any artist, including Elvis Presley, was with The Coasters. We'd be falling on the floor—all of us—and staggering around the room holding our bellies because we were laughing so hard.

Leiber: Billy Guy would say things like, "Man, we just cannot do this song. They're going to fuckin' lynch us in Mississippi, man!" Then someone would say, "Oh come on, they're going to dig us." He'd say, "No, man, they're *not* going to think it's funny. They're going to know we're putting them on!" [Laughter.] Billy was always worried that they were going to see through it. [Laughter.] "These crackers are going to say, 'Hey, these black cats are sending us up!' " [Laughter.] We had a great time.

So what happened with The Coasters?

Stoller: The world changed. . . .

Leiber: . . . Everybody got serious. . . .

Stoller: . . . Everybody got very serious and lost their sense of humor. The black power movement strained a lot of black-white relationships. It polarized things. The music changed. The Coasters seemed to be a relic of a more innocent time.

Let's talk about The Drifters. "There Goes My Baby" was the first session you produced for them. It was such a beautiful, lush production. . . .

Leiber: That was the time Jerry Wexler's tuna fish sandwich went all over the wall. We played him the record while he was eating his lunch. He started screaming at us: "What are you doing with my money!? This is the dumbest—the craziest!—this fucking record is out of tune! Hey, Ahmet, isn't it out of tune!?" [Laughter.] Ahmet says, "Hey, wait a minute! Stoller knows whether it's in tune or not! Is it out of tune!?" [Laughter.] Stoller says, "Well, it's a little out of tune, but I think it's kind of interesting." [Laughter.] "Interesting! What kind of interesting? The fucking timpani are out of tune, man! This is a rotten fucking record! And I'm not going to put it . . ." And the tuna fish sandwich was all over the wall.

Stoller: Ahmet was trying to mollify us. He said, "You know what, fellows? Look, you guys cut great records, but you can't hit a home run every time at bat. You know that." We said, "But there's something in it. Can we work with Tommy Dowd? Maybe we can fix it up." It wasn't recorded where we usually record because Atlantic's studio was booked that day, and it was done . . . it was upstairs on 40th Street off Sixth Avenue. . . .

Leiber: The booth was upstairs, but the recording was down in the pit. There was a terrible time lag in the studio, and a strange echo system. It gave a weird wash to the record. We knew the timps were out of tune. It sounded like two AM radio stations playing at the same time.

Stoller: It wasn't that they were out of tune, it was that they weren't played by a timpanist. He was an R&B drummer and he just played it straight through, and the one pitch went through all the changes.

Now, this was the first R&B tune to feature strings. . . .

Stoller: We had a timpani, four violins, and a cello, with a regular rhythm section which we augmented because I had come up with this Borodin-like line I was playing on the piano during rehearsals. Jerry said, "That should be violins." Stanley Appelbaum wrote the line as a unison for the violins and the cello. Anyway, the timp was in the studio, and Jerry and I have always loved a certain Brazilian beat called the *baion,* which we heard sung by Silvana Mangano in the Italian film *Anna.* It's that BOOM . . . boom boom, BOOM . . . boom boom, which later became the signature of half a dozen years of rock and roll and soul records. It was used extensively not only by us, but after us by Phil Spector and Burt Bacharach.

So Ahmet and Jerry thought you were nuts?

Leiber: Wexler thought it was terrible, god-awful.
Stoller: I think Ahmet thought it was awful, too, but he was trying to be kind.
Leiber: I'm trying to remember who came in and said it was a hit. Was it Nesuhi [Ertegun]?
Stoller: No. I think it was Tommy Dowd. We said let us work with Tommy on it. We just mixed it. It was only three or four tracks.
Leiber: I know that at some point Ahmet said he thought it was a hit. Maybe it was just before we released it. I remember Ahmet saying, "It could be a hit." And, of course, it did become a hit.

Then came more with The Drifters, like "This Magic Moment," written by Doc Pomus and Mort Shuman.

Leiber: Yeah. We started building this rhythm section. By the time we were in full swing we were using like three to five guitars—a twelve-string, a lead guitar, two rhythm guitars . . .
Stoller: And one that went "chang . . ." [Laughter.] Electric, using whole notes.
Leiber: Then we used up to three percussionists and a drummer. We had somebody on what we called the African hairy drum, someone on a triangle, and someone on vibes and marimbas, then a regular drummer.

Wasn't Phil Spector your apprentice during this time?

Leiber: We brought him in in late 1960. Phil Spector was another discovery of Lester Sill. Lester called me on the phone and said, "There is this very talented young kid out here, and he's bored with the scene." Nothing much was happening there [L.A.]. At the time everything was happening in New York. He was just out of high school. Lester said, "He wrote one hit song and he made a record, and he wants to hang out with you guys." I said, "Sure, send him along." And he stayed in my house.

Stoller: We sent him a ticket as a favor to Lester.

What did he do as your apprentice?

Leiber: He just hung around us.

Stoller: To help support him we'd put him in the guitar section. Then we started getting him outside gigs.

Leiber: We had too much work. A job came through. Big Top Records—Paul Case—called us and wanted us to cut Ray Peterson. We didn't have time. I said, "You know, there's a very talented young man who's working with us, and I think he can handle it very well. We'll supervise him and check the mixes." He said okay, he'd take a chance. Phil went in and cut "Corrina, Corrina." The rest is history [laugh].

He must have been heavily influenced by the stuff you were doing with The Drifters.

Leiber: I think he was influenced by our techniques and ideas but he used them in his own way. We used five guitars; he used three pianos. He was influenced by us, but he developed his own thing, which is what anyone good finally does.

Jerry Wexler said he remembered when Atlantic got an early eight-track machine you were saying, you can't make R&B records on multitrack, that the records would lose their soul. Is that accurate?

Leiber: Did I say something like that? I could have. Well, they were too clean. I used to talk about "the rub." Then someone explained that it was on the old tube machine.

Stoller: Oh no, that had to do with the harmonics being different on the tube machines. But Tommy's [Tommy Dowd] eight-track was running on tubes at that time rather than chips. It was later on that we learned the difference between the transistor and the tube machine, the warmth of the tubes, and the slight harmonic distortion that was different.

Leiber: You couldn't make a Howlin' Wolf record, you couldn't make a Chess record, you couldn't get that sound on a transistor machine. At first multitrack techniques drove me crazy because of the possibilities and the alternatives. It bothered me because I was always geared for a record session like I was geared for a performance. It all had to do with capturing the spontaneity of the moment. The idea of having so many extra tracks meant that you had the luxury of making mistakes or not being up for the moment to really nail it in that one take or two takes or whatever. You could come in later and overdub it. Not that we hadn't used overdubs, but we didn't use overdubs normally to get the central performance. We would use them to fix a moment, something that was off. But we always felt the band, the rhythm section and the singer—there was an interaction that was irreplaceable. I don't like to make tracks and overdub a voice. We thought that sounded dead. So the idea that all these tracks were there would create a kind of laziness in terms of performance. That took a kind of urgency out of the moment for me. Recording for me was not as exciting anymore.

Mike, do you agree with that?

Stoller: Well, yes and no. I recall using the eight-track machine with Tommy as if it were an extension of mono, not like the experiences we've had since in working sixteen-track and twenty-four-track, where I've definitely felt exactly as Jerry has described. I've gotten hung up on the process in some cases—lost in the technical possibilities, and the remix possibilities, and the "we'll do it later" possibilities. But the eight-track, especially with The Coasters, where we had the rhythm divided on the tracks—the main thing that it gave us was three tracks to play with the vocals. If a performance was almost there and we missed one line, instead of having to intercut it with another performance, where the rhythm section might not fit perfectly, we could touch up that particular line. We had the luxury of being able to fix it.

You adapted to this?

Stoller: Very quickly. We were helped, of course, by the fact that we were working with a technician who became a great producer,

Tommy Dowd, who understood what we were doing as producers. He was just brilliant. You know, a lot of the engineers we worked with became producers afterward. Tommy Dowd, Brooks Arthur. Phil Ramone was an engineer at A&R Studios. We started working with him in 1959, when we began using orchestras too large for Atlantic's old studio on 56th Street. There were techniques that we used in those early days that you just don't think about now because you can do so many different things electronically. While we were mastering, for example, we were always very aware of the possibility of altering the tempo ever so slightly. But they didn't have all the VFOs, variable frequency oscillators. So we would "speed them a wrap." You took a piece of tape and wrapped it around the capstan, which made the take-up faster. We wouldn't speed it so many seconds, we'd speed it one wrap or two wraps. It was hard to speed it a half a wrap because then you got a wobble [laughter].

Didn't you also work briefly for RCA Victor in New York in 1957?

Stoller: 1958. We moved to New York at the end of '57. We had already started working for Atlantic in California. The RCA thing was arranged by Jean Aberbach through Steve Shoals, who was head of A&R.

Leiber: [At RCA] by the time you filled out a requisition for something, the idea was stale. I got so confused. All the offices looked exactly the same. [Laughter.] I couldn't find my office. I would come to the building, and every day I would go into an office and sit down and I'd be sitting there for ten minutes thinking this was my office and a guy would come in and look at me and he'd say hello, and I'd say hi. He'd walk around kind of uneasy, and I'd start to feel uneasy. Then he'd say, "You're in my office." [Laughter.] I'd get up and I'd go into another empty office. They were these cubicles and they were all furnished the same, the same size. I didn't know where I was. I couldn't make it.

Stoller: We produced seven records in the first four months we were there, and had six Picks of the Week in *Cashbox.* Varetta Dillard, Georgia Gibbs . . . But they never sold any of those records.

Meanwhile we made one record for Atlantic during that period and it was a smash.
Leiber: So we said we're wasting our time because even if we made a hit, it wouldn't be played.

Weren't they greasing the right people?

Leiber: We didn't know what was going on. The records were being sold by the people who sold refrigerators.
Stoller: We didn't know how records were promoted. We only knew that you made them and Atlantic put them out and if they were good they'd be hits.

Let's talk about Elvis Presley, another RCA artist. How did you feel about him before he recorded your material?

Stoller: I heard "Heartbreak Hotel" and I loved it. It was weird and it had more echo than I'd ever heard before, but I loved it. That was in the beginning of '56. Then I went to Europe for three months and I didn't know that Elvis had become the biggest thing going in the States.
Leiber: He came back on the *Andrea Doria.* I had just come back from California. I had been on this hair-raising fishing trip where we were stranded in a little boat off the coast of California for like eighteen hours. It was terrible. We were towed in finally by the Coast Guard, and the rope broke a few times. I had this great wild adventure up my sleeve to tell Stoller. I was checked into the Algonquin and I was smoking a cigarette and listening to the news and I get this news flash that the *Andrea Doria* is sinking off the coast of Nantucket. I thought, Jesus Christ, he's on that boat, I've been upstaged again! [Laughter.] Actually, I thought of that later. I was absolutely horrified. I had just found out that Elvis' "Hound Dog" was an overnight smash, and I had this great news for Mike that we had this great hit record. Then this news came of the sinking ship. I listened all night and I heard there were survivors. I didn't know who, though. Then, finally, I got a telegram.
Stoller: I had some lire in my pocket. We were on a United Fruit Lines boat that had picked us up out of a lifeboat. They wouldn't

send a telegram unless we paid in cash. I had given money to some
other people to send wires back to Italy. I could only afford to send
one telegram and I figured Atlantic Records was the place, because
I knew Jerry and Lester were planning to meet me there. Jerry was
at the dock waiting when we came in . . .
Leiber: . . . with the news about "Hound Dog." I thought he was
wet or something so I brought him a suit. [Laughter.]

*How did you feel about the way Elvis did "Hound Dog?" He
changed the lyrics around and so forth.*

Leiber: The first time I heard it I hated it. I didn't like it at all. My
idea of the right rendition was the Big Mama Thornton record.
Elvis' record was much too frantic. The original was kind of a cross
between a New Orleans buck dance and a blues-rhumba. It was
relaxed and nasty. The Presley record that I loved most was "Love
Me Tender." I thought Elvis Presley was the greatest ballad singer
since Bing Crosby.

What was it like, working with Elvis?

Leiber: He was fast. Any demo you gave him he knew by heart in
ten minutes.
Stoller: He'd sing along with it a few times and he'd know it.
Leiber: Elvis Presley was like an Olympic champion. He had more
vitality than ten other singers put together.

*You didn't feel, as two guys very involved in authentic black
music, that he was some kind of usurper of the black sound?*

Leiber: I wouldn't say a usurper. I felt he was not quite authentic
—after all, he was a white singer, and my standards were black.
Stoller: We had strong feelings about what we thought was authentic. And one of the things we felt was not authentic was a white
singer singing the blues. Why we thought that it was all right for
us to pass, I don't know. Maybe because we were writers, not
performers. But, even so, I did like Elvis right from the git. And
when we did meet him . . .

Was he aloof in those days?

Stoller: No. He was *protected.* He was removed. . . .
Leiber: He was protected by the CIA [laughs].
Stoller: The Memphis Mafia CIA. Colonel Parker. They kept him separate. We met him in a studio at Radio Recorders when we were doing the prerecording of the songs for [the film] *Jailhouse Rock.* It was great, very easy. We were surprised at the kind of knowledge that he had about black music. We figured that he had these remarkable pipes and all that, but we didn't realize that he knew so much about the blues. We were quite surprised to find out that he knew as much about it as we did. He certainly knew a lot more than we did about country music and gospel music.

What was it like writing the songs for the Elvis films?

Leiber: We thought they were dopey.
Stoller: We would write for them, but after a while they got so dumb and so repetitive that we got bored and decided not to do any more because it was no fun.
Leiber: We did more Presley movies than we ever intended to do because we were making so much money. But it got to a point where we just couldn't stand it anymore.
Stoller: It got to the point where it got to be too much like work. The score to *Jailhouse Rock* was written in one afternoon in the Gorham Hotel. Because Jean Aberbach, who was the publisher and co-owner of Elvis Presley Music and Gladys Music [and co-founder, with brother Julian, of Hill and Range Music] came in and said, "Where's the score, boys?" He sat down on a big overstuffed chair and planted himself in front of the door and said, "You're not leaving until I have some songs."
Leiber: We had been running around New York. We were just so excited about everything that was happening that we hadn't settled down to write.
Stoller: We rented an upright piano and put it in the room. We were going to stay in New York for three weeks. We'd been there two weeks and they'd given us this cockamamie script, and we were not too enthused and stimulated by it. So we hadn't started to do anything. But we wrote those in one afternoon. Then the scripts got worse.

Let's talk about some of the records you produced at United Artists in the early sixties. There were some very nice pop tunes like "Only in America" and "She Cried" for Jay and the Americans and one of my favorites, The Exciters' "Tell Him."

Leiber: Well, that one's a *baion,* with triangles.
Stoller: Bert Berns wrote the song and I think they had released a record of it before, on a small label, and it had not been successful. We liked the song . . .
Leiber: . . . And we had this hysterical-sounding group called The Exciters. The girl, Brenda, sang out of tune, but she sang in a wild, exciting way.
Stoller: They just used it in *The Big Chill.*

You did Ferrante and Teicher at United Artists, no?

Stoller: One side, *Lawrence of Arabia* [laughter]. We had them playing inside the piano on the strings.

Your songs and productions, which started out being inside and hip, gradually became more universal.

Stoller: I wonder about that.

"Only in America" seems as universal as can be.

Leiber: Let me tell you something about that. "Only in America" was a song that Mann and Weill wrote with us. Originally it was The Drifters singing, "Only in America can a guy get a break," again a sendup, a black person talking about what a great place this country is for opportunity—an ironic, bitter statement. Now Jerry Wexler heard the thing and he said, "Are you kidding? I'm not going to put that record out for anything!" We'd made what we thought was a hip track with The Drifters. So he said, "I'm not putting that out. I don't need that kind of trouble." So I said, "What are we going to do?" He said, "I don't know. Whatever you want to do." So I said, "Can we have the track?" He said, "Sure." So we made a deal with Atlantic and we took the track and over-dubbed it with Jay and the Americans. *They* sang it. A white group singing it sounds like "Tenement Symphony." It sounds like they meant it. It was no longer ironic, in fact it was downright patriotic. But you're right about some of our other productions. We did start moving more into the mainstream of the pop music business. We certainly were not cutting the blues anymore. There wasn't a large enough audience for the blues anymore. The business was changing.

Stoller: What was happening at that time in terms of black music was Motown was starting. And Sam Cooke and Sam and Dave.

How did you feel about Motown then?

Leiber: At first we thought it was white bread. We thought that Motown was Madison Avenue for black people. We said, "Man, those are white teenage stories. What does that have to do with black culture?" We'd have discussions about that with some black music people from time to time. They'd say, "What? Are you in love with the ghettos? Are you in love with that old regionalism? Things are changing, man. That's not the black image any longer."

Was your Red Bird label a reaction to this?

Stoller: No. Red Bird was a reaction to United Artists.
Leiber: We had broken with Atlantic in '60, '61. We went to United Artists and made a slew of hits. At one point we looked at each other and said, "Why are we making these record companies rich? Why don't we go into the record business again and do what we want to do, and not have to call upstairs for budgets, etc." We opened up a record company, Tiger, and each record got hit picks in the trades and we didn't get one of them played. Nothing was selling. We were cutting people like Alvin Robinson, who was a stone soul blues singer from New Orleans, and we loved him. Still love him. We cut a number of great singers and songs that we thought were great, blues oriented, and we couldn't sell two records. We were about to go out of business. Mike and I had been producing and supervising record production with songwriter-producer teams that we were bringing along—like [Jeff] Barry and [Ellie] Greenwich, and Shadow Morton. Mike had written some arrangements for them with a group called The Dixie Cups. We had

some sessions in the can with a couple of little girl groups that had
nothing to do with our tastes in music at all. It had to do with the
young writer-producers who were now working under our banner.
They were doing what they wanted to do. But we were running out
of money and time because the records we had made were not
selling. Mike, didn't we, with the advent of George Goldner, start
a new label because we thought the other label had the stigma of
flops?

Stoller: Tiger and Daisy were the first labels. We formed them when
we left United Artists. Our first releases came out the week of the
Kennedy assassination. Of course, nothing ever happened with
them. The music business, along with everyone else, went into a
state of shock. By the following year in about March or April, when
we were coming out of that shock, we needed to start releasing some
of these records that had been piling up on our desk. *That* is when
Jerry bumped into George Goldner and made what I consider to be
the best possible business arrangement that could have been made
for us to go into the record business.

How was it the best arrangement?

Stoller: Because Goldner was the best record salesman, *ever* . . .
Leiber: . . . Outside of Jerry Wexler. He had Gee Records, Rama,
and Roulette, Tico . . .
Stoller: . . . He started all these labels. He was a mambo danc-
er. . . .
Leiber: His big problem was gambling. He was a big horse player.
He lost every label he ever had at the track. I met him one night
when he was down on his luck and out of money, sitting with Hy
Weiss, who owned Old Town Records, in Al and Dick's. Weiss was
blowing cigar smoke in his face, calling him a schmuck, and telling
him what kind of fool he was and why, and trying to get [George]
to work for him for like $200 a week. George said he needed at
least $350. Hy had invited me over to the table, using me as kind
of an audience to put George down. Hy would turn to me and say,
"See this schmuck sitting before you. He was worth $20 million,
and he blew it at the track." Then he'd blow more cigar smoke at
him. I'm looking at George and thinking, Jesus Christ, we don't

have much money. I can't really afford to give George $350 a week. . . .

Stoller: But if he'd made $20 million in the record business, he must've known how to do something right. . . .

Leiber: At some moment I said, "George, you want to go into the record business?" He looked at me and he said, "I hope you're not pulling my leg because I wouldn't think it was too funny right now." I said, "I'm not being funny at all. I'm being serious." He said, "What kind of a deal are you talking about?" I said, "A partnership." He said, "A partnership with Leiber & Stoller? What kind?" I said, "Even up. Three ways." Upon hearing this he went into his inside coat pocket and he got out an old Tiffany cigarette case, opened it up, took out a Pall Mall, lit it, and blew the smoke into Hy Weiss' face. He said, "Hy, we're going to see who the schmuck is." [Laughter.] I had told him I had these acetates. He said, "Where are the acetates?" I said, "They're sitting on my desk in the Brill Building." He said, "Give me the keys to your office." I said, "I'll go with you." He said, "No. Don't come with me. Come in tomorrow morning when you normally do and I'll see you." I said, "Are you going to stay there all night?" He said, "I might." I gave him the keys and I came in at eleven o'clock the next morning and he was sitting behind my desk, not a hair out of place, same suit, same tie. He held up this acetate and said, "On my life. On my life." I said, "What are you talking about? Play it." He put it on, and I hated the fucking record. . . .

Stoller: I always liked it.

Leiber: He liked it. He wrote the arrangement.

What was it?

Leiber: [singing] "Going to the chapel, and we're gonna get married . . ." [Laughter.] He says, "This is a stone smash." I said, "George, you're the boss. You put it out. I hate it." [Laughter.] That was the first record on Red Bird. I think we ran eighteen straight hits.

Stoller: Something like that, between The Shangri-las, The Dixie Cups, The Jelly Beans, The Ad Libs . . . But Alvin Robinson, we released records on him that sold 100,000, and his were the kind of records we loved. After a couple of years we felt that we were distanced from the material that our record company was doing. It was doing great, and selling all kinds of records, but we didn't have any emotional feeling for that. Because we wanted to write.

What happened next?

Leiber: We did some outside productions and writing after that. At some point we gave George Goldner Red Bird Records for one dollar.

Let's talk about your work with Peggy Lee.

Stoller: It started in '62. We made a demo of "I'm a Woman" and we sent it out to Dave Cavanaugh at Capitol Records. Not long after, Peggy was appearing at Basin Street East. We went down to catch her act and she was singing the song. The audience loved it, and we went down to the studio about a week later and recorded it.

"Is That All There Is?" almost sounds like a comment on your careers up to that point.

Leiber: Maybe it was. We were thinking of moving on. We were getting older, and were not writing for kids anymore. We were looking for another, more mature audience. We thought perhaps the theater would be the place for us. So I started experimenting with some ideas and Mike and I got together on that. "Is That All There Is?" was one of the first ideas of that genre that we completed.

Was it very successful?

Leiber: Not at first. We did it first with Georgia Brown.
Stoller: I wouldn't say that it wasn't successful. Georgia Brown performed it beautifully on a BBC television show in 1966. But she didn't get to record it, and without record sales it's hard to measure the success of a song. We continued to work on it—we wrote it a

couple of times. Then Jerry presented it to Peggy when she was working at the Copa. She was very taken with it, and Jerry told her that he would produce it with her in L.A.

Leiber: It's funny. I just saw Ahmet the other day and he said, "Hey man, I want you to write some songs for Peggy. We just signed her."

Stoller: When we went up to Peggy's house she was playing an album of Randy Newman doing his own songs, the big orchestra one, with songs like "Linda" and "I Think It's Gonna Rain Today." The orchestrations were so beautiful that we decided to use him on "Is That All There Is?", and he did a brilliant job of arranging and orchestrating it.

That brings up a question I meant to ask before. How did it feel for you as songwriters to work with other songwriters when you were producers or record company owners? Did you feel sympathetic?

Leiber: I think so. Strangely enough, I think because we were such prolific producers, we never felt very competitive. We would sometimes give the back side of a surefire hit to another writer. I guess we thought we could make a hit record anytime we felt like it.

Stoller: It wasn't like we were taking pity on anyone. It wasn't charity. There was enough for everybody.

Leiber: There was so much going on. We had so many opportunities to do whatever we wanted. If a songwriter came along with a great song we'd do it. We loved good songs.

You mean you weren't a couple of pains in the neck who would start rewriting songs?

Leiber: Oh yes, we were. I was very tough on writers. I made Gerry Goffin and Carole King rewrite the lyrics to the bridge on "Up on the Roof." And I had Doc Pomus rewrite part of "Save the Last Dance for Me."

Stoller: We changed the structure on lots of those songs. But we were close friends of these writers and we could say, "Look, Doc, we're going to take this section out, and come out of the instrumen-

tal right into here." And he'd say, "Oh man, that sounds great."
Leiber: To make the song better, to make the record better, to make
the production better, we felt that we had that obligation as
producer/arrangers.

(October, 1985)

Bob Thiele

F ans of modern jazz know Bob Thiele as the man who produced John Coltrane's great ABC Impulse records, as well as those of Archie Shepp, Albert Ayler, and many other jazz greats. His stature as a producer would be secure just on the basis of such outstanding and critically important recordings as Trane's *A Love Supreme* and his avant-garde masterpiece, *Ascension*. But Thiele's amazingly varied career is comprised of much more.

He began recording jazz as a teenager in 1939 when he founded an early and successful independent jazz record company, Signature, whose catalog boasted Erroll Garner, Coleman Hawkins, Lester Young, Pee Wee Russell, Eddie Heywood, and others. At Decca, after much arm-twisting, he convinced his bosses to let him release, on the Coral subsidiary, the first records of a strange-looking young Texan— Buddy Holly. On another subsidiary, Brunswick, he made the debut recordings of soul legend Jackie Wilson. At Dot he recorded Pat Boone's big hits, as well as those of Lawrence Welk. He made records with Steve Allen, and with Allen released a controversial record by Jack Kerouac. At Roulette he put Louis Armstrong and Duke Ellington together.

During the blues resurgence of the sixties, Thiele

made records with B. B. King, John Lee Hooker, and T-Bone Walker. On his Flying Dutchman label he introduced new jazz stars like Gil Scott-Heron and Oliver Nelson. He produced the early hits of a lovely young singer, Teresa Brewer, married her in 1972, and is now making jazz records with her. He has resurrected Signature and is once again creating new jazz, putting out previously unreleased material on his Dr. Jazz label. In this interview he talks about it all.

The Impulse jazz catalog is such a great collection of music. But in this country, when MCA rereleased the records, they issued them without the double gatefold album covers. Did you have any control over or input into the series of rereleases?

No. As far as the rereleasing of the Impulse series, I was completely out of the picture. Undoubtedly someone in the company had a feeling for the Impulse catalog, and they decided, from an economic or financial standpoint, it would make sense to rerelease them at a lower price. So the packaging certainly wasn't up to the original.

But I understand in Britain . . .

Yeah. MCA has licensed to Warner Bros., in England, the rights to the entire Impulse catalog. And it's their intention to use the double gatefold and the original art, and to redo all the masters from the original tapes. So the sound should be better, and of course the jackets will be to the same standard as the original records.

How would they go about remastering the original tapes?

There are two ways of going when you reissue an album. You can use the original metal parts, which should still be at the factory and available to press records. Or you can take the original master tape and cut new lacquer masters for plating. You can always, with the advent of new equipment and the various technological advances, improve upon the original transfer from the tape to the lacquer disc. So in very simplistic terms, you might be able to brighten the recording, add more bottom to it, add more top to it, add more middle range. Whatever you feel would improve it, you do.

I heard that you are moving into digital recording for the first time.

We're going to do it. We haven't done any digital recording as yet. Personally, I'm really at the learning stage. I have engineers at CBS and RCA—I don't mean that I'm taking a course—but we sort of hang out together, and they're educating me as to the proper procedures for digital recording.

Is digital recording something you think everyone is going to have to do from now on?

I think it's fine to do if you can enhance the quality of the music, and if the price is the same as the price of a normal phonograph record. I love to have great quality, and I try my damnedest to make good-sounding records. I probably, through the years, developed less as an audiophile than as a music person. I mean, I still have equipment that can play 78s, and the scratch doesn't bother me as long as the music's there.

John Hammond was telling me—that his wife never really got used to buying LPs.

I don't go that far. When I say I still listen to 78s, I would add that the only 78s I listen to are recordings that are not available on LP. I prefer to listen to an LP. I'd rather listen to Benny Goodman's "King Porter Stomp" on LP than the original 78.

Do you share Hammond's philosophy in the studio, favoring simplicity over fancier, more advanced techniques?

I think that we really have to separate the music. In terms of jazz, when one strives to enhance the music already there—what's being played—I think that you're defeating the purpose of what jazz is all about. You want to capture jazz music as it actually happens. Whereas when we go in and record in England and in various "rock" studios, it's an altogether different approach. I would never take a jazz band into a studio that specializes in R&B and rock because there, the concept is just completely different. You're recording separate tracks for your rhythm section. You may bring in voices for a day and just use them against the rhythm tracks. Bring in horns on another day. Bring in your star vocalist, and put that track on at the end. And all of that can be reversed, too. I've even used electronic drums. I've used all that, but 90 percent of what I do is jazz, and all of the things I've just mentioned have no relationship to jazz music at all. It just doesn't make any sense.

When you look for a jazz studio, are you looking for a place that specializes in more of an ensemble sound?

Well, there are no *jazz* studios, but there are . . . Well, for example, RCA has two tremendous studios here in New York. There's twenty-four-track tape . . . all the latest technical advances available. We recorded jazz at RCA because we're recording something as it happens. We're trying not to do anything to it later on, except mix it and make sure the balance is right. If I was recording at the Power Station—not that there's anything wrong with it; I enjoy making rock records, I enjoy R&B records—but there the whole concept is different. You're laying down separate tracks constantly, and I just don't see that as far as jazz is concerned.

How did you come to Impulse, and what was the concept at its inception?

I went to Impulse probably around 1960. The company was ABC Paramount. I went to work there as Director of Artists and Repertoire, which encompassed all popular music, including jazz. Impulse had actually started by then. I think they had released six or seven albums. Creed Taylor was the producer who made those first records. I don't know the arrangement he had with ABC, but after he made the first six or seven, I came in and they asked me to continue the Impulse catalog. I know I was *living* in the studio. Over a period of three to five years, maybe, I must have made literally two hundred albums.

There was such an incredible roster at Impulse.

I think the roster . . . This may sound corny to say, but I started in the record business when I was about seventeen and I'm still in it, and, either fortunately or unfortunately, I really have never made a record anticipating how it would sell. I think almost every record I've made has been made because I personally liked the music. It's as though I was making records for my own record collection.

When I look at my *record collection, I see huge chunks of it with orange and black spines with little white dots. That's Impulse, and a lot of it is John Coltrane albums.*

That spine was not just a fluke; some careful thought went into that. We felt that there were no records—and to this day there aren't any—where the spine is always the same no matter what the music is or what the cover is. We did those spines for two reasons. One, the consumer would always be able to spot them in his collection. And two, which is more important, the dealers would know where to look for Impulse when they had them filed on their shelves. So that was by design. With my new label [Dr. Jazz], if you look at it you'll find that the bottom half is always yellow. I'm always surprised that nobody else does it. I hate to give away my secrets, but that's one of them.

It's a great idea, and I get a kick out of seeing the spines expand in my record collection.

I remember I was at a Newport Jazz Festival. A guy walked up to me and said, "You're Bob Thiele." I said, "Yeah." He said, "I want to thank you for making those spines orange and black." I thought he was going to say, "Gee, those recordings are great." [Laughter.]

*Let's talk about the Impulse roster. There was Coltrane, Albert
Ayler, Archie Shepp, Pharoah Sanders, Charlie Haden's band, and
of course Duke Ellington, Coleman Hawkins, Quincy Jones . . . so
many great people. When you came to Impulse, were many of
these artists already signed, or did you go out as talent scout and
A&R man and sign them up?*

I actually went out and signed 99 percent of the people. The only
individual who had signed a contract with ABC Impulse before I
arrived was Coltrane. I believe his first album was *Africa/Brass*. It
was number A-6, right in that first group of six or seven albums
to come out on the Impulse label.

*You've said that Coltrane really taught you things about music.
In what way? You've also said he kept you involved in jazz.*

It wasn't that he kept me involved in jazz. He brought me to what,
in that period, was the "new jazz" or "new black jazz." The critics
were giving it all sorts of names. Another classification at the time
was "avant-garde." For his second album for Impulse, we decided
to record live at the Village Vanguard. I was apprehensive, a little
nervous about doing it. I had not known Coltrane before then. I had
heard some of his records. He was turning jazz music around. So
I met him. You know, there was no reason to have meetings before
making the recordings because we were merely recording whatever
he played; it wasn't a question of selecting certain tunes to be
played. We decided to record, I believe, all three nights of his
[stand at the Vanguard]. But it was just at that initial stage, during
those three nights, that I got to know him. He happened to be very
warm, very friendly, and very quiet. He certainly wasn't outgoing.
He was, as I recall it, reticent to talk about anything. But we hit
it off. I mean, sometimes these things happen. I've grown up with
musicians. I deal with musicians. I relate to them, I guess. And we
got along fine, as I began to spend more and more time with him,
and we had our various meetings as to what should be used for an
album, and where we should record, and what musicians to use.
    It was during this period that he was explaining to me what he
was trying to do musically. Initially, all I knew when I heard some
of the music, being an old-time swinger, was that it sounded as

though he was literally leaving the chords. When he was improvising, it just didn't hit me right. But I have a hunch that part of it was that he felt he could go further. I mean, I've really thought about it quite a bit; he explained everything to me, why he was playing the way he played, and how he felt music could go. He always felt restricted playing within the chord, staying within the chords of, say, a Cole Porter song. He was the first guy who really took vamps, and played endlessly on three chords. But those vamps were just devastating. They were truly exciting. I think what I'm trying to lead up to is that it happened naturally. You know, you can go to school and have someone explain a subject to two students, and one bombs out while the other just goes, bam, right along with it. Because I know other producers my age who, to this day, look at me like I'm nuts. They can't understand how I can listen to that music or why people buy it. Yet some of these fellows made some of the finest recordings in the history of classic jazz. And then the curtain came down [on traditional jazz] and it never went any further.

What did Coltrane say to you to convince you, other than just playing?

He explained it technically, as to why one could leave the chords. "Who says there has to be a restriction on what you play?" And the more I listened, the more it sounded natural to me.

When I was just getting into jazz, I picked up Coltrane's Ascension. *I just couldn't listen to it. I parked it for about a year and listened to earlier Coltrane. Then one day I put* Ascension *back on, and it just clicked. It was there. I heard it. It was an amazing experience to hear this masterpiece for the first time, and understand it.*

What you're saying is what I'm saying. You can be technical until you throw up, but how many people ask you, "What is jazz?" or "How do you know when you're listening to jazz?" or "How do you learn to like jazz?" I'm sure you've heard it before. Some of those classic jazz producers know Fats Waller's line, "If you have to explain it, then you don't know what it is." There's no way to explain it. I believe that somehow it's inbred in America, in the people as they grow up. All popular music stems from jazz. Gershwin and composers like that wrote because they heard jazz musicians. They went to Harlem and heard jazz bands. The songwriters of our day were really writing rhythmic popular songs. The song "Margie" swings if Coltrane or Coleman Hawkins plays it. They were writing a form of popular music that definitely had roots in jazz. What can you say? Either you feel it or you don't feel it.

Did Ascension *really cause a furor?*

It did. I did things with Coltrane that other producers probably wouldn't have done, and couldn't have been able to do; I let him record whenever he wanted to record. He had the idea to record *Ascension.* My role, as opposed to working with Duke Ellington or Coleman Hawkins or Count Basie, where I had a tremendous input as far as selection of material, as far as what takes we should accept . . .

But not with Trane?

Not with Trane. I think that my contribution with Trane, as I said, was to let him record whenever he wanted to—even in opposition to the power structure in the company. To the best of my recollection, Coltrane had a contract that called for two albums a year to be recorded and released. Well, hell, we recorded *six* albums a year. And I was always brought on the carpet because they couldn't understand why I was spending the money to record John Coltrane. We couldn't possibly put out all the records that we were making. It even reached a point where I would record late at night so that no one in the company would know where I was, because if I was out during the day they'd say, "Where's Bob Thiele?" Someone would answer, "Well, he's recording John Coltrane in New Jersey." I'd do it at night so at least we'd have peace then.

    Ascension was all his. I had nothing to do with the creation of the music. I was surprised when all these musicians showed up. Very quickly he told them what he wanted them to do and where we were going, and it was just going to be continuous. He did a take. Coltrane always had a tendency to want to do something

again, so we made a second take. When I had everything transferred to cassette, I sent it to him to listen to. I don't remember
which take he liked, but I, by accident, put out the other one. That's
the record that came out first. So I decided, with his approval, to
play a little game. After we went through the initial pressing run,
I changed the masters to the other take. I inscribed "Edition Two"
on the inside of the runout circle on the lacquer. It took several
months before collectors and musicians started to pick up on it and
say, "Hey, what's going on?" So, really, there are two versions of
it out there.

*You were usually involved with jazz musicians who stayed closer
to the melody and within the song structure. Was it a problem as
a producer to record a very long piece like "Ascension" or "A
Love Supreme," which each took up two record sides?*

It wasn't a problem because at that stage I had actually joined in
the movement. It was invigorating. I probably became more excited
and more creative because of those recordings. It really helped me
continue my career. I just became more and more excited about
making records—all kinds of records. But most of the guys who
were producing jazz sort of came to that curtain. They didn't, in
my way of thinking, really progress with the music. I listen to
Coltrane, and I still listen to Bix Beiderbecke, and I listen to Louis
Armstrong's Hot Five, I listen to everything. One of my greatest
kicks is hearing a great Dixieland band. I love all kinds of jazz
music. Coltrane just opened it up, and helped me appreciate the
jazz that was unfamiliar to me until I met him.

Tell me something about the critical reaction at the time to
Ascension *and, earlier, to* A Love Supreme.

I remember most of the critics and the various music magazines
were putting Coltrane down. And there's one time when I did
suggest to him. I said, "Why don't we just go in and show these
guys?" I suggested that we do an album of popular songs, all
ballads. We went in and did *Ballads,* which I think is a beautiful
album, and he loved it. And that started to turn the critics around.
Then, as time passed, I think people started to reevaluate things

like *A Love Supreme* and *Ascension*. They recognized the greatness.

*I've heard all kinds of stories about Mingus. What was he really
like to work with?*

Charlie was an all-right guy. He was always after me to make
records. He always wanted to record. But I was budgeted, and I was
trying to make as many records as I could. . . . In the studio and
musically, there were never any problems. There were [other] problems that existed that I really wouldn't want to get into. In those
days things were pretty hot and heavy. I know I used to have
meetings with Leroi Jones, now Amiri Baraka. I got pretty friendly
with him. There was a white critic around named Frank Kofsky
who I got close to. What happened was that, for the literary frater-
nity, the music of Coltrane and others, like Mingus and all of the
modern group, really represented black militancy. Most of the
musicians, including Coltrane, really weren't thinking the way their
[militant] brothers were. I mean, Leroi Jones could feel the music
was militant, but Coltrane didn't feel that it was. But he didn't go
out of his way to tell Leroi Jones that.

Mingus, though, was different.

Well, Mingus was a little different; in that period I think he was
on the militant side. I remember Stanley Crouch, who is a very dear
friend of mine, who writes to this day for the *Village Voice*. . . .
Stanley and I used to argue for hours and hours about the music
and the black movement. I asked him to write liner notes for a
Duke Ellington album. Duke had put together a show called *My
People* which was basically a short history of blacks in the United
States. When I sent the record down to him to write the liner notes,
I said, "Stanley, before you start this, Duke Ellington is not a
militant. Take it from there." And the liner notes opened with:
"Bob Thiele says that Duke Ellington is not a militant." And then
he went on to write his notes. See, Stanley was very subtle. He
pointed out something to me that I really hadn't thought about until
then, which was about fifteen years ago. When you think of his
titles, Ellington was, in his own quiet way, really trying to show the

greatness of black people in America—"Black and Tan Fantasy,"
"Black, Brown and Beige." There was a record Duke made in 1929
that I picked up later, a thing called "Black Beauty." Now, I was
still a kid when I found the record, sixteen or seventeen years old,
and I thought it was named after the horse. Because there was
nothing going on then about various social problems, and Stanley
pointed that out to me. He said, "Hey, he means what he says,
black is beautiful." Duke, in a way, was the first person to say that.

*You've had quite an association with Duke Ellington over the
years, and you've also been responsible for some unusual pairings
with him: Duke and Coltrane, Duke and Louis Armstrong.*

I think that Duke has probably made the deepest impression upon
me. It's different than Coltrane. Duke was a musician whom I
idolized as a kid, when I first started to listen to music. I'd go out
many nights alone, all by myself, and listen to music. Somewhere
along the line I was listening to Ellington night after night, and he
spotted me and we got talking. Here again, it was a natural thing.
It developed into a terrific friendship. I was always flattered. As the
years went by, we did an awful lot of things together. I got to know
his family; we all became friends. When we did the pairings, I just
told Duke my idea. Anything I ever wanted to do with Duke, he'd
say, "Let's do it, let's go."

*You did the Armstrong/Ellington session when you were with
Roulette?*

Yes. I had always wanted to record Louis. I had only met him a
few times. Louis was amenable. Duke said okay. We did all Ellington songs, as I recall.

*Did you sit down with the two of them and decide which songs
were going to be recorded?*

Yeah. It's always difficult, especially with extremely popular musicians who were always on the road. They were always touring, so
I had to meet with each of them separately. Duke's attitude was,
any songs you want to play, we'll play. So I really had to discuss

the songs with Louis so that he felt comfortable with them and knew what was coming. But there were no arrangements. We just picked keys and did it.

How about the Ellington/Coltrane pairing? That is certainly a much more discordant mix, on the face of it.

Discordant on the face of it, but it worked out beautifully. There again, I think that's one of the great recordings. Duke was from a different era. He could make *anybody* feel comfortable, and he could make anyone think they were his dearest friend. He and Coltrane got along famously. Two points I'd make about the album. Johnny Hodges told me that "In a Sentimental Mood" was one of the best readings he'd ever heard. I think the way this recording affected Coltrane was that, while Ellington's style was to capture music as quickly as possible on recordings, Coltrane could stay there in the studio all day playing the same piece over and over again. I remember hearing him do things where it just kept going downhill, and he would become depressed and throw his hands up and say, "We'll try this again some other time." Probably the first or second playing was a gem, but by the time he did it twenty times, it wasn't a gem anymore. Duke knew that. Duke knew from experience: If you get it, save it. Don't try to destroy it by playing it over again. I really don't remember which tune, it might have been "In a Sentimental Mood," but I was in the booth and they played a song. After the first take, I looked up and Duke was smiling and Coltrane wasn't smiling. I knew just what was going to happen. I knew Coltrane was going to say, "Let's do it again," and Duke was going to say, "That's beautiful." I sort of felt good about it, so I ran over to Coltrane and said, "John, that was it," and Duke said, "Bob, you're absolutely right. John, don't ever do it again here." Then we talked about it. I think I got Coltrane out of that rut of trying to make things perfect. You do lose the spontaneity and the excitement by doing it over and over again. So I think he learned something from that album.

Did Ellington know about Coltrane and appreciate him?

Oh, yeah, yeah. Duke had big ears. He knew. I didn't realize it until
years later that Oliver Nelson played saxophone with Ellington.
Duke hired some great players, not just players from the twenties.

*Let's go back and talk about your earlier days with Signature in
the thirties and forties. You were the first to record Erroll Garner.
You did Earl Hines, Coleman Hawkins, Lester Young, so many
people. How did Signature come about?*

I was a kid. In the middle to late thirties, I was bitten by the jazz
bug. I began to appreciate and understand jazz. I remember exactly
when I became interested—I received a phonograph for a birthday
present. But, you know, I heard literally all of the dance bands
. . . everyone from Benny Goodman to Hal Kemp to Will Osborne.
Somewhere along the line I began to hear some Fats Waller records. I think Fats Waller's records were the ones that sort of turned
me into a jazz fan. I heard some Paul Whiteman and some Frankie
Trumbauer. Through those recordings, I learned of Bix Beiderbecke. About four or five musicians—I just wanted to hear every
single note that they played.

   I began to find that I was listening to records and to live music
in all of my free time. It was almost an obsession. I would come
home from school and go right into a room and listen to records
until dinner time. My mother thought I was freaking out. My father
wasn't sure what was going on. He was the buffer. He said, "He
likes music, so let him listen to music." I can see where, in those
days, it would seem strange. Other kids were doing the baseball
thing and what have you, and I'm up there listening to records.
Over a period of a few years, I probably heard every jazz record
ever made, whether it was Jelly Roll Morton or Johnny Dodds. I
can practically hear all of those records today. I know them like
I know the palm of my hand.

How do you get from that to being a producer?

I guess I had some drive in that direction, like some kids want to
be a lawyer or doctor. I was so involved with records and I was
hearing so much music, so many musicians, that at some point I

said, "I've got to record some of the musicians who are not being
recorded." There were a lot of little labels around in the late
thirties. Everybody was pressing records, all kinds of records. I was
in my last year of high school, probably taking all lightweight
courses. I had an art class and the final exam was to do a design.
I designed two record labels—one was Capitol and one Signature
—because I was going to make some records. Shortly after high
school, I went to a club called the Ideal Spot on the outskirts of
Forest Hills [New York], where I lived. Of all people to wind up
playing there—it was such a strange thing—was a guy from Chicago who played blues and boogie-woogie, Art Hodes. So, I'd go
over there every night and listen. He had a bass and drums with
him. I suggested that we cut four sides, and those were the first
sides I did.

You just went up and introduced yourself to him?

That's right. You know, I don't mean I'm on an ego trip or anything, but there was such a deep love of what I was into, the
musicians and the music. It wasn't just walking up. Maybe over a
period of a few nights of hanging out with the guy . . . Somehow,
they liked me. I always get along very well with musicians.

What did you know about making a record?

All I knew was that you hire a studio and get an engineer, and you
put up three mikes, and that was it. It went from microphone to
lacquer disc; there was no tape. So we recorded Hodes first, and
I remember flipping a coin to see which label I'd use, because I had
the two designs, Capitol and Signature. That was the beginning of
Signature Records. I had the records pressed in Pennsylvania, at
the Scranton Record Company. Anybody could get records pressed.
They shipped the records to my father's house. I didn't have
distribution. I really don't remember how I advertised; I must have
taken a couple of little ads in *downbeat* or something. I would sell
directly to dealers. In those days there were some great ones. I'd
have one or two dealers in each of the major cities. There was
Schirmer here in New York, and there was an outfit called Mar-
coni's on Madison Avenue. In those days, those buyers would buy

one or two of almost every record that came out, especially for their collector customers. I would get orders, wrap the records in the bathroom, run the gum tape through the sink, wrap up my cartons, mail them out at the local post office, and bill the customer. In New York, I'd deliver the records myself. I sold every store on Broadway. In those days, 1938 or '39, there must have been fifteen record shops along Broadway from 42nd to 57th Street. Loaded with record shops. I'd go in and deliver my records and get paid for them.

You went on to record top people at Signature.

I recorded Yank Lawson, Pee Wee Russell, and Eddie Condon; I did some things with James P. Johnson, and he's a perfect example of how I worked. I heard some of his records. About the same time, 1936 or '37, a dear friend of mine named Dan Priest became as much interested in jazz as I was, so at least there were two buddies who could go out and hear the music together. We decided to put out a jazz magazine, called *Jazz.* There was no outlet for jazz writing then, and I remember some of the critics at the time, Charles Edward Smith and Charles Paine Rogers. These guys were really intellectual, and they were deeply interested in the history of the music. They wound up sending us articles because nobody else would print them. In fact, the first book on jazz—which I think was the greatest—was written by them, along with two others. It was called *Jazzmen,* a great book. Anyway, the first issue of this magazine had a feature story on Scott Joplin. The author had dug up the famous picture—you know, whenever you see a picture of Scott Joplin, it's the only picture anyone has. But here were these kids, and we come out with a magazine, and we're bringing the world the music of Scott Joplin. I said, "Who the hell was Scott Joplin?" The author said, "He's the greatest ragtime piano player, the greatest composer of ragtime." But he referred an awful lot in the article to James P. Johnson and other rag players, Willie the Lion Smith, people like that.

I listened to a few James P. Johnson records, and found out that he lived on Long Island, near Forest Hills. I said, "I'm going over to see James P. Johnson." I had his address and I didn't call; I just went up to the door and knocked. This little gray-haired lady

answered the door. I said, "You don't know me, I'm Bob Thiele,
I just wanted to meet James P. Johnson." And she said, "Well,
come on in, son." He was a hulk of a man. I don't want to say he
was ugly, but he certainly wasn't handsome. He had a very big
head. He came down the stairs, and he wound up playing piano for
me for about an hour. He sat there playing all his compositions.
And I became a friend of his. I recorded him with Yank Lawson
and Pee Wee Russell and people like that.

Then, when the war came, I ended up in the coast guard. I was
stationed at Manhattan Beach, Brooklyn, for practically the whole
war. I guess I can consider myself lucky that I was stationed at a
base in the United States, but in a way, it was bad because I was
too close to home, so I wasn't in or out of the service. Near the end
I remember Shelly Manne was in the band down there, in the coast
guard. That's where we met. Shelly and I became good friends, and
we'd go into town every night and listen to jazz. It was at that point
that I got to know Coleman Hawkins, and we recorded him. And
I got to know Dicky Wells and the fellows in the Basie band. We
did a thing with Dicky Wells and Lester Young.

Signature folded right after the war, didn't it?

What actually happened is, my father sort of kept that going. He
had had nothing to do with the music business. He happened to
like music, and he was proud of the fact that I had a little business
going and was selling records. A normal parent reaction. So he said,
"When you go in the service, don't worry about the records you
have. If we get orders, I'll ship the records for you, and I'll order
records as we need them." We had ten or twelve records, all 78s,
and when Coleman Hawkins' "The Man I Love" came out we had
my father's office listed as the address. It really became almost a
popular recording. The dealers in Harlem were coming down to his
office to buy the record, and they'd pay cash. That really impressed
him. He said, "He's not only got a business going, but they're
paying cash for the records. This kid's got something on the ball."
After the war we got the bright idea to expand and make it a real
record company. Through his help, and various friends, we actually
sold stock in the company, we started to build a record company.
Then it became such a big business, it was too big for me to handle.

I had no business experience. Psychologically, I wasn't ready to be in an office at 9:00 and run a business. I started to, like, fall apart. I was listening to jazz at 4:00 in the morning and boozing it up; then I was supposed to go in and run a record company. It finally went out of business, bankrupt, in 1948 or '49.

After Signature, you were independent for a while, and then in the early fifties you went to Coral Records.

In those days, really, there was no such thing as an independent producer. Either you worked for a company or you had your own company. I wasn't doing anything at the time. I had a couple of jobs that really didn't mean anything, just working to make a few bucks. I was hired at Decca as an assistant producer to work on the new Coral label that was formed by Jack Kapp, who was president of Decca. He felt that the independent record companies were getting too much activity, selling too many records, and he wanted to get in on it. Rather than use Decca, he formed Coral Records and put Coral through independent distributors, not Decca distributors. So Coral was in direct competition, with all the little fellows that were trying to make it in the record business.

This was in pop music, and rhythm and blues?

Yeah. It was an all-purpose record label. Pop, rhythm and blues, jazz. So I guess I went to work there in the early fifties, and I started out as an assistant producer. Certainly by '53 or '54 I wound up as head of A&R. Those were sort of my glory days, from a pop standpoint. For a period of eight or nine years, I had hits flying out of there. It was unreal.

Tell me about Buddy Holly. He was your biggest smash there.

Murray Deutsch, who was the general manager of a music publishing house called Southern Music, came to me with some dubs of a group called The Crickets. You know, Coral certainly wasn't as important as Columbia, RCA, Decca. Murray had received these dubs from Norman Petty, who produced them in Clovis, New Mexico. You sent them to a music publisher in those days and said,

"Look, you can publish the music, but will you please try to have these records released by some record company?" Murray came to me and played "That'll Be the Day." I flipped. I said, "Hey, this is terrific. We're going to put it out." I found out later, by the way, that he had gone all over the place, and everybody said, "dumb sound." It's true.

In those days at Coral, I had a recording budget, so much money per quarter. It's different than the record business today. If a record is being presented to Columbia, for example, the first person to hear it might be a lawyer or an accountant, or it might be a guy in the music department. Then that record is played at a meeting that involves maybe nine people; sales, marketing, lawyers, accountants, everybody gets involved. How they actually get records out, I don't know, but they do. Columbia and all the companies seem to be doing the right thing. But in those days it tested with one man. Every record that was made, every song, every artist all came under the jurisdiction of the one guy, the head of A&R. You were the one guy in that company. The president of the company didn't care who you recorded or what songs you did, as long as there was a profit, as long as you were selling records. So when there was something new, you always had to get approval—not approval of the amount of money you were going to spend, but that it would fit within your overall budget. But [with Holly], I was so excited, I wound up playing the record for a lot of people in the company, and everybody said, "Forget it! You just don't put this kind of a record out." I remember the president telling me, "You can't put it on Coral. It'll hurt the image of the label. We have some great artists on Coral, and here you're coming out with this horrible thing by The Crickets." I believe, now, that they let me put it out for two quite simple reasons: One was that I was of value to them, and they didn't want to really upset me. I was sort of an emotional guy at the time, and I would quit at the drop of a hat. I'd walk in and say, "I quit." Then I'd regret it, but I'd go through the motions, I guess. What really solved the problem was that they owned the Brunswick label. I told them, "If you're so concerned about the image of Coral, put it on the Brunswick label." And they said, "Go enjoy yourself." Well, I remember we were at a convention in the Midwest somewhere. We used to check with the office every day. The sales manager said, "Bob, I don't know what happened, but we got an order for sixteen thousand records from Philadelphia on 'That'll Be the Day.' "

Had you had a chance to meet Buddy Holly at that point?

No, at that point I hadn't met him. Murray Deutsch and I were invited to Clovis, New Mexico, to receive whatever—a Western hat and a key to the city [laughter]. So we flew down and that's when we met Buddy Holly. We stayed there about two or three days, and got to know everybody. I suggested we record and keep The Crickets going, but put Buddy Holly on Coral, even if it's with The Crickets. Buddy Holly on Coral and The Crickets on Brunswick.

What for?

I guess I was really thinking commercially. Buddy was the personality, and we didn't really want to bust up The Crickets and Buddy Holly. So I felt we'd get more exposure, more of a run for our money, by having it get out there two ways.

How did they decide which records would be credited to Buddy Holly and which to The Crickets?

The main guy who was doing the producing at the time was Norman Petty. He lived in Clovis. He really found these kids. He really decided. We'd say, "Look, we want a Buddy Holly record for the next release, and then we'd like a Crickets record." And he'd go in the studio there, and he'd make the records. That's how that was done.

Did you get involved with Buddy as a producer?

Only once. Buddy and I got to know one another pretty well. He was a terrific kid. Very unassuming, and a real gentleman—he always had a suit and tie on. So opposite of what it is today. He always wanted to record in New York. As I've said before, Norman Petty was jealous of the fact that Buddy wanted to get to New York and make some records there and that he wanted to work with me. Anyway, he did get to New York, but we wound up with only two

sides. We did a thing called "Rave On" and a standard, "That's
My Desire," which didn't come out until about three years ago,
when Steve Hoffman at MCA found it. "Rave On" was tremendous.
We did that on Eighth Avenue in a hot studio at the time. I didn't
want to use the Decca studio, so we used Bell Sound. At least at
Bell, unlike at Decca, we could isolate musicians. It was a dead-
sounding studio, the sound wasn't traveling all over the place. I
knew that's where I should record him.

Were you in the movie, The Buddy Holly Story?

No. The interesting thing is that the A&R producer in the movie
turned out to be a black guy. I didn't quite understand where all
these facts came from, but it was based on John Goldrosen's book.
Maybe a year or two ago I got a call from Goldrosen. He said he
had to see me, and that he was writing a revised edition of the book.
Well, he was amazed at the story of how things happened. If you
read the revised edition, you'll read exactly what I'm telling you,
and more. I mean, there were all sorts of shady deals down there
in Clovis, and I don't want to say it.

*I'm surprised that Brunswick was considered the "B" label. For
me, Jackie Wilson was the great Brunswick star. How did he come
to your attention?*

There was a manager of artists, Al Green; I think he was out of
Detroit. He'd been around for years managing black artists. In
those days what would happen is, you'd get a call from Al Green,
and he'd say, "I'd like to come by and play you some music, and
introduce you to some of my acts." And that was our job. We saw
the people who had reputations and could present some new talent
for us. So he came in and he had a vocal group he wanted to sell
me, the Dominoes. So I went to the Apollo Theatre one night to
hear them. I saw Jackie Wilson with the Dominoes and I said to
myself, "To hell with the Dominoes, let's take Jackie Wilson." In
those days there were a lot of cut-throat approaches to things, I
admit. I said to Al Green, "I don't want to sign a vocal group, but
I'd like to sign the kid." Well, you know, all he saw were the dollar

signs, and he said, "I don't care about the vocal group either. Take Jackie Wilson, you got him." So, I'll never forget, Al Green was staying at the Taft Hotel in New York, and I wanted to get the contract signed. He had had it a couple of days, and I was to pick it up at his hotel one morning. So I rang the room and a young man gets on, a kid eighteen or nineteen years old, and he says, "Mr. Green died last night." I said, "Oh, my God, that's terrible!" He said, "But I have a contract here that I was supposed to give you this morning." So he came down and gave me the contract. And that kid was a fellow named Nat Tarnapol, who later became Jackie Wilson's manager. He even wound up at Brunswick because Decca—after I had left the company—in an attempt to keep Jackie Wilson, gave him the label. They gave him Brunswick; that was part of the deal.

Berry Gordy wrote his first songs. Did you ever deal with Gordy?

No, I didn't know who he was. But we wound up with these songs and we went in and recorded. The thing that was different was that Jackie was an R&B artist, but we didn't record him as an R&B artist. Rhythmically we did. It was an R&B sound. Little Richard or Fats Domino had four or five guys and a couple of saxes, and boom, that was it. But we used a regular sixteen-piece orchestra. We had a big band for him. Somehow—and his acceptance proved it—somehow that overall sound not only appealed to the black market, which was a specific market in those days, but it also got into the white market quicker than if we had made out-and-out R&B records.

On the other hand, some people have said, "He's from Detroit, he was involved with Berry Gordy. If he had signed on at Motown, he might have had a much greater career. . . ."

He might have had a greater career if there was the proper control exercised over his personal life. I think that had a lot to do with it. That's a subject you can't really go into.

Sure, you can.

Well, we know he got involved with drugs. I don't say that he had the best guidance in all areas. I'm not talking about recording, because I'm not going to say we were making lousy records. We were making good records. But I would say, in all other aspects of his career, I think he was misguided. I don't think he was treated properly. From a financial aspect, I can't even talk about it. But knowing the business as I do, I'm sure he wasn't seeing all the dollars he made, even though he got some new clothes and a new car and things like that. But he was also getting drugs. So maybe Motown would have been better. . . . I don't think in the strict recording sense. . . . I think it would have been better in a guidance sense. Because as I know the story, and you do too, Berry Gordy and people like that, they really controlled the lives of those artists, which was a new approach at the time.

After Brunswick you went to Dot, around '59 or '60. Now you were producing Pat Boone, The Mills Brothers, all kinds of middle-of-the-road people. Then, from that, you went to producing a Jack Kerouac album that Dot president Randy Wood recalled for being obscene. Was the Kerouac album a reaction on your part to doing all this middle-of-the-road music?

No. I've said this before: I enjoy the recording business, the recording industry. I love to record. I love to make records by all kinds of artists. I always say this jokingly; if you called me tomorrow and said you had the greatest polka band in the United States and would I record them, I'd say yes. I enjoy working with performers and artists. Jazz is certainly my true love. It's my main thing. But in those days, when I had a hit record with the McGuire Sisters, that was pretty exciting. That was great. Buddy Holly records. I enjoyed making the album with Pat Boone. After all, Pat Boone was a nice guy. There was no problem. It was up to me to assemble a large orchestra. I think we recorded him with about twenty-six or thirty guys, here in New York. We did standard tunes. Pat Boone was discovered by Randy Wood. Here again, it's something I can't understand, but I guess it applies to any business—jealousy is always rearing its ugly head. Here I am, recording Randy's boy in New York, and Randy is out in L.A. And at the end of the session we called Randy, and Pat got on the phone and said, "Boy, I'm so happy here. We're having a great time and the record sounds great." The next morning, Randy Wood was in the recording studio. He flew in. He probably said, "This is all I need. Bob Thiele will leave some day, and take Pat Boone with him."

Did that affect the session, after he showed up?

Oh, no. He let us go on. And The Mills Brothers, they're great guys. [Their music] may not be as deep as some great jazz, but boy, it's fun, and it's a pleasure. You know, making records can be a good time.

How did the record with Jack Kerouac come about?

Well, the same thing would happen as what happened at Coral. Because of my luck or ability to make pop records, I was able to do my labor of love, make jazz records. If I was unsuccessful making pop records, then I wouldn't be permitted, you might say, to spend money making jazz records. When I went to Roulette, it was basically the same approach. Even when you think back to the days at Impulse—I mean, I had a few hit records there. I remember they brought in Frankie Laine, who hadn't had a hit in years, and we had a hit. So I kept the jazz thing going. But at Dot Records, Randy Wood and I didn't get along. Outwardly it looked like we were very friendly, but I don't think we really appreciated or respected one another. Here was a guy from Gallatin, Tennessee, a producer, who could go in and make records. He did all these Little Richard hits with Pat Boone. He produced all these things. I'm sure he wanted me around to produce The Mills Brothers and people like that. I don't think he felt that comfortable with the black performers. But there are white record companies and black record companies, and then there are the companies who produce it all. I'd hate to think I was going to go through life only being permitted to record white artists or black artists. So I got involved in the soundtrack of that Red Nichols life-story picture, *The Five Pennies.* I got to know Danny Kaye, and got Wood involved. I had had a big hit with Debbie Reynolds at Coral, "Tammy." So I brought Debbie Reynolds to Dot. And the crowning achievement, for Randy Wood, was that I was able to get Lawrence Welk to leave

Decca and come to Dot. Of course, they got along great. Lawrence
Welk doesn't drink and he doesn't smoke and he doesn't swear,
and neither did Randy Wood. So they got along famously, and I
sort of just slipped by. I was losing my friendship with Welk,
because I drink and smoke and curse.

So I made a few jazz things at Dot. Wood said, "Okay with me."
We did some albums with Manny Albam, a terrific arranger. I did
some things with Yank Lawson and Bob Haggart. We made a great
album, with Steve Allen, of the music of *Porgy and Bess.* Steve met
Jack Kerouac, and I knew who Kerouac was, and he said, "Why
don't we record him reading his poetry, and I'll noodle on the
piano?" So we did. I put the album on release, and Randy heard
it and said he's recalling it, that he wouldn't let his ten-year-old son
listen to this album. I said, "It wasn't made for your ten-year-old
son." So I quit. Steve and I took the album back and formed a little
company called Hanover Signature Records. Steve would record on
the Coast, and I'd record here in New York, and we put that album
out again. We had a fair amount of success. We did a thing with
Don Elliott and a fellow named Sasha Berland. I don't know
whether you remember it or ever even heard of it, but we sold close
to a million copies of this record, "The Nutty Squirrels." A dynamite record. I'll tell you, it's terrific. It was bop done like The
Chipmunks [laughter]. Don Elliott, who passed away recently, a
great mellophone, fluegelhorn, and vibes player, and Sasha, who
worked in an advertising agency, created The Nutty Squirrels. It
was like scat, but speeded up. Then Steve and I recorded Les
Brown and we did Ray Bryant, the piano player. We had a great
session with the clarinetist Tony Scott, and Bill Evans on piano,
but unfortunately the tapes have been lost forever. The company
only lasted about a year and a half.

Then you went to Impulse?

Yeah, then to ABC.

*Okay. After Impulse, while you were still at ABC, you started
Blues Way. You recorded B. B. King there, John Lee Hooker,
T-Bone Walker. Were you always a blues fan? Or was this a
response to the rediscovery of the blues in the sixties?*

Well, it might have been. I can't really say. I have to go back to my early days of collecting records, back to the thirties and forties. I used to have certain dealers in New York City who would order records for me, and in those days they were race records. But I was listening to—as most of the classic [jazz] producers were—Roosevelt Sykes, Leroy Carr, Kokomo Arnold. I've always had a love and appreciation for the blues. I guess there was that revival happening. I remember going to see Eric Clapton at the Fillmore East. Before he started to play, he made a speech to the audience, saying, "Before we play and before you start listening to us, all you people have to go out and buy records by people like B. B. King and Muddy Waters, because these are the guys that really started it for all of us." I felt, why not record all these great blues artists? But let's put it on a special label. And I still feel, today, that one of the best ways to get jazz music out there, or to get blues out there, is restrict the label to a certain kind of music so that John Coltrane wouldn't be coming out on ABC in a release with Johnny Mathis and Peggy Lee or whoever. So I came up with a name, Blues Way. ABC approved it, and then I proceeded to go out and record T-Bone, Joe Turner, Eddie "Cleanhead" Vinson. In fact, some of those records . . . I've listened to them recently, and I think they really surpass a lot of the records that those same people have made since then. You know, Norman Granz did some things with Joe Turner and Cleanhead. But boy, these records that we made, I think, are truly great records. Again, I was doing something that I loved to do.

Why did you leave ABC and go out on your own again with your company Flying Dutchman?

Well, to be short and sweet, I quit ABC. I had written a song with George Weiss specifically for Louis Armstrong. And Louis had just had a big hit, "Hello Dolly." At that time things were very crappy throughout the world. Vietnam was going on; there was a lot of turmoil all over, including right here in the States. I wanted Louis Armstrong to say what a wonderful world, it really *is* great. I mean, you look around and people are really shaking hands, and saying I love you, you know? So we finally wrote the song. I went down to Washington, D.C., and played it for Louis. And, in his inimitable

style, he said, "Pops, I dig it. Let's do it." We took him into the
studio. We used about sixteen strings and a rhythm section; this
was a ballad. Then the president of ABC came into the studio just
to say hello and have his picture taken with Louis Armstrong. He
was sort of a crude individual, and he said, "What the hell are you
doing? Louis just had a hit with 'Hello Dolly,' a Dixieland tune,
and you're doing a ballad!" He says, "I'm ending the session." He
threatened to throw Louis out and me out, and I was screaming.
I remember one of my friends in the publishing business was in
tears, holding the studio door and saying, "Please don't go in and
keep disturbing Bob, let him finish the record." So we got the
session finished; the next day I quit. As emphatic as that sounds,
a couple of the vice presidents there said, "You know, stick
around." They called me at home. So I lasted a bit longer; I stayed
on and then finally did leave the company.

Now, I had to stay in the record business, so I formed Flying
Dutchman and was able to get back to recording and doing just
what I pleased. Flying Dutchman was a jazz label. I formed a lot
of little labels. I knew I'd like to make pop records, so I had a
subsidiary called Amsterdam. And I think I had another one. Then
I wanted to do a blues label again, so I came up with another name
and called it Blues Time. I received a letter from ABC threatening
to sue me because it's too close to Blues Way. I didn't even have
to call my attorney. I just wrote a letter back, and I said, "You know
I only graduated high school, but blues is a generic term. I'm sure
you can't sue me for using blues in a title." And that was the end
of that.

*Let's talk about Flying Dutchman a little bit. You had some
great, important jazz people there, Gil Scott-Heron, Oliver Nelson,
Gato Barbieri. Did they achieve a substantial amount of
commercial success with the records they did for Flying
Dutchman?*

Yeah. I think that Flying Dutchman did very well in the initial
stages. We sold quite a few records. The records and the label's
general activity certainly helped Gato Barbieri and Oliver Nelson.
It certainly helped Gil Scott-Heron, as well.

*This was really a new breed of guys. Were they people that you
were familiar with as a fan and wanted to record?*

Some were and some weren't. Oliver Nelson was probably one of
my closest friends, so I was certainly familiar with him. Gato I first
heard when I did Charlie Haden's Liberation Music Orchestra. Gil
Scott-Heron actually walked into the office, and somehow we were
able to see one another. He wanted to give me a book of poetry that
he had written. He knew that we had recorded Jack Kerouac, and
he asked if I'd be interested in putting out an album of him reading
his poetry. So I read the book and I said, "Let's do it, I think the
poetry is great." Later I found out that he could sing, and he could
write some songs.

Why did Flying Dutchman fold?

The record industry is a very, very tough business. Major companies handle their own distribution, while the small labels go
through independent distributors, who are not basically music people. The old gag was that these distributors were so great they could
sell shoes as well as records. Unfortunately, what would happen is
we would ship records in response to orders, but the cash flow
situation always was a problem. There was always a reason why you
couldn't be paid. I'm sure many musicians think, "That guy up
there is having a ball spending my money." If they only knew, or
if they tried to do it themselves, they would learn why record
companies come and go. I have a label right now called Dr. Jazz.
If that label was not distributed by CBS, I would not be in the
record business.

You're that discouraged by independent distributing?

Oh, yeah, I'm completely discouraged by it. Herb Wong's Palo Alto
Records went bankrupt, and they have a catalog of fifty or one
hundred records. There is no way that I can think of for a small
record company to make it, unless it's operated by an entrepreneur
such as Norman Granz or Carl Jefferson, with Concord Records,
who can bankroll it.

IN THE GROOVE

You're trying to circumvent this now with Dr. Jazz's distribution deal with CBS. It seems also that you're into a different kind of product, releasing records by more traditional jazz artists than you did at Flying Dutchman.

Actually, the Dr. Jazz catalog is made up of a few reissues; the *Classic Tenors* album with Coleman Hawkins, the Ellington, the Lester Young were originally done on Signature, which I still own, fortunately, so I can make them available again. But as far as new recordings are concerned, the financial aspects enter into it. I could give you a list of nine LPs I'd like to make right now, of players out there that I would love to record. If I was working for Impulse or if I was working for Columbia directly, I'd bring in these artists and record them. A perfect example is that I brought Arthur Blythe to Columbia Records, and then I went on to do other things.

He seems to be doing a much more traditional kind of thing than when he first came out or when he was on the India Navigation label.

I have to be honest, I haven't heard his latest records, but I know the things that we did were far out. But maybe now they're not as avant-garde. Maybe everyone is changing musically. I don't think it's by direction. He's playing what he wants to play.

You're married to Teresa Brewer and you're recording her again. You recorded her at her early stage at Coral. What's it like working in the studio with your wife?

It's terrific.

You're getting her into more of a jazz thing, too.

Yeah. That was certainly by design. As you said, I made practically all her hits in the fifties. Since we've been working together again, I really tried to study the situation. She's what's classified as a pop singer, from the era of people like Pat Boone, Patti Page, Rosemary Clooney, Perry Como, you name them. But she always thought the songs themselves were stupid songs. She got locked into what she calls "itsy-bitsy-poo" songs like "Chewing Gum" and even "Put Another Nickel In"—which is really her claim to fame; people still want to hear it. See, Teresa can swing—that's natural. I'm getting into what Fats Waller said again; if you have to explain it, then don't even attempt to, because the person asking will never understand. If you said to Teresa, "You know, you can sing jazz," she would say, "I don't really know what you are talking about, why do you say I'm a jazz singer?" Mel Torme swings, Frankie Laine swings. Frank Sinatra doesn't swing, Tony Bennett doesn't swing, [yet] they attempt to make what I call swinging records. I knew she could swing. When we did the album, the first jazz album with Count Basie, if Count Basie wasn't happy, and if the band wasn't happy and didn't feel she was swinging, that would have been the last jazz album she ever made. Duke heard it, and we were at the Rainbow Grill one night, and he came over and we were kidding around. He said, "You recorded with Count Basie, when are you going to record with me?" I said, "Tomorrow!" And Duke was standing there, and it's all so easy to say because it happened, but I can't explain it much further. He said, "Teresa, you're blessed. You swing, and that's what it's all about." She can and she does.

When we record with Stephane Grappelli, she'll go in and we'll do eight sides, eight songs in two or three 3-hour sessions. All live, two or three takes, and she's out. Well, you know those things don't happen unless you sing jazz. As Duke says: It don't mean a thing if it ain't got that swing. And Teresa swings.

And that's the reason why you married her [laughter].

You know, the funny thing is, Teresa and I were somewhere, and you know how friends sit around and get arguing about which is a better record and who is a better singer. So we were discussing one of the current popular singers. I was saying, "This guy sounds awkward to me." Somebody asked, "How can you really tell if somebody swings?" And Teresa said, "Watch him when he walks across the stage or when he moves his body." Then I thought for a minute, and all the motions of a lot of the singers who are supposedly singing jazz are stiff, awkward movements. Their arm movements, their legs, everything about them. There's nothing graceful about their bodies. To me, she made a hell of a point. The grace has got to be there, and that loose, swinging feel.

(February, 1985)

Clive Davis

E verybody in the music business has an opinion
of Clive Davis, the former head of CBS Records
and current president of Arista: He's marvelous. He's awful. He's a genius at finding and developing talent. He's a genius at self-promotion. He's a
visionary. He's an egomaniac.

Opinions can be readily argued; facts cannot. Part
of the reason for Davis' sometimes inauspicious reception in the music community stems from his role
in the shift of power in record companies from
"music people" to lawyers and professional managers. Clive Davis was president of CBS Records for
almost eight years, yet the Harvard Law School graduate admits to having no musical background whatsoever. Nevertheless, under his guidance it became
the most important record company in the business.
In his fascinating book, *Clive—Inside the Record
Business*, he tells of his eye-opening experience at
the 1967 Monterey Pop Festival. After that epiph-
any, Davis turned CBS from a musically conservative
company into the corporate leader in rock 'n' roll by
the end of the sixties, by signing top acts like Janis
Joplin, Blood, Sweat & Tears, the Winter brothers,
Santana, Chicago, Laura Nyro, and Sly and The
Family Stone. He successfully negotiated to keep

218

Dylan on Columbia, and not long before he was to leave, he signed Bruce Springsteen at John Hammond's urging. As his confidence grew at CBS, he began to take a more active role in the careers of many of his artists—tailoring their images, picking hit singles, occasionally even going into the studio with them. His success was dramatic, almost unprecedented.

His ouster from CBS in 1973 was even more dramatic. He was accused of misusing company funds. No criminal charges were ever filed and nothing proven, but he lay low for a year and a half and worked on his book. He fielded and turned down lucrative offers including ones from Island Records' Chris Blackwell and from Robert Stigwood.

Instead, in 1975 he began a totally new enterprise, Arista Records, in partnership with Columbia Pictures, which had had little success with its Bell Records. One of the only three artists he kept from the Bell roster was Barry Manilow. Under Davis at Arista, Manilow became a superstar; Arista also hit with other easy-listening acts such as Melissa Manchester and Air Supply. But Davis also won praise for supporting a line of avant-garde jazz discs, and for signing innovative rock artists such as Patti Smith and Graham Parker. From scratch, Arista became a major force in the record industry.

Far from making him more circumspect, Davis' troubles seem to have made him even more outspoken, and he has assumed the role of corporate spokesman on issues varying from record pricing

and marketing to the death of rock 'n' roll. No matter
what Clive Davis says or does, he'll never be unim-
portant—or uninteresting.

*You have been personally involved in signing and bringing out
records by such a wide range of people, from Neil Diamond and
Barry Manilow to Johnny Winter and Patti Smith. I couldn't
possibly relate to such a broad range of music. How do you do it?*

Of course, a lot is dictated by necessity. Commercial considerations.
My roots are really in AOR [Album-Oriented Rock] in the sense
that I began with early signings of Janis Joplin, Santana, the Winter
brothers, even Blood, Sweat & Tears—who became a little middle-
of-the-road later in their career, but when they began were very
avant-garde in the fusion of jazz and rock. And Chicago of course,
Ten Years After, Pink Floyd, and Billy Joel. But I found after I
started Arista that over this past ten-year span, up until relatively
recently, there were very few American artists, American rock
groups, other than one or two heavy-metal ones, that were breaking, and broke big. So out of economic necessity I had to turn to
see if I had any other kind of talent to explore. In Arista's era I
worked much more in the song area to supplement AOR because
I could not live off only American groups. No company could.

What do you mean by song area?

Finding songs for entertainers such as a Manilow, such as an Air
Supply, such as a Melissa Manchester. We're talking now from '75
to, say, '83. Except for The Cars, whom we almost signed. It's a
dramatic story. . . . We had a memorandum of agreement all
initialed, and thought we had them locked up. At the last minute,
Elektra offered more money and got them. But I was there, and had
them and loved them, and they had, in effect, agreed to come to
Arista, interestingly enough. Of course, we had Patti Smith and
The Outlaws at that time. But a lot of the industry's success was
with foreign groups. And we as a young company did not have
subsidiaries in Australia, let's say, to give us Men at Work, or in
Canada to provide Loverboy or Rush, or foreign groups such as

AC/DC, those foreign bands that were breaking here. There were very few major, original American groups. And here my career had begun with the original groups that I mentioned. So you had to survive by taking established artists, as I did; by attracting to a new operation groups like The Grateful Dead and The Kinks or The Alan Parsons Project, along with the discovery of The Outlaws and Patti Smith. We had to exist by doing something other companies were not doing.

I was never really disco-oriented, so I didn't do what Neil Bogart did with Casablanca. I did it in the pop area. We uniquely married songs with popular entertainers and had terrific success with Manilow and Air Supply and Melissa, to supplement building an AOR base of artists that had varying degrees of success. I was even in the avant-garde with Stiff Records and Ze Records and Lou Reed, and Graham Parker to supplement Patti Smith. But AOR radio was so conservative they were really only into the oldies with Led Zeppelin and The Stones. I had to turn to [pop singers], apart from black artists and jazz artists. We had to be catholic in what we did because if I continued primarily with a base of AOR artists, we would not have survived the holocaust that occurred after The Bee Gees came out with *Saturday Night Fever.* We had to broaden our base from the beginning, and we were uniquely successful. We were one of the very few companies that were very song-oriented, and for entertainers like Dionne Warwick and Aretha Franklin and Barry Manilow and Air Supply—whether they wrote or not—we came up with the hits that propelled their careers.

Are you saying that the move into the pop-song area was something you would not have done if you did not have to do it?

I like pop music, personally. Right now the market dictates a lot of what you do, and right now the market is *not* receptive to pop acts. So therefore, apart from the pros like a Neil Diamond and a Barbra Streisand and a Barry Manilow, you're not finding singer-songwriters. So I might like, and I do like, James Taylor or Jackson Browne, but you don't find companies signing artists like those today because the market is not going to play it on the radio. I tested the market substantially in the mid-seventies with avant-garde artists that I felt comfortable with, because I love originality.

I worked with Dylan; I didn't sign him, but I was there. I was at the signing of Bruce Springsteen. And I signed Joplin. I was there for the *original* talents. That's what gives me the greatest pleasure. I love a great song. I do not demean being able to write pop hits, but I do like to be with the hallmark of originality. Unfortunately, America has really not come up with a great original talent since Springsteen—except for Prince. It's formulated. There's a lot of corporate rock.

A lot of the New Wave acts are British. It's interesting hearing you talk of the importance of the song, because that seems to me to be at the heart of the New Wave movement. That return to the song instead of just long, indulgent guitar solos. Yet it doesn't seem that Arista has been that involved in the so-called New Wave.

No, that's really not true. It's hard to really say what you classify as New Wave. With foreign acts you're only as good as the subsidiaries you get the talent from. We did get The Thompson Twins from our English company, and we did get Haircut 100, who had a nice sound with that first album—then they broke up—so we had a little of that. But because we did not get from our English company the likes of Culture Club or Duran Duran, we did go out to make deals with separate private entrepreneurs, and so we were able to get A Flock of Seagulls and we were able to get Heaven 17. If you talk about the original New Wave, we had the queen and the king in Patti Smith and Lou Reed, and certainly at a quality level we had Graham Parker. So I think we've been there and in AOR qualitatively, even if it wasn't in mass numbers. Mass numbers we have with The Thompson Twins, who are a platinum act. A Flock of Seagulls, over two albums, sold about 1.2 million in the aggregate. And I'm looking for rock 'n' roll acts because I think America is ready for its own now.

What I'm saying to you, in answer to your question about the universality of the acts I've been involved with in one capacity or another, is that a lot is dictated by commercial considerations. And because American AOR dried up for the most part, and was not prolific as it was in '67 to '72 or '73, to become a sizable label we had to go into pop and black music, which relies more heavily on

the song, and not AOR play, which has a harder rock edge. We
built up. . . . we certainly had the biggest growth of any company
in the business, and I would say in the pop or black areas we were
either number one, two, or three every year. That's what accounted
for our ability to survive and to diversify and grow.

*You must have been right at the forefront of breaking black acts
on pop radio and butting heads with MTV to get black acts on
there. Was that a frustration?*

Candidly, no. I never came to that with MTV. I don't think MTV
avoided black acts, any more than an AOR station. How many
black acts does WNEW [in New York City] play?

Good question.

They don't play them, not because they're against blacks, but
because it doesn't fit their format. Their format is hard rock, or rock
'n' roll, and there aren't that many black rock 'n' roll acts. You
can't ask them to play Dionne Warwick or Ray Parker. Yes, one
or two Ray Parker records, maybe. But you've got to understand
the other person's problem. It's certainly not racial prejudice. It's
based on segmented formats. Once you understand the problems
of MTV or radio you recognize that it would be silly. It doesn't fit
their format. I never bumped heads at all with them. I did bump
heads with AOR radio because of their conservatism, and their not
playing Lou Reed's *Street Hassle* or not playing some groups in
Middle America or the South. It's shocking, not playing some of
the avant-garde stuff. I think that's terrible. Until KROQ [in
Pasadena] and WBCN [in Boston] showed that new music can play,
you were there in a bastion of oldies but goodies. It was terrible,
except for harder rock stuff. Even now—where's the new Dylan?
Where's the new Springsteen? Where's the new Dan Fogelberg or
Jackson Browne? It's horrendous to me that there's no new artists
coming along with music that is lyric-oriented!

Are you blaming this on the stodginess of AOR radio?

Yeah! Absolutely.

They don't encourage these sounds?

Absolutely not. It has to be shoved down their throats pretty much. Yeah.

It seems that it still hasn't caught on. If you want to hear New Wave in New York, you've got to tune in to WLIR on Long Island.

Well, for your definition of New Wave. Big New Wave, in the broader sense, has become mainstream music today.

True.

I mean, Duran Duran and Culture Club and The Thompson Twins are Top 40, primarily. They still don't give the exposure to Elvis Costello or X. No, they don't. Graham Parker is great! He doesn't get the kind of play in the South or Midwest that he should get. Nowhere near.

Will they ever break nationwide, except for the New Wave acts that have crossed over to pop success?

Today, first of all, AOR doesn't have the strength it did five years ago. Contemporary Hit Radio, the equivalent of Top 40, now dominates. It's a shame that the new artists who are literate and lyrical and articulate and intelligent, lyric-oriented as distinguished from harder rock-oriented, don't have the avenues for exposure of their music; ergo, record companies shy away from it. How long can you keep banging your head up against the wall if you're not going to get exposure?

In that line, let's talk about Patti Smith. You seem to have a very special relationship with her.

I do because she was one of very few originals. You know, when you start a new record company and you're able to come up with an original who breaks all over the world as she did . . . She did it in her own style and her own way, with her own charis-

ma, with very few compromises and condescension, with true
poetry and excitement. She was very warm and personal and
would always drop in, so we established a personal friendship
and relationship. Then when she got hurt and her neck was in a
brace for a year she lived right here at One Fifth Avenue, and I
would go down there to visit her. Because she's bright. She's
a Renaissance woman. She's an artist in her own right, not
only as a poet, but she's an artist from an artistic point of view.
She was literate; you know, she lived for years with Sam Shepard.
She was a delightful, stimulating person to both talk to and be
around.

What's happened to her now? I understand she got married.

Enigmatically—not enigmatically because she got married; she's
certainly entitled—the enigmatic part is that in her marriage and
in her pursuit of domestic and personal happiness, she really
dropped out of the jungle of musical warfare, so to speak. She's had
a child. She did reappear. . . . I had no contact with Patti, not even
a phone call for over three years. No one did, except her mother.
It wasn't that I was phoning her; I didn't ask for product. We were
so close, I figured, if she's happy, who am I to even remotely bring
up the subject of music? Then, several months ago, we had a tenth
anniversary party for Arista. We took over the Museum of the City
of New York. I didn't even invite her; I didn't have her address
or her phone number. The photographers were there. It was a
major event, if you will. All of a sudden there's this incredible stir,
and who walks in unannounced, no advance notice, but Patti with
her husband Fred. She had heard about it through her manager.
She came in and threw her arms around me and said, "I just had
to do this for you." I didn't ask her anything about recording. She
showed me pictures of her child. She seemed happy. She was
overwhelmed by the attention because there were a lot of TV
cameras and press there, clicking away. She was a little shaky
because of that. Because it was really a return from absolute isolation, it appeared to me. But she was extremely warm. She said
she'll come back.

Where's she living?

Detroit.

You used the term musical warfare. Rereading your book, it does seem like warfare. Is it, really?

Well, it can be. I mean, on a day-to-day basis it's not.

It sounded like it in the book.

Well, I'll tell you. That book coincided with an explosion of original talent in every area. I wish there was such an explosion today. You get the warfare when a hot new artist comes along, and we all go after that artist at once. But since there are so few of those today in America, the opportunity for that kind of competition at the artist-signing level is not nearly what it was from 1967 through 1973. The biggest new, original talent, in my opinion, is Prince. To my knowledge he was first offered to Columbia, and I don't know what happened there, but they did not get him for whatever the reason, and then he went to Warner Bros. So it wasn't that anybody knew of Prince. He was part of a local group that was creating noise. It wasn't that everybody was going after this hot new group; I mean, it doesn't happen. Now it happens in the banking deals to some extent.

How do you mean?

Well, if you hear that a Bowie is free, or a McCartney or an Elton John or The Rolling Stones, then there's competition, obviously. I'm sure that Atlantic wanted to retain The Rolling Stones.

You call them banking deals because of the vast amounts of money involved?

Yes. Very few of those deals have ever made money for the label. They usually are deals where the artist uses the competitive interest of the companies, and walks away with an enormous sum of mon-

ey. . . . I would think that the history of the last seven years should
be a clear message to all record companies to stay away from these
banking deals, because they just don't make money.

Why do record companies pursue them? Is it a prestige thing?

Part of it is that. Part of it is miscalculation—not recognizing when
an artist has peaked, and thinking it is going to go on. Of course,
certain artists do go on for a long time. But I would say the history
of most of these deals is that the company has lost considerable
sums of money.

*One thing I have never understood is how different record
companies can come up with such widely divergent offers for the
same artist. I just read somewhere that one record company tripled
the offer made by another company for a certain artist.*

There is a different mentality at almost every record company.
I'm amazed at some of the deals that I hear of. I can't even believe that a rational businessman would offer those amounts of
money.

Let's talk about The Cars.

Well, that was a brand-new group, that wasn't a banking deal. I was
signing them for the standard terms of a new artist, which at the
time probably was $25,000 and a recording budget of $100,000
to $125,000.

This was around when, '76?

Probably, yeah. It's not that different today. There is a black artist
I'm launching, Whitney Houston, that I'm very excited about. But
we're talking here now about rock, as opposed to black and pop.
I am very excited about the black roster that we've built here. It's
spectacular, I think. I mean, working with Aretha, and having the
success we've had in relaunching Dionne Warwick . . .

In front, from left: Jerry Wexler, Alan Freed, Ahmet Ertegun. In back: Buddy Johnson, *Cashbox*'s Norman Orleck, Ella Johnson, Big Joe Turner, Lou Willie Turner, and Jackie Freed. At a *Cashbox* award presentation on the Alan Freed Show, 1956 or '57. You had to stigmatize the music, and call it what it was, otherwise it never would have seen the daylight. It would have been lost—blotted out by the Ames Brothers and Patti Page. (Courtesy Jerry Wexler)

With Aretha Franklin, mid-1970s. When you're dealing with a singer like an Aretha Franklin, with a backup band of the best studio musicians, you get right down to it pretty quick. You grab it while the bloom is on. (Courtesy Jerry Wexler)

With Solomon Burke at the Atlantic Studios, about 1960. "Who's the best soul artist?" "Solomon Burke with a borrowed band." (Courtesy Jerry Wexler)

With Willie Nelson. It was no problem signing Willie. It was not a heavy deal. Nobody wanted him. (Courtesy Jerry Wexler)

Jerry Leiber and Mike Stoller, Los Angeles, 1951 or '52. *Leiber:* I think we wanted to be black. Being black was great. The best musicians in the world were black. The greatest athletes in the world were black, and black people had a better time. We lived a kind of black existence. I'd say eighty percent of our lives were lived that way. (Courtesy Leiber & Stoller)

Jerry Leiber, Lester Sill, Atlantic records sales manager Lou Krefetz, and Mike Stoller outside the office on Melrose Avenue in L.A., late 1956. *Stoller:* Jerry Wexler told me we were the first independent producers. We were record company owners who were persuaded to give up their company and become producers on a royalty basis. (Collection of Lou Krefetz, courtesy Leiber & Stoller)

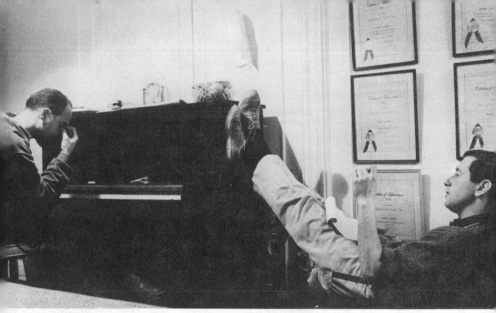

At work in Jerry Leiber's study on 72nd Street in New York, 1959. *Leiber:* Mike would jam until I would just get struck by some notion. Then I'd start yelling some kind of line. If Mike dug it, he would pick it up. *Stoller:* It was like spontaneous combustion. (Courtesy Leiber & Stoller)

With Peggy Lee at A&M Studios in L.A., 1975. *Leiber:* We were thinking of moving on. We were getting older, and were not writing for kids anymore. We were looking for another, more mature audience. (Courtesy Leiber & Stoller)

Bob Thiele with McCoy Tyner. I was *living* in the studio. Over a period of three to five years, maybe, I must have literally made two hundred albums. (Courtesy Bob Thiele)

With Buddy Holly. I was so excited, I wound up playing the record for a lot of people in the company, and everybody said, "Forget it!" I remember the president telling me, "We have some great artists on Coral, and here you're coming out with this horrible thing by The Crickets." (Courtesy Bob Thiele)

With Louis Armstrong and Duke Ellington, 1960. There were no arrangements. We just picked keys and did it. (Courtesy Bob Thiele)

With Earl "Fatha" Hines. In terms of jazz, when one strives
to enhance the music that is already there—what's being played
—I think that you're defeating the purpose of what jazz is all
about. You want to capture jazz music as it actually happens.
(Courtesy Bob Thiele)

Clive Davis with Janis Joplin. Joplin was a vibrating, charismatic, exciting, exhilarating live performer from the first day I saw her. I knew I had to have her. (Courtesy Clive Davis)

With Paul Simon and Art Garfunkel. If I believe someone's great I will trumpet that, unless it interferes with the artist's integrity. To me that is not hype. It is setting the stage for an appropriate understanding of the magnitude of talent. (Courtesy Clive Davis)

With Miles Davis. To participate in the creative process . . . It's accepted in my particular case because of my track record, and it's usually not accepted for most people. I was there for the *original* talents. That's what gives me the greatest pleasure. (Courtesy Clive Davis)

With Pia Zadora, Barry Manilow, and Morgan Fairchild, 1983. We uniquely married songs with popular entertainers and had terrific success with Manilow, Air Supply, and Melissa Manchester. Arista had to broaden its base from the beginning. (© 1983, Ebet Roberts)

*I want to get into that in a minute, but before we do, tell me—
when you're going to make an offer for an artist, what do you
look for?*

A new artist?

Either new or old.

It's vastly different. In the established category, sometimes the
talent is just there. The question is how much money they're
asking, and whether you think they're going to go out of style. You
have to make a judgment, creatively, as to where that artist is at.
Because sometimes artists and their managers ask astronomical
monies. You've got to believe they can retain their superstardom.
Or are they going to diminish in popularity?

With a new artist it depends on the category of music. If it's rock,
I look for originality. Also, today you've got to look for hit songs.
Very few artists break from AOR today. Years ago, and for many,
many, many years, you *could* break from AOR play; the category
was sufficient to sell millions of albums for Pink Floyd without a
Top 40 single, or Bruce Springsteen, or other artists. Today, you
gotta have a single, so you're also looking at their song sense, and
looking at their musical-composition sense—apart from charisma.
So, in the rock area, it's either commercial appraisal of material or
looking from an originality point of view. In the pop area you're
listening for hit songs. In the black area you're listening for where
the material is coming from, whether there will be hit songs; plus
the artists' ability to entertain, and the kind of vocal ability they
have.

How about stage presence?

Stage presence is more in the rock area, and the black area, too.
It really varies so much. I didn't look for stage presence when I
signed Springsteen. It was just pure originality of lyric content. He
was very uncharismatic as a rock personality when he was signed
in '72. He really was not a major performer onstage. He didn't
move around. He was totally different than he is today. He devel-

oped into the best rock 'n' roll performer alive over the years, on his own. But nobody knew he would, neither John Hammond, who brought him into my office, nor I, who then appraised him. I said no to ten or twelve or fifteen or thirty John Hammond acts—and then said yes to Springsteen. That's why I feel, candidly, very close to the signing process involving Springsteen. Because I said no to a few acts, the previous week, that John might have been interested in, and this one was different. His lyrics were piercing. I can remember going on closed-circuit TV just reading his lyrics, saying you're not going to break him because of his musicality, but his lyrics are spectacular, and listen to this imagery, and I recited his poetry to the Columbia sales force. Yes. And I had the videotape sent out to be shown to every retailer. Because that was the approach we were taking. And he didn't break right away. He came, really, out of the folk/rock poet tradition, but he has developed into the most incredible live performer. Joplin, on the other hand, was a vibrating, charismatic, exciting, exhilarating live performer from the day I first saw her. I knew I had to have her.

Talking about getting on closed-circuit TV to your Columbia sales force, is that a big part of your job? Keeping your promotional people and salespeople and marketing people motivated and excited about acts?

I leave that to others within the company, but it's part of it, yes. But I find that today the sales and promotion forces are so sophisticated, much more sophisticated musically. Originally, it was a great part of what I had to do, because when I inherited Columbia they were all so middle-of-the-road oriented, into the music of Mitch Miller and Andy Williams, who was a great seller, and Tony Bennett and what have you, that a lot of orientation was required. Today, not that much orientation is required, and they pretty much pick up on their own, whether someone is a really great talent or not. Most of my time, 80 percent of my time, is spent in the creative arena, at the artistic level of finding new talent, finding material for established talents who don't write for themselves, and watching an album evolve. All these cassettes on my desk are either songs for artists or albums in preparation. I'm monitoring, listening to them, helping pick the singles, editing the record, and in a few specialized cases, going into the studio to produce it, if it's a song I found for a pop act or a black act. That's 80 percent of my time.

Do you think you are different in that way from most other major record-company presidents?

I think that it's probably different from most. It's not singular, but I think that a lot of executives who have been very successful in their own right operate in their own style, which is not quite as creatively oriented.

You're an interesting case. You don't come from a musical background. You're Harvard Law. How did this creative career happen?

By accident. By necessity. I don't know, it's a talent that I've developed, and I didn't know I had it, and I didn't get into the business because of it. It seems to have worked, and it keeps working. I love it and it just keeps paying off, and it's thrilling, and so I do it. I mean, I'm not trying to be either modest or immodest in answering, I'm just trying to answer in the nice spirit that you ask it. It came out of survival and necessity. I didn't know I had it at Monterey, I didn't expect to ever sign an artist in my life. I would have preferred to operate as most—to hire a head of A&R, to make it. But my heads of A&R were signing no rock groups. We were marginally profitable. I sat there in the midst of a revolution, and was lucky enough to be there.

You seemed to really be getting off on the whole thing.

I did. My whole life changed. I went to Monterey for fun. I went there because a few friends were running the festival. Abe Somer, an entertainment attorney who represented a lot of major artists, was on the board; Lou Adler I had a label deal with, and he was on the board. Simon and Garfunkel and The Byrds were going to perform, and I thought I would have fun. It was the first pop festival. I never thought I'd see new talent; it wasn't billed as a new talent thing. If I hadn't been there, I don't know when I would have signed my first artist. But I knew I had to, and I was motivated to, and I did. And when it hits out of the gate that way with everything you sign, from Joplin to Blood, Sweat, Santana and what have you, it then gives you confidence to keep trusting your judgment, and then you start living it. Then you start liking it. Then you start getting, if you can, an intuitive feel for it. And that is what I, through evolution, developed.

We were talking about how you get involved in the creative process. You've certainly never been shy about talking to an artist, whether it's Horowitz or Ray Davies, about what you think they should do to change their direction and perhaps become more commercially viable. Has this usually worked out for you?

Do people resent it? Yes. It is the most troublesome thing to do, the most emotionally difficult thing to do. It is a double-edged sword in every case when you do get so involved. It's hard to translate this to the public. I've never been asked this type of question, and it's a great question because it really is the most troublesome part of the way I, at least, personally perform my job. To participate in the creative process . . . It's accepted in my particular case because of my track record, and it's usually not accepted for most people. And yet, even that is accepted so begrudgingly that you run a delicate line between being a meddler and a participant. It's a very, very, very difficult thing to get into.

You do it only when you feel it's absolutely necessary?

Without question.

You felt it was absolutely necessary to talk to Ray Davies about a change in direction away from the concept albums he was doing?

Well, he solicited that, in order to see what label would be best suited for The Kinks. He wanted my ideas on that subject. He recognized that his sales had fallen way down. It's much easier when people have fallen way down from where they had been, and then they come to you. Then you're welcomed with open arms. So that when Dionne came here or when Aretha came here . . . I'd always heard that Aretha was a terror. Her sales were not what she or anybody would have wanted at Atlantic. So when she came here, she had heard about me, and, of course, I had more than heard about her. And she wanted to work as a creative team. So it's not in those cases that it's difficult. But in the vast majority of the cases, I'm not God's gift to creativity or to my artists. You take the artist because of *their* talent. So the only areas I get involved in, with the true originals who write their own material, like an Alan Parsons or a Patti Smith, are whether their song is a hit or not and whether my Top 40 ears perceive any of the currently written material as a hit. So I'll come in as a friendly partner. There, it's been peaches and cream.

The problem is in the areas where an artist doesn't have a Top 40 hit, and you've got to tell them that, from what they have written, there is no Top 40 hit and therefore they've got to use outside material. Then it is war, usually. If they don't write, then they're willing to accept that, depending on your relationship.

When you get to that point with an artist, I suppose they don't really have a choice.

Oh, look, I can't tell you the battles.

Sure you can!

There *are* battles. And even when you've done it four or five times in a row, if they write or have written any hits in the past . . . Well, say, Melissa Manchester. I really have been very fond of Melissa, though she's no longer on the label. But for years you see an artist going in one direction; she wanted to be a triple-threat star, and you see her as a pop star, because her talent, outside the pop area, for going into R&B, folk or jazz, is not there. So you suggest that she stay with pop. If that doesn't fit her image of where she wants to go, it's very traumatic. If she's written, as she did write, "Come in from the Rain," a beautiful song, and "Midnight Blue," a beautiful song, you sort of suggest that the hallmark of her writing points her in the pop direction. But she wanted to be Linda Ronstadt or Joni Mitchell, you know, the first white-black-jazz-rock 'n' roll star. You've got to let them carry through their dream, until you see it falling into a noncommercial area. Then you say, "There

are just no hits, and if the album comes out, it's going to sell 50,000
to 75,000 copies. You must do (for example) 'Don't Cry Out
Loud.' " Then she says, "I hate 'Don't Cry Out Loud'!" And you
say, "But you must do it." And then you do it, and she does it. Then
the next time an album comes around with all her own material,
and you say, "Well, there's no hits; I gave you 'Don't Cry Out
Loud.' " Well, there's resistance. Even though you keep doing it.
I understand that it's not personal. It just happens with any artist
who also writes. Now, in the cases where they write well, they don't
need me for any of this, and I would never presume or even think
about it. They need me for a sense of marketing or career development. But in the creative area where artists don't have hits or are
not writing hits for themselves, then you do intrude and it's never
easy. They never like any piece of outside material you first play
for them. It does become, depending on their outlook toward you,
usually more difficult, always painful, never appreciated as much
as you would like. It's the most painful area that I have to work
on.

*Let's talk about something totally different. Let's talk about hype.
Do you feel that hype is sometimes something you just have to do
for an artist?*

I really have difficulty with your premise, because first of all, you
take your lead from the artist. With Dylan it was very clear to both
of us that there would be no interviews and no discussions. That
just the announcement of a Dylan album was sufficient, and anything different from that would be untoward. There was never any
hype for Bob Dylan. I have never shied away from trumpeting
something as strong, with sensitivity to the artist involved, if I
believed in it. But the word hype itself, to me, is an overstatement.
I don't believe, in music, that this is like selling a movie, or that
we're going to sell it to the public like a piece of product. I am very
sensitive to the underlying creativity and take the lead from it. I
don't believe that an advertisement, if we're talking advertising
now, with just a picture of an album, in most cases, is sufficient.
It's sufficient now for Springsteen, for Prince, it always was for
Dylan. On the other hand, certain artists need background, like
The Alan Parsons Project. Maybe you define as hype the fact that

when we launched The Parsons Project, I analogized it to Ingmar
Bergman and said here is the first somebody who is assembling a
cast of musicians and vocalists, and is coming up with material, and
is like the first director à la Bergman. To me that is not hype. It
is setting the stage for an appropriate understanding of the magnitude of talent. If I believe someone's great I will trumpet that,
unless it interferes with the artist's integrity. The most important
thing is to be sensitive to an artist's image, and the integrity of what
they're doing. I'm not saying this because it's a cliché or it sounds
good, but I don't believe in being derelict. I believe that there is
an art of career development.

*You're a very outspoken person. Do you ever get other record
company executives angry at you for things you've said? You will
be very specific and criticize something if you feel it's not good for
the industry.*

I think that there is always a double-edged sword with visibility.
If you're very visible, and other executives are not, you can be
accused of being on a personal ego trip. There's always that fallout.
I, in the trade press, have stuck to issues. And yeah, there have
been examples where . . . I don't take on people as personalities,
or I attempt not to. There have been times over the years when
people have trumpeted the dying of the record industry, the death
of the record industry, the fact that music is dying. And I did rise
on several occasions. Once, when Bill Graham was going out of the
Fillmore business, he kept saying that rock is dying, or the press
kept saying the Fillmore's closing and rock is dying. I took an
active role in showing the diversity of music, the strength of music,
and put on shows at the Ahmanson Theater mixing and matching
Miles Davis and Loudon Wainwright and The Mahavishnu Orchestra and the range of talent to disprove that. It did get personal a
number of years ago, when a number of executives went on "20/
20" to say that the aural record was dying, it was all going to be
video, that the record business was dead. They were actually singing us out of business because it was a bad time, and it looked like
video was going to take over. I couldn't believe it! That they were
not only issuing statements to *The New York Times* to that effect,
but also to "20/20," and I said it was crazy. I wrote an open letter

to Joe Smith [of Warner Bros. Records], who happens to be a very
dear friend of mine, saying, "Hey, this is crazy. I don't believe that
it is true. I think it is hurtful to our business." I'm sure there were
some misgivings there, but it was never done on a personal level.
It was to tell these people not that we should hype our business,
but that they were creating a bandwagon idea that we have an
obsolete product here, and we don't. Then I gave separate editorials
saying that you can't hum a video game, and the video game fad
will be over at some point. I think that where I've chosen to make
an issue of these points, the record will show, hopefully, that I've
been proven correct.

*But you don't have to do it. I'm sure there are other people who
share your feelings who won't go out and put themselves on the
line. . . .*

Well, that's where my legal background, which I don't use in any
of my creativity, gives me . . . I don't fear public speaking if I'm
asked to appear on the "Today" show or "Good Morning, America" or to speak on a controversial issue. . . . So often, and until
fairly recently, record executives were pictured as finger-snapping
and wild-eyed. There was always the Phil Spector "dem, dese, and
dose" types. It was an amazing picture of the record executive as
compared to the Hollywood types or television types. They're all
different, perhaps, in their way. But I did feel . . . I saw my
colleagues—whether it be Jerry Moss [of A&M] or Mo Ostin [of
Warner Bros.] or several other people—as bright, articulate, intelligent business and creative people who might, for whatever reason,
not be public speakers. I mean, Mo Ostin is marvelously talented,
but he is somewhat shy in public, and Jerry Moss is a very private
person who is more comfortable not speaking. I grew up not feeling
there was any awkwardness in that. So that the lot sort of fell to
me. I don't think I'm a ham. I think the record industry needed
defense in certain areas, and the reaction was good, and so I've
done it. Not to be a martyr, not to be a hero.

*People have said that the reason for your problems at Columbia
was because you were so out there, so . . .*

Visible.

. . . That that's what created this sort of "Twilight Zone" batch of problems for you there.

I don't think there was a negativity to me at Columbia. What happened is that there was a brand-new president [of CBS Inc.] who had only been there for six months, and we didn't even know each other. You know, I was always considered a candidate for that job and I never wanted to be. I was asked to be the head of their studio and other divisions there, but I am not one to move on to other tasks for the sake of a corporate ladder. I know what I like to do, and I'm gratified that I've found a career that I love. So that even though I've invested in a Broadway show, and hopefully will do one or two or a few movies over a period of years, I love the record business. I'm not the comedian yearning to be the dramatist, or setting up false challenges for myself. I had enough of a challenge coming out of the law proving that I had creative talent, and showing, after I was head of what became the world's largest record company, that I could do it from scratch on my own, in a brand-new enterprise. That's enough challenges, aside from doing well in a very competitive business. My prime interest now is to stay in a field I enjoy, and I enjoy this, so I stay in it.

When Alan Hirschfield left Columbia Pictures in the wake of the David Begelman scandals, which David McClintick wrote about in Indecent Exposure, *how did that affect you at Arista? [Columbia Pictures was the founder of, and major stockholder in, Arista Records; Hirschfield was Columbia's president and CEO.]*

Are you asking me, businesswise or personally?

Both.

Well, Alan was a very close personal friend at that time. He believed in me and really was the main reason why Columbia Pictures financed the beginning of Arista. I was affected by it personally because he was a close friend who I felt was not treated well, and treated unfairly. I thought that he was on the right side of the issue, and that it could have been handled better by both sides. I'm not saying I agreed with everything that Alan did. But on the other hand I think that the position in *Indecent Exposure* was pretty accurate. And I did feel a certain sense of alienation from the board of Columbia Pictures, and I motivated, pretty much, the sale of the . . . I was the co-stockholder, with Columbia Pictures, in Arista. I really felt, probably, disenchanted and alienated, and I felt those things probably a little more keenly, having gone through the trauma of corporate alienation myself.

Seeing this situation . . . I would not be a passive observer. I came up with a purchaser of the stock of Arista, and recommended very highly to the board of Columbia Pictures that we both sell our interest in Arista to Bertelsmann [the German-based firm Bertelsmann A.G.], the company that bought 100 percent of the stock.

This was in . . .

In 1979, I believe. So I would say that I was affected personally.

So that the sale of Arista to Bertelsmann was in a way the direct result of Columbia Pictures falling out with Alan Hirschfield?

To me. I mean, I could not cause Columbia Pictures to sell the stock if they didn't want to, but on the other hand I think that, as the head of the company, my recommending it as well as having expressed alienation and disenchantment over the Hirschfield issue pretty vocally, I'm sure that that was a contributing factor.

Well, both you and Hirschfield have both succeeded as well as you could possibly turn out, after your respective crises in business. [Hirschfield is now an investment banker and a consultant to the entertainment industry.] Do you feel vindicated?

On all the legal issues I feel exonerated. You never get the press for the exoneration as for the initial furor. So it's a wound that never fully heals. It's a . . . the pain you go through you never quite make up for. But in hindsight, it did open up opportunities. The opportunity to write a book, which I never, never, never would have thought of doing. The opportunity to start a new company. The

opportunity to broaden my horizons, and to really respond to the
challenge of starting a new company and have it live. It recently
finished its first decade. If it goes not a day further it will still be
an exciting accomplishment.

*Truthfully, though, isn't there an aspect of "living well is the best
revenge"?*

I never viewed this as a personal feud. It was never a personal feud,
it was a wound that occurred. There were things that were done that
I was very upset about that I've written about in my book from the
point of view of [Columbia Records] rewriting history. A corporation has got to show that no one man is indispensable, and that they
can go on, and the stock shouldn't go down. That does have a
tendency of happening, and when you're on the other side of it, you
are hurt and you fight back. But you're fighting back against an
institution. I personalized it to one or two people. So that now the
wound is dealt with and recalled. On the other hand, you integrate
it into your life. If you're saying now that . . . I don't feel glad about
it, no. But it had its other upside benefits that I never would have
been able to experience.

*But you know, there's almost a backlash. When you become the
underdog, everyone's on your side again. And people must have
been saying, "Boy, I bet he's just sitting there thumbing his nose
at them now, because he's a success on his own."*

It's funny. I'm not saying that I'm bigger or smaller than that. I'm
saying that there were, apart from that incident, people who would
bet against someone who was a lawyer and a president of a large
record company starting his own business. There were an awful lot
of people saying, "Hey, he can't do that." And yet those who knew
that I was not just a president, that where an artist was signed
. . . I looked at thirty artists and said yes to Joplin, and yes to Blood,
Sweat, or yes to Billy Joel, or bought the Pink Floyd contract before
they broke, etc. . . . So much has happened since I left Columbia.
When I started Arista, [Columbia] gave me a million dollars [for
mail order rights] for the Columbia Record Club. Four or five years
ago, the Martell Foundation, which is dedicated to the memory of

a CBS employee's son and is the industry's main charity, honored me as their Man of the Year. The president of Columbia Records at the time, Bruce Lundvall, spoke to the company and said it was like the McCarthy witch-hunt era, and that I led a lonely battle for the industry . . . and only because of my reputation and my standards and morals and integrity did I come out of it the way I did, and it was of great benefit to the industry. And it was of tremendous note that the award was not only given to me by the then-president of Columbia Records, but that it did, in effect, hopefully speak for CBS. Because knowing that I was the honoree that night, Tom Wyman, the new president of CBS, came and was very warm to me thereafter. So that, you know, there's no war going on. It was an unfortunate coincidence of events, and I was unfortunately brought into it without foundation. It did cause trauma, and it did cause pain, and that won't ever be forgotten. But it has given me the opportunity to do other things. It has worked out great, and it has given me great satisfaction, not so much from a thumbing of my nose at anybody, really, because I don't personalize that to CBS. In fact, the first day I opened my doors at Arista, two dozen CBS executives came with flowers and drinks. And so many executives from CBS have come over at one time or another to work for me. CBS artists have gone on TV specials and honored me. So that aspect of it doesn't continue today.

Today it seems the record business is really dominated by CBS and Warner Bros. How do you, as the president of a large independent, feel about this, and the problem it obviously causes?

Thank God you said large independent. If you had said small, I would have felt very insignificant [laughter]. Look, you have realistic dreams. You can be so large after ten years. I feel fully able to compete with CBS and Warners. We immediately, I think two or three years after the founding of Arista, became the alternative to those two major companies for an artist to consider. Many artists that have been looked at or bid for, whether it was The Alan Parsons Project, or The Kinks, or Hall and Oates, at different stages of their careers, have chosen Arista. So I feel fully able to compete with CBS and Warners. Over this period of time we have become a so-called large independent, although almost everybody distributes through a branch today. And we're 50 percent owned by RCA, who bought their interest in the company from Bertelsmann because they've established joint ventures with Bertelsmann all over the world, as a global plan. I feel that we are a legitimate alternative to CBS and Warners, and can focus the spotlight better than they can. I fully believe that over the next decade, after America starts breaking its own artists again, that we have large growth opportunities in front of us. I'd hate to be head of a large company that has to replace the volume for artists that are currently so big, once they are not quite so big. To come up with that volume and budget of 10 percent bigger every year.

If you were asked by someone thinking about starting an independent record company today—the way you did with Arista —or a total independent with their own resources, what advice would you give them?

I think that there are very few people who could do it. I think that if the person has the goods to do it, I would encourage that person to do it. The goods, meaning . . . I mean, David Geffen, with his talent, did it and could do it. So if he were thinking of doing it today, I would say do it because David Geffen has an ear for creative talent. If there is someone unknown to me who really is a budding, talented, creative entrepreneur, I would advise that person to do it. Yes, it can be done—more so today than five years ago. Properly bankrolled, not on a shoestring, yes, I do believe it can be done. Unfortunately there aren't too many people around who show the kind of talent that I would bankroll to do it. That's the problem—the dearth of executive talent, which I'm surprised at. I would have thought that there'd be more budding creative entrepreneurs who could do it.

But you don't think it's a closed shop?

I don't believe it is. No.

(February, 1985)

Phil Ramone

P hil Ramone may be the quintessential pop record producer. Undoubtedly one of the top hitmakers of all time, he is perhaps best known as the man behind all of Billy Joel's zillion-selling records. He has also helped create hit records for a fair number of the pop world's upper echelon, including Paul Simon, Barbra Streisand, and Chicago. His newest star is Julian Lennon. Ramone is a true hands-on producer who learned his craft as an engineer for legends like Leiber & Stoller and Bacharach & David. His great commercial success has earned him respect in the music business, but it hasn't all been a traipse through the tulips for Ramone. Many critics have excoriated the records Ramone produced for Billy Joel, and Joel's most warmly received effort, *The Nylon Curtain,* was—believe it or not—a relative commercial disappointment, with only a few more than a million units sold. Ramone and Julian Lennon also faced widespread skepticism at first, although the quality of their work ultimately quieted most critics. Here Ramone discusses his reaction to all this, and tells the story of his rise from child violin prodigy to pop production whiz.

You were a child prodigy violinist at three, and you entered

Juilliard at thirteen. How did you go from this formal classical background to pop and rock 'n' roll?

When you learn about classical music there are so many rules, and there is so much structure. When you're a teenager, you're rebellious against certain things. In the classical world . . . you don't do this and you don't do that. You don't play baseball, you don't play tennis, you play the violin. You don't listen to other music except that which comes in the package that is preprogrammed for you. I got into trouble because obviously I listened to other music. Here I was, a scholarship kid who had to live up to all these marks. I was one of the few people who had the Gershwin scholarship; you had to win it every year. I came from a very poor family, beyond poor.

What did you do for money in those years?

I worked at anything. Because I was cute and a moppet, I got various offers. I'd go and do a television show, play in a club or whatever.

This is when you were ten or eleven?

I was on the road by the time I was twelve. The so-called vaudeville style of theater was resurging then, in the early fifties. People said, "He's cute and he plays fiddle, and he does a little joke and he can sing." Boom, I'm starting to play gigs. In order to preserve my classical world, my violin teacher would say, "You have to learn to read better, so you must play chamber music." I played chamber music with doctors; there was a society. There was also a little society where they made classical recordings in a boutique manner. We'd record in stereo in this guy's Riverside Drive apartment or little classical halls like Judson Hall. Any gig I could get I would take, whether it was playing that or playing in a club down in the Village, in a rhythm section, trying to learn how to write jazz.

You were a twelve-year-old kid playing in jazz clubs in the Village?

Yeah. I electrified the fiddle, put it through an amp. I loved Stephane Grappelli. The attitude of the typical violinist is that he's
going to be Jascha Heifetz. I understood the instrument, and I also
understood my own limitations. If I wasn't going to be a Heifetz,
I wasn't going to settle. Also, I thought the instrument, because of
its ancient quality, had so many ugly rules about it. You never
electrified it. Why? I was into Charlie Parker when I was like eight
or nine years old, and I had to literally hide out because it was
against the rules. I had a teacher who taught me a few jazz and
blues licks. Through him and other friends I'd get to sneak into
record dates, and watch jazz dates in the studio. By the time I was
fifteen I was into the studio.

*Did that get you fascinated with the guy on the other side of the
glass?*

Yeah. In 1957, '58 there were still a lot of jazz dates being done.
I'd go anyplace. To get in I'd clean the studio up, do anything to
be around it. Whatever they wanted, I would do.

How did you begin to work as an engineer?

Friends who were playing club dates or gigs tried to open a demo
studio in their apartment. That's where I started really getting into
it. A friend of mine named Bill Schwartau, who I really idolized,
was an engineer. Through him I got to meet Tommy Dowd and
other famous independent engineers who weren't at Columbia or
RCA—you couldn't get into those studios. Eventually a couple of
guys hired me to work as a musician on a Harry Belafonte record;
some musicians said I played real well. That's when I first went into
the RCA and Columbia recording studios, playing in a section,
scared to death. Eventually I got to go into the control room. All
I cared about was to get into the control room. I was fascinated.
I'd be at those playbacks and I'd say, "Wow!" I had recorded a lot
since I was eight or nine, and I had transcriptions and acetates,
recordings of concerts, and the sound was awful, disgusting. I
didn't play that well, in my opinion, but even when I did play well
it still didn't sound good to me. So I begged these guys, when they
opened this tiny little demo studio in their apartment, I asked them

if I could do anything. I'd work for nothing, and eventually when they made enough money I would become a part of the thing. I started in this kitchenette kind of situation.

What kind of studio setup was it?

The living room had a piano in it and some tiles and a carpet, and a couple of condenser mikes; in those days, '58 or '59, it was really the ultimate thing to own a Telefunken. I learned how to record mono and then two-track, which was in its beginning stages, and then to find echoes. We shellacked one of the bedrooms, painted it for weeks until it had the right sound. Because money was tight, what we did to delay the echo was to take the feed from the tape machine, run it into that bedroom, and then return it. That is not great technique. But I'd seen this guy at Columbia run his tape machine into these huge vaults of echo and slap, and other sounds, and I said, "Oh, this is what I got to learn." Because half of what you do in the studio is the mixture of echoes, reverbs, slaps.

I got hold of an album, I'll never forget, it was called *Elsa Poppin and Her Pixieland Band.* Some French guy and a French engineer made it, probably in 1953 or '54. It did what George Martin and other people did later. There were seven or eight machines out of sync, in sync, and all of it humorous. One part would slow down while another part would go out of sync and the guy would giggle. I sat there for days, months, listening to this and trying to figure out how he did those things.

Did you learn mike placement and other recording techniques by playing on sessions and watching, or by experimenting with engineering?

Both. From playing I learned immediately from the playback what was happening. I would do dates in other people's studios for only one reason—to learn what the engineer was doing. I'd say, "Do you mind if I come in here?" It was sort of an unwritten law that musicians never went in the control room. Only the concertmaster or the contractor did. I used to watch them doing mike placement, that was the key to good technique in the fifties.

My reputation grew very quickly. By the time I was twenty-one

I was engineering for [Burt] Bacharach & [Hal] David, Quincy
Jones, Leiber & Stoller, Ellie Greenwich, Jeff Barry, Neil Diamond,
Doc Pomus, and Mort Shuman. There were maybe four independent studios that had any reputation. A&R Recording Studios,
which I was a part of, was really starting to happen, because when
Bell Sound and a couple of the others were overbooked we got the
spill.

Rock 'n' roll people like Leiber & Stoller were making records
to sound great on a mono station. Then I befriended Tommy Dowd
and people like that who were into stereo. But I had to have more
than two tracks. I befriended a lot of interesting people—people
in the computer business and other areas of technique—to try to
lock up two machines. I had heard about this eight-track machine
that Atlantic and Les Paul had. Eight tracks on one piece of tape!
I mean, if you saw the machine today, you'd laugh. It was literally
like a van, a truck, it was so huge. But they could erase a track
or put one in, take one out. It was against the union rules to do
this.

You're kidding!

No, you were never allowed to overdub. In '60, '62, I don't remember when, the rule changed. Now, when I say it was against the
rules, you were supposed to record the singer and everything was
supposed to go down exactly as it went. You weren't supposed to
replace the vocal.

Why?

Because the union said any time you replaced the vocal, all the
musicians had to be paid. I had to make a speech in front of a whole
group of musicians and say that the union had to realize that
multiple track was going to cause a certain kind of problem. I built
booths because I couldn't control a singer's level against a huge
band. Very difficult. Only the big engineers in those days knew how
to do that, because they had space and they'd build screens around
these people.

You were working in eight-track at this point?

No, we were still three-track. Then it went four-track almost a year later. To get control of a Diahann Carroll record for Atlantic . . . They said to me before the session, "Diahann sings very quiet and sweet, not loud." And we've got like a thirty-eight-piece band behind her. Some friends and I built a corner for her out of truck blankets and two-by-fours. The session was with Nesuhi Ertegun, and I'll never forget it, it came out so much different than any session I had ever done. There wasn't that leakage into the vocal. You could change the balance. You could also turn her channel off, and get a stereo mix, which you had to do in four-track. You had to have the band in stereo. I used to put the vocal on track two and the rhythm on three, because I learned the outside edges of the tape were dangerous due to the wobble of the tape. You tried to avoid strings and stuff on the outside, but you could put horns there and you'd never hear any waver on the tape.

This was really pioneering.

Yeah. Especially when they went to multi-track. Creed Taylor was really the leader of the pack. He was another client of mine. I learned a lot from him. I was doing jazz records with Creed and at the same time he was doing rock 'n' roll. He was also working at Verve, so I got into all this bossa nova stuff. He gave me a lot of freedom. He let me run the tape machine at double the speed, waste tape. I followed and read about everything that had to do with recording technique. I wrote to people. I wrote to this guy in France. I wrote to George Martin and got a very nice letter back. I listened to Beatles records and said, "You know, this guy is doing this on a four-track machine. Maybe he's got two four-track machines, but he's doing something no one else is doing." And records were coming from Nashville that used to kill me, they sounded so good. Nashville was really way ahead of its time. People don't realize that. I traveled the country a lot. So when I went to Nashville or someplace, I'd run into a studio and learn about how they got a sound.

Most of the producers I've talked to, like John Hammond and Jerry Wexler, have not really been trained technical people. You,

*of course, are. How important do you think it is for a producer to
also be a technician?*

I think whether you're an active technician or a person who uses
his ears and finds a great engineer to work with, it's a real team
effort. It just happens that I was fortunate enough to have been an
engineer first. I think in this day and age, where young people have
a chance to record at home and make great demos and work with
multiple-track stuff, it's impossible to be a good producer without
having some technical knowledge or some technique.

Anybody that hangs around me will tell you that I'm shopping
all the time for new sounds and ideas. I'm not out to copy anything,
but if Emulator makes a new drum kit . . . Like, we heard a new
thing last night that I liked, so I sent my assistant Joe to the store
in the morning to check it out, to see whether it's interesting
enough to either rent or buy. Everybody has this tendency to be
so precious about the past. It's the future I care about, and what's
happening at this moment. I remember doing interviews about CDs
five years ago. I was a big nut-case on wanting to see that CDs made
it. The audience, meaning people who care about new things, are
going to reach for better sound, better quality. Because when things
cost more, people expect better. When an album cost five bucks
fifteen years ago, if you only had three cuts that were good, and
four were mediocre and the other two were throwaways, it didn't
matter. You didn't go broke buying a record. When kids put down
ten or eight bucks for a record, they expect and deserve a really
well-produced one.

*When you were an engineer working for other producers, didn't
you ever say, "Hell, I can do this better than that schmuck, I
don't need this guy to tell me what to do"?*

I think that I got my chops by working with really good producers.
Bad producers were the guys who were not around. They were good
for me because they left me alone, and let me do what they didn't
do. There were guys who couldn't talk to musicians; it would insult
their intelligence, because musicians are the hired help, and they're
just supposed to get it done in three hours. Not thinking that the
musician, if you gave him another ten minutes, might play the most

incredible lick you ever heard. Some producers used to walk in, play you last week's hit, and say, "This is what I want. I love the sound on this guy's record and that's what you better give me. I don't want anything of yours." I used to get frustrated because they didn't want me to do what I thought would be more inventive, a new kind of effect. Guys that wouldn't let me do that, I got rid of as clients, when I had the freedom of choice. I mean, guys like Quincy Jones and Bobby Scott were adventuresome; they let me alone. They would go out and conduct the band or work with the artist, and they knew they could trust me in the control room. There was a big transition from behind the glass to beyond the glass. It's probably the most important transition one makes.

Can you explain the financial arrangements between you, the artist, and the label?

It's changed over the last five or six years, but basically, if they don't sell records, I don't get paid. A lot of producers demand heavy front money and a high royalty, but I'm not getting paid by the day. I don't get an hourly rate. If it all goes well, then I start to see some profits. That structure—if you want to talk about insecurity, that's how you live. You get paid quarterly against actual sales minus returns. We're one of the few businesses in the world that takes back merchandise. Record companies say, "We shipped half a million records," but it doesn't mean anything.

The fact is that a producer can be paid well. If you have a hit, it's marvelous. But you have to wait. And you have to go through all of these discounts, the free giveaways, the this, the that. There's hundreds of clauses in a record contract, and it takes a long time to learn all of the routes to making a decent deal. Producers only in the last few years have gotten better deals. Up until five or six years ago you were nailed to a price and a delivery [date] and a cost. Even today, in many contracts, including those of most newer producers, it says, "If you do go over a certain budget, you pay."

Let's talk about some of the people you've worked with. You and Billy Joel have been together since 1978. All of the albums you worked on have gone platinum plus.

I think the reason we work well together is that it's all one could ever hope for in a relationship. He trusts me implicitly. He gives me all the freedom I want. And we're totally honest with each other —musically, as human beings, and with the group of musicians we use. There is a total, absolute belief in saying what you think, immediately. I don't lose my temper very easily. Part of my technique is that I let the musicians get in a playpen and scramble away for hours.

How does a Billy Joel album come together? Does he come to you with a list of songs?

Generally, yes. For the first album I did with him, *The Stranger*, he had three or four songs. The band—Liberty DeVitto, Doug Stegmeyer, Russell Javors—had been with him for years. I believed in the band; I think that probably got me the gig. The thing I saw at Carnegie Hall when I went to hear them was that this was a very well put-together rhythm section. Billy's past records that I was handed were all studio-produced records with studio musicians. I don't care whether a guy is a studio player or a road player. Eventually a road player with enough chops will become a studio player.

I want to get at the essence of your working relationship.

With Billy, yes, we're supposed to make a hit record, we're supposed to have a hit song, but neither one of us will sit in the studio and believe that that's what we're aiming at. We all have the feeling that it *could* be a hit, or it *feels* like a hit record. Those words are part of our vocabulary. But you can't go in the studio and try to make a hit record. If you try to make a hit record you will probably fall on your ass.

I think The Nylon Curtain *got the best reviews of all the Joel albums, yet it didn't sell as well as the rest. Is that frustrating? How do you explain it?*

I love being teased about that, because everyone overlooks the fact that the album sold a million records. Of course, he had sold 4 or

5 million before but it was like going from being a .400 hitter to being a .300 hitter. So success is a relative thing. I hope such a "poor" seller happens to me every time out. Also, if it wasn't for *The Nylon Curtain,* I wouldn't have recorded Julian Lennon. Through that album he decided that he wanted to work with me. He loved it.

I want to talk about Julian Lennon more a little later. First let me ask you about An Innocent Man, *which sounded like Billy's attempt to capture the songs of his youth. Do you really think you can do that? Can you make records today that sound like the classics of the fifties and sixties?*

No. You know, when you analyze *An Innocent Man,* there's another level of it that is not looked into. What Billy felt was that at his particular vocal age, before his voice changed in his mid-thirties, he could still hit those high notes. He loved songs like "Spanish Harlem" and "Under the Boardwalk." It was part of his background. He wrote an original album and original songs. We did not go out simply to salute the sixties.

Did Billy Joel feel he'd gotten too far away from what rock 'n' roll really is, and that he had to get back to it with an album like An Innocent Man?

It was no more a process than *The Nylon Curtain* was a process. It's where Billy was at a particular time in his life.

But there are outside influences. . . .

Of course there are.

For instance, Billy has obviously been plagued throughout his career with rock reviewers tearing him to shreds—selling millions of records, but the critics really killing him. That's got to have an impact on someone.

You'll remember he wrote a song "It's Still Rock and Roll to Me." The punk age was happening and he was being buried. Billy Joel

was middle-of-the-road. Critics were really nailing him. Of course
it affects you. I mean, he would read a review onstage, and then
do a medley of rock 'n' roll tunes.

*Doesn't the criticism contribute to the creative process when he
comes to you and says, "Phil, I want to make a rock 'n' roll
record"?*

He *is* a rock 'n' roller. He's just as much rock 'n' roll as Bruce
Springsteen or anybody else you want to name. But because he's
able to cross over, people decide . . . It's so different every five years
in the music world, and he has survived eight years of success, plus
the five years before that, which people forget. He was a cult
musician. He broke out of that, he hated that identity. *Piano Man*
was not Billy Joel alone. Billy Joel is an eclectic musician and writer
who is as capable of writing a Broadway show as he is of doing a
pure rock 'n' roll concert with the funkiest, punkiest band that ever
walked. He can sing the blues with everyone else. They nail you
because you're successful.

*Do they? Do you really think they have it in for you because you
sold five million records?*

Anybody. I think right now if Michael Jackson were to make a
record he'd be in for it. What can he do to top his 30 million–
seller? Billy's been on tour. He's sitting now and trying to write
and go back through the process. He's not saying, "I'm going to
please this critic." They can't be your guiding light.

*You're saying there's nothing crass about the way you and Billy,
or others you work with, make an album.*

No, there isn't anything crass about it. You don't go into the studio
saying this better be a 5 million–seller or our careers will be over.
Maybe they *will* be over, if we go in and try to make something
that's stylistically "right" at the time.

*Let me ask you about another New York songwriter you've worked
with, Paul Simon. He and Billy are both New York kids, they're*

*both singer/songwriters, but I'll bet they're very different in the
studio.*

Absolutely. Paul has grown up in the studio; he was kind of born
there. Paul is meticulous and likes to be a part of everything, and
yet hates the waste of time and the time it takes. He's part of
every inch of his records. It was only after five or six years of
working with Paul that he would leave me alone and go out to
dinner or take some time off. But when he was in the studio he
spent every hour with me. We coproduced. He had come from the
years of discipline that he and Art Garfunkel had spent with Roy
Halee. Roy was an employee but he became part of the production. All those wild sounds that Roy Halee created with them
were outlandish, bizarre, rebellious, against all the rules. Nobody
took as much time to make an album. Clive Davis, and whoever,
obviously trusted them.

When I met Paul Simon, and he started his solo career, he was
a guy who had totally lived his life in the studio. Yes, he had
performed, but the difference was that Billy's real world was to play
in clubs and sleaze joints, then concert halls, and finally arenas.
That's where 90 percent of Billy's life was. The studio became fun
to him later. When Billy and I started making records, the nicest
compliment to me was, "I really had a good time in there." Paul
treated it as part of his daily activity.

*There's been a lot of talk about how long it takes to make rock
records today, with all the indulgences involved. In the old days
you'd make a record in a couple of days; now it can take months.
Is that usually the artist's fault, or the producers?*

You can give credit to both sides. When people made a record ten
or twelve years ago, you were given $12,000 to make the record
and it was $3.98 in the marketplace. When the big million-dollar
deals were made, and albums went to $6.98 or $7.98—Billy's
records always seemed to come out just as they were raising the
price, and both of us were scared. When kids buy a record, they
have the freedom of choice to pick among tons of records. It's quite
amazing that they pick yours.

Are you saying that fear contributes to the increasing length of time it takes to produce an album?

Of course. I don't know if you understand how huge the profits are for the record company if you happen to have a hit. Yet, on the other hand, so many dollars are inside the production of a record, if it's a flop, it's a real loss. And that situation creates madness both from the artist's and the company's point of view. I'll promise you this, the business end decides where you are going. If you don't sell, you are not there.

I think the key problem is that someone invented the word demographics. We've created a monstrosity. Sometimes you get a message from the record company saying, "Look, we really have to make sure we're on Contemporary Hit Radio or that we have an AOR hit." I say to them, "The more you channel me, the less I know where it's going to go." What happens if I break in the R&B market, or on the dance charts? What difference does it make?

But you're the big hit-maker producer. If there has been any criticism of you it has been that you pay too much *attention to demographics.*

I don't pay any attention to them at all. I can't. I'm demographically over age. I don't belong anymore.

But you're making records for people who are under forty.

I make records for musical reasons, and it just happens to be that I'm one of those people who is never looking back. I love kids. I don't particularly cater a record to a fifteen-year-old, but I am interested to know if he likes it.

All right, let's talk about Chicago, a group that you worked with that has been a real hit-making machine for more than fifteen years. They have eighteen or nineteen albums, and don't you think they've followed a formula to guarantee them AOR radio success?

No. They went through a drought. They had a hit recently. But until David Foster came along . . . I mean, I made a pretty good record

with them. I did number twelve, their first album after Terry Kath
died, which was a major trauma. I had worked as engineer on some
of their stuff before that. But they're not a formula machine. They
were considered, at the time, a dead issue. Once Terry had died,
people were going to give up on Chicago. It took a great deal of
strength and inner desire for them to make sure that they didn't
fall apart, and that everything was a part of their musicality. The
record business treats certain acts after a certain time as being over
the hill.

So did you retool them?

I tried to. I think I was part of the health process. As I said, we
didn't have a smash hit. We did okay. I think we sold a couple
million records. Then they went into this period when they themselves admit they allowed too many people in the band to write,
trying to get, quote, a hit.

*Let's talk about a record that required a lot of work on your part,
Julian Lennon's* Valotte. *I know that some record companies had
apprehensions about doing the record to the extent that they passed
on the project. They thought it might be exploitative of John's
death. Did you have any apprehensions about that?*

The only apprehension, before I met Julian, was to find out if he
was genuine about what he wanted to do, if he was there to be taken
seriously as a songwriter. Once I heard material, scraps, and pieces
of songs and I got to know him, I knew that the time spent would
be, to be honest with you, the hardest time I would ever spend in
my life, and the most fun. He is a guy who is genuine, absolutely
honest about himself, and he happens to be the son of John Lennon. It's not a disgrace; if anything it's an honor. The criticism I
get is that he sounds like his dad. He doesn't *try* to sound like his
dad. He can't help it. It's in the genes, folks.

But the kid is good.

He's a talent. He's a serious songwriter. He has a great sense
of humor. He's a genuine human being with a desire to make

it. My only question with anybody is, "Do you want to make it?"

Why do you think the record companies that did pass were apprehensive about him?

First of all, his demos were nothing to be heard. He hadn't really spent enough time in the studio. The people he did spend time with wasted his time. I think they were hanging on to him because he was Julian Lennon. Nobody realized this guy was serious until he went to this place in France and started to write and make these little home-grown demos which were really good. Obviously, Ahmet Ertegun and Doug Morris at Atlantic realized that this was not a toy. When I heard the demos, I heard what I wanted to hear, which was a songwriter. My only basic desire when I met him was to see if our personalities would be okay. We hit it off. He's very shy. We both looked at each other and said we were out to make a quality record. The deal between the record company and us was very simple. If we didn't like what we made in a couple of months, we would go back and recut it and do better.

That happened, didn't it? Ahmet [Ertegun] heard the first three or four cuts of the record and said it was too downbeat. Did that surprise you?

No. Ahmet Ertegun is a guy who is really aware of the music world. When he said it was downbeat I said, "Just give me a chance." Because we had just spent three weeks in Alabama at Muscle Shoals, and this is what was coming out of Julian at the moment. I said, "Unless you let this out, you won't get an up tune." Some of those songs are not on the album. So what? I'm used to the writing process. I've been through it, with ten years with Paul Simon and eight with Billy. There are some songs that don't finish, or become part of something else, or a verse becomes an up verse for something that was originally written as a ballad. That's what my craft is, to work with people and change things. You must indulge a certain amount of this. For Julian, it was the first chance to really pour out what was in him.

Ahmet realized that?

Oh, yeah. He was worried, like anybody would be. It's an investment, and he expects me to make a record in a certain amount of
time. But I said to him from the very beginning that this is not
going to be a three-month project. It's going to be six months.
There's a great sense of humor in Julian. He's not a down person.
He has come out of his shell.

How were you able to bring that out in the studio?

By letting him take chances. Leaving him alone sometimes for
hours with a drum machine and a keyboard. He realized that I was
going to let him do that, that I wasn't going to sit there and demand.
What I kept preaching to Julian and myself was that if they don't
like the record, fine, but only because they don't like *this* record.

*I think it would be interesting to talk about your work with
Barbra Streisand here. She was a middle-of-the-road artist for
many years. . . .*

She's a person who has the chops that any producer would like to
work with. You're dealing with a fine artist, and a great singer, and
a person who is sensitive to the delivery of a song. Barbra has
turned a corner, and wants to make a transition. She's not going
to sing worse, she's going to sing better. She doesn't want to be
passé.

*What does she want from you as a producer? What does she say to
you when you're going to make a record?*

I don't know if she says to me what you think she says to me. It
always boils down to something you did that she likes. Obviously.
That's why you're a hired hand. It's like her wanting to work with
Miloš Forman or somebody like that because he makes a certain
kind of movie. Barbra likes to be in control of a lot of elements.
She's still human, and understands that you have to trust somebody
to do something. The one thing you can't do with Barbra is formu-
lize something and think she's going to fit it. I think people have

done that with her, and those records are there to be heard, and they're not the most popular. She can't do a Madonna record, nor should she. She's Barbra Streisand.

What is she like in the studio?

Barbara can deliver a song. I think that's one of the things I'm good at, picking a song or finding a song. She is meticulous about songs. One of the things I think she enjoys with me is that I go for the immediate. I go for the performance. That magic. But in case it goes wrong here or there I'm ready to move, at any moment at any time, and change everything. What people get upset about is that she'll say, "Yes, tomorrow this is what we're going to do between the hours of 10:00 and 5:00." Then she walks in and the mood has changed, the chemistry has changed; the actors or musicians are all there, and she feels something else that may be totally different from what you had planned. And if you're not a freewheeler like I am, you're going to get crazed.

I like to create an arrangement within the room, with three or four musicians. Now, for Barbra that's not always a thrill because she likes to hear it all. But there's a way around that: You get two keyboard players with synthesizers that sound synthetically like strings and horns. Nobody wants to have to do what she used to, which was to go through all the parts with an arranger while thirty or forty musicians are sitting out in the studio. That's how electronics have made a marked difference. That was a major step for her because she loves to change. "Oh, I like that line. What did you just play? I want that." Fine. I've got plenty of tracks. The engineer knows that what she's saying is the essence of what she really wants. Then perfection for her is going 180 degrees each way. You have to have extremely strong will, and you have to be honest with her. Ninety percent of the people with a star like that tend to not be honest.

It's nice that you're in such a strong position.

It's not that. Look, that's this week's news. I could be history tomorrow, or in a matter of hours. This business doesn't allow you the privilege of looking at your charts. If you start believing that stuff you're a has-been in my book, because you're not working at your craft. You're not going to the clubs. You're not going downtown to the Village or Soho. You're not listening for the next Bob Dylan to come along. You're not listening to the street. If you lose that you become a polished producer. "Hey, on my last record I did this." Good night. You might as well kiss it good-bye.

(March, 1985)

Chris Strachwitz

C hris Strachwitz has never produced a smash hit record. In fact, if one of his records became a big hit he'd probably wonder what he did wrong. His company, Arhoolie, is pleased when a record sells in the low thousands or even hundreds. But the eclectic Arhoolie catalog of around three hundred records is far more important than its sales would indicate. Since 1960 Strachwitz has recorded and made available some of the most important blues, country, regional, and ethnic music. Whether it's country bluesman Mance Lipscomb, zydeco master Clifton Chenier, the yiddish group The Klezmorim, norteno star Flaco Jimenez, or J. E. Mainer's Mountaineers, Strachwitz has pursued the purest music in America. The distinctive music in the Arhoolie catalog has withstood the advances of popular music that have threatened to obliterate it, and Strachwitz has made a near-heroic effort over the years to preserve it. Moreover, although he doesn't profess to be much of a businessman, he has managed to make Arhoolie a profitable business, and to branch out with his own distribution company, Bayside, and his wonderful retail store and mail order firm, Down Home Music Co. in El Cerrito, California. He even managed to back into a couple of minor hits when he recorded Country Joe and the Fish's "Fixin' to Die Rag," and Fred McDowell's "You Got to Move," which was covered by the Rolling Stones. But his story begins with a wide-eyed trip down South in search of his idol, Lightnin' Hopkins.

Who inspired you to do your own recording?

I met Sam Charters, who lived out here [in the Bay Area] and would go down South every summer. I met Bob Geddins, who was making all kinds of rhythm and blues records here. He recorded for Trilon, Downtown, Big Town, Geddins, Irma—he had more labels than you could shake a stick at. Every month when I used to go visit him he would be someplace else. There'd be a sign on his old place saying done moved, try this and this address. And I'd go and they'd be sawing away building his studio all over again. I don't know how he ever got anything done. That's how I first met Big Mama Thornton. She was a big shape lying on a sofa in a studio. The other man who really inspired me was a guy named Jaxyson. He put out records on the Jaxyson label. It was written Jaxyson, but it says under it "pronounced Jackson." He had a little repair shop next to the old Lincoln Theater on Seventh Street in Oakland. That was the heart of the black ghetto in the thirties and forties. I was always hunting for records. I was just a record-collecting freak.

You were what? A teenager?

When I came to this country from Germany in 1947 I was sixteen. I came up here in '53. I went to school in Southern California until then. From about '53 on is when I got the idea of making records. So those guys had probably the most influence on me. Because I had always thought that records were literally made in some huge factory where artists walked in one end like mice in a cheese plant, and out come the records on the other end. I had no idea how they were made. But Mr. Jaxyson, he just had a record-cutting machine, and he literally recorded guys that came off the street in the forties.

But how did you get the idea of jumping in your car and going down South, into the field, to record?

I was totally addicted to Lightnin' Hopkins ever since I heard his first records on the radio. I remember Sam Charters in about '57 would go down South. He'd come back with a trunkful of old records. Stuff I'd never seen before like old scroll Victors—you know, Memphis Jug Band and stuff like that. I was staying with some people here as a student, and he would come over and listen to Lightnin' Hopkins. We didn't know where Lightnin' was from. We were total romantics. There was an article in a French magazine that said perhaps Lightnin' Hopkins is from Mississippi, but we weren't quite sure. Maybe it's Texas. We didn't have the sense to call up one of these guys like the Biharis [of Modern Records], which we could have done if we had any ingenuity. Anyway, one summer I got a postcard from Sam saying, "I found Lightnin' Hopkins!" That was like a revelation to me. Like the Book of Moses [laughter]. I said, "My God, he actually exists." The next year, I believe it was in '59, I had an older sister who was working in Albuquerque, and she needed her car driven down there. So I said, well, that's halfway to Texas. So I drove it down there and took a bus to Houston. In the meantime, Sam had also told me about a guy named Mac McCormack there, who was acting as Lightnin's agent. Sam said, "Lightnin' is very suspicious, he's very hard to deal with." But Sam did record that first Folkways record with Lightnin' at that time. So I took a pilgrimage to Houston. I stayed at the YMCA. I met Mac and he took me over to meet Lightnin', and that was just like meeting God.

This trip was just as a fan, then.

Absolutely. I just wanted to hunt records and visit Lightnin' Hopkins. That year I didn't do any recording at all. I had made some tapes before. Jesse Fuller in his house. And I had recorded some guy, John Hogg, he was a relation to Smokey Hogg, in Los Angeles with a fellow named Ken Mills who later started Icon records in New Orleans. I was also a New Orleans jazz freak. George Lewis was my other idol—I used to tape-record him. I used to go to the Beverly Cavern at night with Frank Demond, who is now trombone player with the Preservation Hall Jazz Band, when he and I were going to Pomona College. We used to go every night. I almost flunked out of that school [laughter]. And that was before they had freeways in L.A., man. So I was already into taping stuff. But I don't think I had the idea of starting a label until I went to Texas.

Meeting Lightnin' Hopkins was the revelation?

Yeah. I had never heard of anything like Lightnin' in these joints. I knew all kinds of records had been made, but I thought nobody had captured this man the way I saw him at Pop's Place. He was just moaning some blues about how he hardly could go to work that night because it had been raining so hard and his shoulder was hurting, and the chuck holes were all full of water. He made it into poetry, all rhymed up. He saw us coming in, but he kept going with this same drone. It was just a drummer behind him. And he sings "Woe, this man come all the way from California just to hear po' Lightnin' sing." It was just a verse thrown in there. And he would sing to the women in front. But rhyming it all the time. I had never encountered anything like that. Just making up this stuff. A real folk poet. That is when I decided I wanted to start a record label to record Lightnin' Hopkins in those joints. Unfortunately, that never came about because I didn't have any money and I had shitty equipment. The next year, 1960, when I was teaching school, that was the first time I took a tape recorder down there.

Let's talk about that first recording trip down South.

I had bought a Roberts tape recorder and a microphone, an Electro-voice 664, I think it was. I had met Bob Pinson, who now works for the Country Music Foundation. He was working in a factory in the Santa Clara Valley. He came from Texas and wanted to catch a ride with me. I was teaching school in Los Gatos down near San Jose. So I decided to go down to Texas to record Lightnin'. I didn't have much money, but I saved what I could from that first year of teaching. I think I was making $7,000 a year, which was big money. I think I had $2,000 saved up for the trip. I had an old

'39 Plymouth, I think it was. It broke down in New Mexico. All the oil came out, and the damn engine burned up [laughter]. Man, I had to pay $500 or something. I thought, man, we're getting the blues right here [laughter]. But we drove into Texas. To me that was very romantic. The whole country became like an opening up of the Pearly Gates. Here's this blues world. I liked country music, too. Now Paul Oliver, who I had corresponded with, had sent me a long list of people who he knew were from Texas—legendary old blues guys. He'd written these books about blues, but he'd never been there. Black Ace and a whole bunch of guys like that were on that list. We got to Dallas and Fort Worth. I liked Little Son Jackson's records, and Bob said he thought Little Son Jackson was from there. We looked in the phone book—I think his name was Melvin Jackson—but we couldn't find him. Bob had the bright idea of going to the library and looking in an old phone directory from the fifties. And there it was, Melvin Jackson, with an address. We called him up, and asked him if he was the blues singer. He said yeah. So we went over, he was working at an auto parts place. He was a little shy guy. I was really enthusiastic. But he was the first to throw a wrench at me with this money business because he'd made commercial records. So he used to get something like what Lightnin' got. Lightnin' got $100 a side, per song.

As an advance or a flat fee?

It was a flat fee. To me it was a lot of money. For an LP I needed twelve songs. I couldn't possibly pay him $1,200. I think I finally told him this is just like one record. But I must have been persuasive. He said "Okay, I'll make some numbers for you." I brought an acoustic guitar with me, although I don't play a note. And he didn't have a guitar so it was a good thing.

Where did you record him?

At his house, in his living room. I just had that one microphone, and I balanced it between that guitar and his voice. He had a very low voice, so it prepared me for what was to come with Mance Lipscomb. He sang quietly, but played very loud guitar. After that I left Pinson, and took off on my own.

Were you still following the list you had?

Yeah. But those were just names, and I don't think they meant that much to me. The people that meant something to me were people I'd heard records by. There was a guy on a Talent 78 I had, his name was Little Brother. I remember I saw a bunch of black guys on the street playing dominoes, sitting on the curb. I just asked them, "You ever hear of a guy named Little Brother?" At first they just looked at me. I later found out they usually think you're a bill collector or some government agent or some damn social worker. I said, "I have some old records by him." All of a sudden one of them said, "Yeah, he used to hang around with Black Ace." I knew Black Ace was on that list. I said, "Where can I find Black Ace?" He gave me the name of a tavern, and he said, "He comes in there every afternoon at five o'clock." He says, "You can't miss him because he's got Ace written on his shirt." So I thanked them and went to that beer joint. This black man walks in with "Ace" written on his shirt [laughs]. I asked him if he was Black Ace. He said, "That's what they used to call me." He still had a steel guitar, but he didn't have no strings. I didn't record him then because he said he needed some time. He hadn't practiced. I told him I was going to meet Paul Oliver in Memphis and come back through Texas.

Why had these guys recorded, and then not recorded for some time?

That music was fading very quickly. Little Son Jackson was almost a rhythm and blues artist, like Lightnin' was. In the early fifties that kind of low-down blues was selling really well to black people who came from the South. Especially out here in California, there's a lot of them from Texas and Louisiana. They were making pretty good money here in the war industry. So they were willing to buy the records and they were willing to pay to hear these guys. Bill Quinn—he was another inspiration to me, he put out Goldstar Records in Houston. His personal taste was schmaltzy German waltzes. Lightnin' went to him and said, "Mr. Quinn, I need me some money." Whenever Lightnin' needed some money he'd find a record man who'd record him. However, by '60 black music was changing fast. It was going to soul music.

How many recordings did you actually do on this trip?

I did Black Ace. Little Son Jackson. Mance Lipscomb. I met Mance
that same summer. There was actually a story to that. Lightnin'
made a record called "Tom Moore," a very stark ballad about:
"There ain't but one thing this black man done wrong, but move
his wife and family on to Mr. Tom Moore's farm." It's a really
strong protest song about the mistreating of the field hands on Mr.
Tom Moore's farm. So Mac said, "Let's drive up to Washington
County [Texas]. I think that's where Mr. Tom Moore lives." So we
went to Navasota and Mac walked into a feed store. He asked,
"Does Tom Moore live here?" They said, "Yes, *Mr.* Tom Moore's
got an office over the bank building. Mac was pretty brash at that
time. I was scared. I didn't know what the hell we were getting into.
He calls up Tom Moore, and he invited us up to his office. It was
a nice big office and he had pictures of his plantation all over the
wall. We talked to him for quite a while. Mac wanted to know all
kinds of stuff about how big his plantation was. I was amazed. Mac
asked him if there was a black hand who played for the people on
the plantation. Tom Moore said, "Yeah, there's a guy, I don't know
his name, but you can find out if you go down to the railroad station
and ask for this guy Pegleg." So we asked Pegleg, "Who's the
guitar picker around here?" He says, "Oh his name is Mance
Lipscomb. You can find him out on the highway cutting the grass."
He also told us where he lived. We didn't find him on the road,
but we went to his house, and that's where we met Mance Lipscomb. He had just come off a tractor. I made a record that same
evening. That became the first Arhoolie record, Arhoolie 1001.

That was quite a memorable trip.

Everything that happened on that trip was like that. I went from
there to Louisiana. I had heard about Cajun music from Bob Pinson, who had played me something by the Hackberry Ramblers on
Bluebird. So I asked at a service station in Lafayette for some Cajun
music. The man there sent me to a bar. I remember there was a
very attractive girl as a bartender. I asked her if she ever heard of
any Cajun music, and she just started laughing like crazy. She said,
"Yeah, that stuff is crazy. My boyfriend and I went to this place

about halfway to Breaux Bridge called the Midway Club." Sure enough, I got there and they were going full tilt. It was Aldus Roger and his band. They were playing a song I loved: "God Didn't Make Honky Tonk Angels," the Kitty Wells hit that J. D. Miller wrote. One singer would sing in French and the other in English. All these old couples were just two-stepping along. Waltzing away. It was a neat sight. They were all really friendly. I didn't record Aldus Roger. I think I was sort of scared of that. I thought that was too big time for me. Also, I couldn't handle it with my one microphone because they used amplifiers and stuff. On a later trip I went to Hackberry, which is just south of Lake Charles, because I figured that was where the Hackberry Ramblers were from. It's just a dinky town, maybe fifty people. I asked a lady in a little cafe there if she'd heard of the Hackberry Ramblers. She said, "Yeah, that's Luderin Darbone; he lives right back in Sulphur on Darbone Street." I said I'll be damned. So I walked to his house, and I think the next day was Sunday and he got all his boys together and we made a tape in his house.

When you came back with all these tapes, did you have to do a lot of work on them before you could put them out as records?

I didn't know nothing about that. What was on the tape was what would go on the record. When I would take it to the guy who cut my masters, he would fiddle sometimes with it. He'd say we can boost this a little or take some of this out. He just had a couple of tone controls. I don't think he did much. I didn't know what I was doing. I was kind of dependent on these people to know what they were doing.

How did you decide whether to record someone on site in the field or in his home versus in a studio?

Money [laughter]. That was the biggest thing. I didn't have no money, so if I could record him in a house that was a natural. Studios cost me ten or fifteen dollars an hour at that time. That was a lot of money. The first year, I don't think I did any studio recordings at all. The next trips I did a couple in little funky studios. Also, if it was acoustic stuff, I didn't really see any sense in a studio. I felt that the only time I needed a studio was if I had a piano player or something. Or if there were several musicians.

So all you had in the field was your Roberts tape recorder?

Yeah. It was bad. In the second or third year I went down it started overmodulating everything, over-recording. One whole summer of stuff I did was wasted. There were some good piano players I recorded in Houston, and that's all useless. I was really pissed. When I found out that shit was of no use, I looked up Jack Lauderdale of Swingtime Records. I figured I had to get out something. He had some wonderful Joe Turner and Pete Johnson stuff that he'd issued on 78s, also some Lowell Fulson. So I bought the masters. I picked the most uncommercial stuff. He just sold them to me for $250. All those sides. He said, "None of those ever made me no money."

Who was your most exciting or satisfying find on these trips?

Oh God, every time was something different. I guess Mance Lipscomb in a way, because it was such a dramatic thing. But I'll never forget meeting and recording Fred McDowell in Mississippi. I believe I heard about him from one of Alan Lomax' records. He came out on that Atlantic series *Roots of the South.* Lomax had made some field recordings. Fred McDowell was the man on those records that just knocked me out. So I wrote to Lomax and he told me he was from [Como] Mississippi, and he gave me a route number. I went to the post office, and they said, "You go up Highway 61, and make the third or fourth left turn and it's the second ranch on the right." He loved music and he was such an open person'. Afterward Fred told me Lomax apparently didn't give him nothing but five dollars and a couple of Cokes, I think, to play for him all night long. So I paid him, I guess, a couple of hundred dollars. He just thought that was great. I stayed in his house that night. He and his wife stayed in the living room and they let me have the big bed. They were just so sweet. We made that record the same day I met him. I had a Capps condenser mike. It was a nice-sounding omnidirectional mike. You had to put it in a good place to catch both the voice and the guitar.

Did you have a new recorder by then, too?

Oh yeah, I had the Magnecord by then. That's been my war horse most of those years. That's the same kind I heard later that Bob Shad and the Biharis had, too. I still have it but it kind of gave out on me. I remember another trip I went all the way back to North Carolina. One of my favorite old-time fiddlers was J. E. Mainer. I think I also found out from Lomax that he was from Concord, North Carolina. I looked in the phone book when I got there, and sure enough there was J. E. Mainer on Poplar Road. I drove out there. I first said, "I'd like to get your story." I didn't really know what to do with him. I just wanted to meet the man. Then I said, "I'd like to get a couple of pictures of you." He said, "Oh, that'll be five dollars, please." [Laughter.] Then he said, "You've got to buy me a bottle." So I went down the road to visit the lady with the bootlegged whiskey. The first year I just talked with him. The next year I went back with a German couple and made a film for German TV, and I made a record. I loved that record. It was a Sunday morning. I hung my microphone from the ceiling, and he had his son and daughter, and another guy on bass, and a mandolin. I just lined them up in a circle under the microphone. Him right in the middle because he was the fiddle and he did most of the singing, so I figured he ought to be the loudest. That was LP 5002.

Some people might think you were exploiting these guys. Did that ever enter your mind?

No, I don't think exploiting ever entered my mind because they didn't seem to have any such feelings about it. Except guys like Lightnin' and Little Son Jackson, who had made commercial records, and they wanted a lot of money, and I couldn't afford it. But also I wasn't making any money on it. That was the other thing. I didn't really start breaking even—I remember talking to Jack Holtzsman of Elektra at some folk festival, and he told me it took him seven years to break even—I told him it took me a lot longer

than that. But it never dawned on me that I could be exploiting
them. I was just having fun, and they were having fun. It was just
a mutual enjoyment thing.

How did you get the business going?

The Folkways label was kind of my format. I even took their
process of sticking the cover slick onto a black jacket. I stole that
from them. They seemed to be a neat label, although they were very
expensive. I couldn't afford many of them. But I liked the way they
packaged them. I remember Wayne Pope, my friend who did all
the layout and art work, and his wife and I would sit at this table
with sponges and wet these goddamn cover slicks down, all 250 of
them. The pressings had come from the pressing plant separately.
Mac had written the notes.

Who is the top-selling Arhoolie artist?

Clifton Chenier. He's the best-seller. I met him through Lightnin'
Hopkins on one of my crazy trips down there. I just liked to hang
out with Lightnin' wherever he played. I remember one night he
said, "Chris, do you want to go see my cuz?" I said, "Who's your
cousin?" He said, "Cliff, Clifton Chenier." The name rang a bell
because I think I had a Specialty record by him, and maybe a
Checker. To me that was rhythm and blues. I wasn't all that
enthusiastic, but if Lightnin' wanted to go there—I was just like
his little dog. I said, "Sure, let's go over and see him." So we went
over to Frenchtown in Houston. I'll never forget. We walked into
one of these little beer joints—hardly anybody in it, there was two
couples dancing. There was this man with his accordion and just
a drummer. He didn't have no band at all. He was playing these
really low-down blues. Mostly in French, but some in English, too.
Clifton came up to me afterward and said, "Oh, you making records? Come on, make me one!" He desperately wanted to have a
single. This was three or four years after his Checker record which
he toured behind. It did okay. But he hadn't had anything since
then. This was about '63 or '64. So we went to Bill Quinn's
Goldstar studio the next day and did the single "Ai Ai Ai" ["Under-
neath the Evergreen"].

How did you come to do the first Clifton Chenier album?

I went back the next year, 1964. The Houston distributor had actually sold a few of the single. I think a thousand, but at least I broke even on it. The next time I took him in the studio he made several zydeco pieces. He also did a tune which I called "Louisiana Blues." He came running out of the control room right after he cut it and said, "I gotta call my old lady." He said, "Baby, listen to this one," and they played it back to her over the phone. I remember during the recording of it Bill Quinn was standing behind me and he said, "Chris, this thing will sell down here." And it did. It had this real low-down sound. I asked Clifton what he was going to call this number. He said something in French. I didn't know what the hell he was saying. I said, "How do you spell that?" He said, "You can write it any way you want to." I finally said, "Why not just call it 'Louisiana Blues'?" He said, "That's good enough." It had this phrase—"Tout les jours les même choses"—either every night is the same or every night is not the same with your old lady. It's a catchy phrase. I probably should have called it "Tout les Jours les Même Choses" except no one would have been able to say it, including me! That one sold pretty good, maybe four or five thousand. It got onto a lot of jukeboxes and the black stations actually played that.

But the reason his records are big sellers for you now is the white audience, no?

Definitely. But at that time he wanted me to get a single out so he could get some work. It did succeed in that.

Did you have him under contract?

No. I don't sign anybody up on an exclusive. I record for one record. That's been my contract ever since I started. I always try to tell an artist I can only do so much for you. If somebody else comes along and offers you more money, go for it, but I wish you would let me know. Because if it's RCA or Mercury I say go because they'll make a lot of money and they'll help me sell mine. But if it's my competition, like Delmark Records or some other little

dinky one, then I must confess I would try and tell them no, don't
do that. Because they can't do any more than I can as far as getting
their name out there. But I remember the record that Fred Mc-
Dowell made on Capitol. That put Fred McDowell's name more
places than I ever dreamt of. And he became a real going concert
artist after that. *I Don't Play No Rock and Roll* was the name of
the album.

You had a couple of artists who left for larger companies, no?

Yeah. Big Mama Thornton, after she recorded for me, she recorded
for Mercury and Vanguard. Of course everybody was after Clifton.
I remember talking with Jerry Wexler about it. He wanted him for
Atlantic. Except it was just impossible for me to agree to it. But
I learned something—I hate to be the middle man.

Why did Wexler come to you to get Clifton?

Well, Clifton told him I'm the man who makes his records. He met
him at the Ash Grove in L.A. Clifton called me and said, "This man
wants to cut some records, why don't you talk with him." I went
over and met with Jerry. He wanted to sign him up for five years
and would guarantee him one record. I said, "Well, will you guarantee so many a year?" No, he wasn't willing to do that. I said,
"Are you at least willing to pay him real well?" He said, "No, I'll
pay him what you pay him." I said, "What's the point in that? And
I have no guarantee of you issuing anything after that. What are
we going to do if we want some local material? He needs to have
jukebox numbers out there every year." Jerry said, "Well, I'll let
you do that." But he was just totally noncommittal about it all. So
the whole thing finally went down the drain. I told him Clifton told
me what he wanted. Clifton told me, "I need a new trailer." He
needed roughly $3,000 or $4,000 worth of equipment and stuff.
Wexler wasn't willing to give that up front. So that blew that.

How about other Arhoolie artists?

Actually the first one, Mance Lipscomb. About a year or two after
I put that out this lady calls me from L.A. and says she's from

Reprise Records, Frank Sinatra's new record company, and they're interested in Mance Lipscomb [laughter]. I said, "Really, how come?" She says, "Well, he sounds like a very interesting folk artist." So we actually did make a deal. Reprise Records actually recorded enough material for three LPs. That was the biggest money Mance ever made at the time. Of course, they didn't keep them in print very long. They issued one, and reissued it a couple of years ago. So that did help.

Can an independent company do anything to keep their artists?

I'm not sure they should. See, I never really looked at it as a business. I only recorded something because I liked it. If I even *thought* it had a commercial potential, I'd probably reject it. I was really anti anything that was really popular. Ralph Gleason always told me, "Chris, you don't have a record company, it's your hobby." And that's true. I never went at it as a businessman. When I first met Bruce Iglauer [of Alligator records] he said, "I like your label, but you don't do anything for your artists." I told him that's not my forte. I like to record things that I hear that I like. I'm not going to be a manager or agent or booking person for somebody and be tangled up in their whole life like that. I don't like that part of the business. I hope they'll find somebody who can do that for them. Iglauer's been really good at that. He's done a lot for his artists. I realized I'm not a good bargaining man. I leave that to people who are good at it.

You were saying that Clifton is your best-seller. How many records will he sell a year?

Maybe five thousand the first year and between five hundred and one thousand the following years. But they keep selling.

Do most of your records continue selling?

No. The country blues stuff is almost dead as a doornail. Like that old stuff I did in Memphis with Fred McDowell and Furry Lewis. That totally stopped selling. Maybe I'll sell about forty a year. I've actually this year for the first time in my whole history withdrawn about fifty items from my catalog for distribution in this country. I felt they were clogging the pipeline. That's only in this country. I still ship them to distributors overseas, and I'm going to start selling them to stores who want them at a fairly low price. But you have to get them directly from me. There's no money in it if you do it through the distributors. Now being a distributor myself I know they're clogging the pipeline. My sales guys will take them out there to the stores, the records sit there, eventually come back, and the whole cycle goes over and over.

How many records do you maintain in the catalog now?

I think I have about three hundred. But in the U.S. now there's about two hundred and fifty.

Isn't it pretty expensive to maintain a large catalog of records?

It sure is. I'm beginning to realize that. And it's becoming more so all the time. Not only is it expensive to maintain it—by just the simple fact of stocking them and having them on my shelves and the shelves of a distributor—if they don't move . . . I'm really fortunate that I've gotten into all aspects of selling records. Not only making them, but wholesaling them, and retailing them. Because that's the only way I've found out—I'm not very good at learning out of books—what the problems are. It's very, very difficult to maintain items that don't sell.

Do you have a distributor for Arhoolie?

I have several distributors. The one I own, Bayside, is my only West Coast distributor. For the rest of the country I've got The House in Kansas City. Then Rounder Records is my other excellent distributor back East. They're sort of a similar operation to mine, except they're bigger. They came along later than I did, but they've done a lot. I also have Floyd's in Ville Platte, Louisiana, but he can only sell my Louisiana/French music, and I have some good distributors overseas.

Why are you not able to service the whole country through your own Bayside Distributors?

There are several reasons. The main reason is that most of the big chain stores who sell most of your records depend on a salesperson coming in to do their inventory. They will not order on their own. Only the specialty stores do that. And if you don't have a local sales rep you don't sell no records. My sales guys go to Tower, which is our biggest account—60 percent of our sales are through Tower Records, and they go in just like a big grocery store. They say you need this, you need that. As long as they've got a budget for them that month, they'll put them in. If they don't sell, the shit comes back.

Let's talk about the plusses and minuses of selling records through stores versus mail order.

I started off in mail order. I started the International Blues Record Club before I had a record out. I solicited money from people who sent me five dollars for a record. When it finally came out I finally sent them some records [laughter]. I made my first money to buy my first tape recorder and stuff by selling 78s through the mail. I did it through a British publication called *VJM*, I think it stands for Vintage Jazz Mart. I would advertise 78s and people would bid on them. I would pack them up, send them the bill, they would send me the money, and I would ship over there. The first Arhoolies I sold pretty much to that same audience. They were collectors. At that time there were very few blues LPs around.

How did Down Home Music come about?

I'm the main owner of Down Home Music. I started it some years ago when an upholstery shop moved out and I had all this space. So I said I want a real record store. I hired a guy and opened a little store. I had all kinds of records in there but no customers. I had met Frank Scott, who had a really good store in L.A. So I called him up, and it was just the right time and the right place, and so he's the man who really runs it. People can always find this

stuff here. If you want "The Bullfrogs of North America" on
Folkways, we got it for you [laughter].

You must get customers from all over.

We had some guy from Germany who came with two empty suit-
cases he filled up with $1500 worth of records. B. B. King bought
over $1200 worth of records the first time he came. Los Lobos have
been here. All the musicians come through here. When we opened
the store George Thorogood played. Ry Cooder will call up and
want to know such and such.

*You have a catalog of three hundred records—blues, country,
Yiddish, Cajun, Polish, Hawaiian, everything—how do you get a
record store, besides your own, to carry all these different kinds of
records?*

There are very few record stores in the world who carry this kind
of an extensive repertoire. I think we were very fortunate on the
West Coast that Russ Solomon started Tower Records. He had a
philosophy right from the start: He said if it's available through a
domestic distributor, I'll carry it. And he's pretty much stuck to
that until very recently when there's so much stuff, and so much
stuff that doesn't move—like the bluegrass section has really
shrunk in Tower. But Tower is an unusual chain. The specialty
stores—I can almost count them on the fingers of one hand for the
whole country. It's very difficult. That's why I'm amazed that I sell
anything at all. Who would put an Alex Moore out there? Who
would put a Black Ace in a store?

*Now before we totally get the blues for Arhoolie, we should also
point out that a number of songs published by your Tradition
Music have been covered as hits, or have become hits. Tell me the
story of Country Joe McDonald's "Fixin' to Die Rag."*

I should tell you first that I didn't know nothing about this aspect
of the record business until I met Eddie Shuler in Lake Charles,
Louisiana. I've got to give that man credit. He was one of the record
guys I looked up on one of my early trips, because I knew he

recorded all that Cajun music. I brought him some tapes and he said, "What do you want these damn tapes for? Get their songs." I said, "What are you talking about, get their songs? I got their music; that's what I want to listen to." He said, "No, that ain't what I'm talking about. Get their copyrights." It still didn't click at all with me. He said, "Look, if some famous singer likes one of the songs your guy is singing, you can make a whole bunch of money off the copyright." He explained to me that the song itself is worth some money. You have to publish it and let the world know you're the publisher, and if somebody records it they've got to pay you, at that time two cents, for every record sold. Then you split that with the composer. It didn't dawn on me. But I did start that. It stuck in my mind. Now Country Joe and the Fish were dragged into my house by Ed Denson, who was their manager at the time. It was just before this big peace march in Berkeley. Ed Denson called me and asked if I had my tape recorder ready. I said, "I'm leaving for Europe tomorrow." I was going over to Germany with one of the American Folk Blues Festivals. I said, "Well, bring them over and we'll make a tape." I hung the microphone from the ceiling—my good old Capps condenser. In came this motley crew of characters, I'll never forget it, shaggy-looking guys. I did it just like J. E. Mainer. I put them all around in a circle. They had a washboard beater and a guy with a guitar. "One, two, three, what are we fighting for? Next stop is Vietnam." I thought it was sort of a catchy tune. They did it pretty fast. I think they did about two or three takes of each of their songs. I gave Ed the tape. Joe asked me on the way out, "What do we owe you for the tape?" I said, "You don't owe me nothing. Just let me have the publishing rights." He said okay. It was just a verbal deal. Well, the shit hit the fan when they went to that Woodstock thing. Some rock 'n' roll band didn't show up on time. And Bill Belmont, by that time Joe's agent-manager, grabbed this guitar and said "Joe, go up there and sing 'Fixing to Die.' " Apparently he did, and it became part of the movie, and part of the record, and the money started rolling in.

Had you formalized your arrangement by then?

I'm not even sure. I guess we did have a piece of paper. I think Joe wanted to renig on it, but Ed Denson said, "I overheard that.

You told Chris. That's a verbal agreement, and that's binding." So Joe agreed to that [laughs]. That's how I bought this building. I remember the money literally started rolling in. I couldn't believe it. I think we each made close to $50,000 on it. I put my down payment on this building, $15,000 or $20,000. It only cost me $55,000 for the whole thing. It was weird because it was not just the record, but the movie, then records overseas. It just came in from all directions. From BMI, from everywhere. It was weird. It was kind of nice to suddenly have some money.

Joe would have said it's karma [laughter].

Well, he also said, "What the fuck did Strachwitz ever do for me?" [Laughter.] Actually, a couple of years ago I gave it back to him. I don't have that copyright anymore. Unfortunately, it's been his only really big selling song. The next time I made some money on a song was that song on The Stones' *Sticky Fingers,* "You Got to Move."

When did you first record the song with Fred McDowell?

It's on that second record I did with him. But I wasn't the first. You know Pete Welding had recorded it before. But Pete was so nice he didn't say nothing. I told him I made the copyright for Fred. Let me just tell you that with Joe McDonald the first money I took was to copyright all of the friggin' songs I had recorded. It costs money. You've got to have somebody write the lead sheet for each of the songs. So somebody has to listen to the tape, write down the notes, transcribe it on the paper. That's going to cost you about five or ten or fifteen bucks per song just to do that. Then you got to send it to the Library of Congress and have the copyright registered. That costs you another ten dollars or so. That's a whole bunch of money when you're dealing with a whole bunch of songs.

And if nobody bothers to copyright a song . . .

. . . Then you can easily lose them. I was lucky that a lot of these people say we know you and we know we should pay this so we better. But, see, if some cold, cruel business guys would have been at the other end they'd say, "Fuck you, guys, you didn't register. This is a public domain now and we ain't going to pay nobody." I think they could have easily done that with "You Got to Move." But The Rolling Stones—Mick Jagger was really neat. On the first record that came out they told Atlantic to put Fred McDowell's name on the record. They didn't know who the publisher was or nothing. They said, "We learned this from Fred McDowell, put his name on there."

They just did this on their own?

Yeah. So all hell breaks loose. I start collecting money for it. All of a sudden I got a call from Manny Greenhill, a long-time friend of mine. He said, "Chris, what are you doing!? You're stealing my song!" I said, "What are you talking about, Manny?" He said, " 'You Got to Move'—you know that's Reverend Gary Davis' song!" I said, "What are you talking about? It's not Fred Mc-Dowell's? As far as I know and you know it's a p.d. [public domain] song. But The Stones say it's Fred's song, so it's Fred's song." Well, he said, "That ain't right." So I wrote to Fred McDowell, saying, "Fred, where did you learn this song?" He said, "Man, I learned it out of a churchbook, a hymn book." Oh God! I said, "Do you have a copy of the hymn book?" He said, "Yeah, I got it right here." He sent it to me. I was hoping it would have a date on it. If it had a date at least that would establish it and he would be the arranger of a public domain song.

If the date was early enough.

Yeah. I think almost anything that has been published. I don't know. Anyhow, the book came and there was no date in it. I wanted to prove to Manny Greenhill that it wasn't Reverend Gary Davis' song, that it was a public domain thing, and that they're just the respective arrangers of it. My lawyers finally told me, "You can make a deal with Manny." I finally got together with Manny Greenhill, a sensible man. Instead of fighting each other for the few dollars that were in this, I said, "Let's get together on this and make both of these guys the composers of this song. This is purely Fred McDowell's arrangement, the way The Stones do it with that slide guitar." Reverend Gary Davis does not play slide guitar, he picks it. It's basically the same song, though. I suggested if somebody records it the way Fred does it, let's have Fred get three-quarters of the money, and if somebody records Gary Davis' version, then he should get the bulk of it. He said okay.

Didn't you have problems with Alan Klein [the Rolling Stones' manager at the time], too?

Oh yeah, he's the one who caused us to have a lawsuit over it. He had his name in there right from the beginning, and the British society had already collected [royalties] in his behalf. We had a hell of a time getting it back from him.

So you sued Klein and won?

Yeah, we did. It wasn't that difficult, but it was difficult to collect the money back from the guy. It was Jagger's niceness to put Fred's name on that record that saved us. Just before Fred McDowell died I went to Mississippi and I had a check for over $7,000, and that was the most money he ever saw in his life. There's more money in copyrights than in selling records, but I enjoy packing records more than I do filling out copyright forms.

Why do you think there is so much great American music that the majors won't release here, but will license to foreign companies like Charly and Ace?

The biggies here don't even consider anything that sells less than fifty thousand a record. They just don't even want to fool with it. At least they are willing to license now. This is a new thing in the last fifteen years or so. Before that, if you wrote to them [about licensing their material] you wouldn't even get an answer. They would just sit on these things, like hens on their eggs. In the last fifteen years, apparently to protect their ownership—I think that's one of the reasons—they are willing to license them. That reinforces their ownership of them. Whether they are the actual legal owners or not is a whole other ballgame. You take the stuff that comes from the old Paramount label. Fantasy claims they bought the Riverside label, who claims that they bought the Paramount stuff. Also, Jack Buck says, "I bought the Paramount stuff." Even if two people gave money for it, how are you ever going to prove it? There were no masters. They were all dubbed off of 78s. Especially when you're dealing with some small label that was owned by maybe some disc jockey or some jukebox operator that was sold to somebody else down the line who was bought out by somebody else. . . . How can you ever tell who was the actual owner?

How about royalties?

I should say something about this business of royalties. It's not an old concept. I think the practice of it is fairly recent, since the sixties or a little bit earlier. In the union contract, to the best of my knowledge, there is no mention of a royalty paid to the leader or the sidemen. You pay session money, and that's it. There are several companies I know—Delmark is always willing to say so: "I go by what the union says. I pay union scale. I pay no royalties." Okay. So there is apparently no [royalty] requirement if you are a union musician. Of course, I am not a union label, 'cause almost none of the musicians I record belong to the union. I feel morally there's an obligation if something is a big seller; I think that people who created the material should share it. So I feel morally there is an obligation to furnish artists with statements saying how much they sold. How much to pay? When I started I took my example from Prestige, for whom I did some sessions. They sent me a contract, and they were paying twenty cents an LP at that time, and I think that's what I used at that time. Most of the people I now pay roughly fifty cents royalty per record. There's usually some advance I pay them. I think people ought to be paid for their time. Although not all of them really demand it, but I always do. On one Clifton record, actually his best-seller, he said, "Chris, I don't want no royalties. Just pay me my five thousand flat." And I did. That's one he's losing on because it turned out to be his best-seller. But maybe I'll just pay him royalties on it anyway, since I've covered my five thousand advance.

Let's change the subject a little and talk about your personal tastes. At first it seemed to be mostly blues and country and jazz, but now you seem to be getting more into regional and ethnic music.

I had a liking for most of it right from the start. I heard Mexican accordion music when I was in high school over a station near Santa Barbara. There were some kids in school who called me the Crazy Mexican or something. I loved the sound of the language. Spanish is still music to my ears, even though I don't understand much. The radio has been the real educator for me. When I was going to Pomona College I heard a radio station in Los Angeles that had this weird-sounding German. I speak German, you see. But I couldn't quite understand all of it. I finally asked a friend of mine what this was. "Oh," he says, "that's Yiddish!" [Laughter.] But I didn't like the music they played on that show. It was all these squeaky clarinets and sort of hokey stuff. Jeff Alexson, the guy who runs Kaleidoscope Records, came over a couple of years ago saying, "Oh, Chris, you gotta hear this little band at the Freight and Salvage [club in Berkeley]. They're just great." I went down there. Here was this band of two fiddlers, a flute, an accordion, and a bass, and they were playing this neat Central European stuff. It was the Klezmorim in their first incarnation. I thought that was a neat sound. To tell you the truth what also really got me turned on was I saw they were mostly Jewish young people playing their own music and I felt this was neat. Because all along I had met people of Jewish extraction who always wanted to play blues or old-time string band music. I myself can identify with them, because I don't want to play German music. I think it's corny and schmaltzy and full of shit. But I thought, here are some Jewish kids who really want to play their own stuff. And the music was so wonderful. I just fell in love with it. I said, "Let's go make a record."

What about Polish music?

It's sort of a similar thing. First of all where I came from—it was Germany at the time, but it's now Poland. I always liked Poles. During the war when I was a youngster we had Polish workers. There were forced laborers in our village. The Nazis would round up whole blocks in Warsaw and bring them in to work the fields. Those were the only people I really associated with. They were our stable hands, and the only guys our own age we spent any time with as children. We both sort of spoke a pidgin German. They were just really nice people. Down-home people. They really reminded me of Southerners or Mexicanos. Dick Spotswood, who did that series for the Library of Congress of old reissues of American vernacular music, played me records of Polish and Ukrainian music. Especially the extraordinary Ukrainian fiddler Pawlo Humeniuk. It was a wonderful country sound with just a bowed bass behind him. The Polish stuff was very much like it. So I put that stuff out. I always did like polka bands. That was a very popular kind of music back in the fifties. Down in Texas they have what they call Bohemian bands. They're Czech. They settled there in the last century and still play a fiery brand of European brass band music that has a definite Southwestern swing to it.

Do you have a feeling that any of this could possibly be commercial music?

I think Los Lobos are certainly showing that norteno music can be commercial if you mix it with rock and roll. When Les Blank made that film on polka music called *In Heaven There Is No Beer,* one of the disc jockeys in that movie says, "I don't know if [popular acceptance]'d be all that good. We would probably all sound like Lawrence Welk." That's true. When you take an ethnic music and try to make it popular for everybody, you're going to grind out all the good stuff usually. What's left over is usually the mush. There's a lot of regional and ethnic music today. But I haven't even touched a lot of it because I know I can't sell it. Like the Bohemian music from Texas, for example. There's a whole Indian music thing. The Yaquis, and the Papago Indians of Arizona—they play a sort of brand of norteno music, but they don't sing, they just play instrumentals with saxophone and accordion together with drums and bass. That's their dance music. That's just going strong as ever. It's all over the place. I remember in the sixties I talked to one of those Czech polka leaders, Joe Patek, at a dance in Houston. He said, "At the moment it seems to be going down because the youngsters all want Beatle music." But I think it's all come back. The same thing with the Mexican stuff. There you have guys tell you, "The youngsters go to school with the Anglos and in school they all want the

Anglo music. But once they graduate and come back into our
society they come to our dances again." Things are changing, but
there is still very strong regional music. It's a social thing, a social
music, all of these forms.

What's been the greatest satisfaction for you?

I enjoy recording this music. The reason I do it is I get such a
pleasure from doing it, that there must be others out there that will
share that joy. I think they do. Like [norteno star] Flaco Jimenez
has just been in Europe. It gives them great joy and pleasure to
meet a new audience. Mance Lipscomb and Fred McDowell had
pretty harsh lives, but they really enjoyed their last years. They
enjoyed meeting this totally new world that's out there. I enjoyed
going on those blues shows to Germany because it was such an
amazing thing to see the reaction of the Europeans all applauding,
and these guys had never been anywhere but the beer joints, where
people threw bottles at them or some woman screamed at them. All
of a sudden they were celebrated musicians! There's so much good
music in this world I just like to put some of it out there so people
can hear it. I always feel that the big music industry pushes the stuff
that they have their interest in, and I figure somebody's got to be
there fighting against it, and putting some of the real shit out there
instead of all that overdubbed and produced crap.

(December, 1985)

Phil Ramone: smoking-hot producer. So many dollars are inside the production of a record, if it's a flop, it's a real loss. And that situation creates madness from both the artist's and the company's point of view. (Photo by Joe Gaffney, courtesy Phil Ramone)

Chris Strachwitz preparing a mail order. I had always thought that records were literally made in some huge factory where artists walked in one end like mice in a cheese plant, and out come the records on the other end. (Courtesy Chris Strachwitz)

At Down Home Music, 1982. I never really looked at it as a business. I only recorded something because I liked it. If I even *thought* it had a commercial potential, I'd probably reject it. (Photo by Jim Larager, courtesy Chris Strachwitz)

Toots and Chris Blackwell. I felt reggae was the white liberal market. I always hoped that it would sell to black America, but it never did. (Courtesy Island Records)

With Ahmet Ertegun. I think the key is as an independent company you should be narrow, honestly, in what you're doing. . . . If an independent company has one person's taste, if that taste is reasonably commercial you'll stay in business. (Courtesy Island Records)

With Grace Jones at Compass Point Studios. As an act gets stronger and more powerful, the less control you have. So if you want control you should pay the penalty if you're wrong, and also be able to get the reward if you're right. (Courtesy Island Records)

Chic (left to right): Bernard Edwards, Alfa Anderson, Nile Rodgers, Luci Martin, and Tony Thompson. Disco music employed much more sophisticated chord changes than any other type of pop music I had ever played before. (Courtesy Atlantic Records)

With Tom Waits and Island A&R administrator Holly Ferguson. When I started making records it was in mono, so you made the decision right there, whether it was a good take or not. I still adopt that kind of approach. (Courtesy Island Records)

Nile Rodgers. I make records. I'm not really capturing what I consider in my head great live performances. I'm making a contrived thing for a specific type of artistic statement—a record. (Photo by Berry Berenson, courtesy Warner Bros. Records)

Chris Blackwell

C hris Blackwell is a fascinating figure in the history of the music business. He is both the most modern of men in terms of taste and technology, and one of the last of the old-fashioned record industry entrepreneurs. His career began in Jamaica where, as the sole importer of American rhythm and blues records, he provided an invaluable link between the sidewalks of New York and the streets of Trenchtown. He began producing and importing Jamaican ska music to England, where he built up his fledgling record company, Island. After hitting it big with Millie Small's "My Boy Lollipop" he began signing seminal British rock bands, especially The Spencer Davis Group, which featured fifteen-year-old Stevie Winwood. When Winwood formed Traffic, he signed with Island. Soon, many of the best British bands of the late sixties joined the Island roster, including Jethro Tull, King Crimson, and Emerson, Lake and Palmer. He also inherited the finest of Britain's folk movement, such as Fairport Convention and John Martyn. In 1970 he helped underwrite the excellent reggae film *The Harder They Come,* starring his artist, Jimmy Cliff. Then came his most important artistic find, Robert Nesta Marley. He became close to Bob Marley and other reggae artists, and almost singlehandedly broke reggae music as an international sensation. Moving his home from Jamaica to Nassau in the Bahamas, he set up the lavish and popular Compass Point Studios. In the mid-seventies he signed Roxy Music, then a host of top New Wave artists such as The B-52's, Grace Jones, Robert Palmer, Malcolm McLaren, and U-2. He also tried to do for African music—namely Nigerian phenomenon King Sunny Ade—what he did for reggae. Now he's moving actively into film, and he hopes to break the latest new black sound, go-go music from Washington, D.C., through a film he has produced called *Good to Go*. This is his first retrospective interview.

How did you meet Miles Davis in New York in '59?

I was very friendly with a songwriter named Sid Shaw. He was very friendly with Miles. I hung out with him all the time at all the jazz clubs, most of which are not around anymore. I can't say I hung out with Miles a lot; the person I hung out with was Sid. I would spend time with Miles, maybe five or six occasions over the course of a year. But they were so burned into my head that I felt I'd spent a year with him.

Were you in the music business then?

No. I was teaching waterskiing in Jamaica. I wasn't really doing anything much—just hanging out. But I was a very, very keen jazz fan. My jazz interest started at school with boogie-woogie piano-type records: Pine Top Smith, then Jelly Roll Morton records, then all the way up through traditional jazz, to the contemporary traditional jazz that was being played at the time. I compressed it into about five or six years as my tastes evolved through these different styles of jazz until I was in New York, when Miles had his unbelievable band with John Coltrane.

At the time that was the music on the cutting edge. Your tastes have always seemed to be on the edge.

I was never interested in pop music. I never bought any pop records. The first sort of close-to pop records I bought were R&B records. Even Chuck Berry records were not my thing. I'd like the odd Little Richard record, but I was never a huge fan of Elvis Presley. The music I always liked was jazz. By definition, almost, jazz is on the cutting edge of music, because that's what jazz has always been—breaking new ground.

Let's talk about how you got started in the record business.

Before I started making records I used to import records into Jamaica. The first record I made was with this jazz band that played in Jamaica at the Half Moon Hotel. It was led by a jazz pianist, Lance Haywood, who came from Bermuda. He plays in New York now. I liked what he was playing, and I figured that at worst we could make the records and sell them at the hotel. I made the record, took the tapes to New York, and got them mastered. I got some artwork designed and the covers made. Then I took the masters to Jamaica, and had the covers printed in Jamaica. I went to the pressing plant and watched them press the record. I picked them up and took them around to the shops. They didn't buy any —hardly any. We also sold some in the hotel. But I just liked the whole process of seeing something all the way through. I made another record with the same artist, adding the brilliant Jamaican guitarist, Ernest Ranglin, and it didn't do well either. But I'd got the bug. It was after that that I found myself in the record business. I'd go to the pressing plant, and I'd press up my 250 albums, and I'd see the press next door was a singles press. I became very aware that there were lots of singles being pressed, lots more than the albums. I saw another sort of excitement—the excitement that happens when you have a hit record. It was a whole different thing than just the whole process of actually making a record. Then I started to hang around all the Sound Systems.

You should explain what the Sound Systems in Jamaica were. They were basically traveling disc jockey parties, right?

Yes. They were like traveling discos. The Sound Systems were owned by the various liquor distributors. What would happen is this: There would be these various Sound Systems run by guys called King Edwards, Duke Reid, Sir Coxsone Dodd, Prince Buster—all these characters in Jamaica. They were liquor distributors as well. So suppose somebody wanted to have a dance. They would book these guys, and they'd come and play, the people would charge the admission, and these guys would then also supply the liquor. There became a great competition over who would book which Sound System, and which Sound System would draw the most people. There'd be Sound System wars to see who could get everybody to leave the other's party. These guys would play music through huge boxes of speakers. It was before stereo, but they'd have three or four speakers. It had a very bright treble. You'd hear them five or ten miles away. They still have Sound Systems in Brooklyn. I was sort of the singular white character hanging out at these. It was a whole sort of netherworld. Middle-class black Jamaicans didn't go there, white people certainly didn't, it was just a Jamaican street thing.

Was this a Rasta [Rastafarian] thing yet? Or hadn't that come along yet?

Not really. Rasta was there, but Rasta hadn't really evolved as much as it did in the seventies. But at this time whoever had the best amps and speakers, and of course the best records, would draw people. So what I used to do was come up to New York and buy 78s for sixty cents or something, scratch off the label, take them down to Jamaica, and sell them for fifty dollars. Because if this [Sound System] guy had a hot record and that guy didn't . . . it became worth that kind of money. I'd scratch the title off because if they could see the title they could also buy them for sixty cents. So that's how I first started in the record business. Then, after a bit, the Sound System guys and myself, at around the same time, said maybe we should make some records ourselves. You'd make the record and just release a certain amount on a blank label—a blank label had value as if it were scratched off. Obviously, since it was a record made in Jamaica, people would know how to get it, but by making it blank you could charge, let's say, twenty dollars for the first hundred or so. Then you'd hold back the release and that was called "pre-release." Then after a bit you'd release some more, let's say a thousand, at a quarter of that price. Then you'd release it to the general public after that. Also, around this same time Sound Systems in England and New York started for Jamaicans who had emigrated. So these records would be imported or people would come down and buy a whole pack of the new key release records. I was one of the first people in Jamaica to make records for this market. Before that, records made in Jamaica were calypso records, or records made for tourists.

So was it the records for the Sound Systems that you saw when you were at the pressing plant making your Lance Haywood records?

Yeah. That's where I met these Sound System guys. They'd wonder what this white guy was doing in a pressing plant. I got to hang out with them, and they'd say, "Why don't you come along to the Sound System." I discovered the whole netherworld music scene in Jamaica from people I met in a pressing plant.

So the next three records I made each went to Number One in Jamaica. I thought, "My God, this is unbelievable. This is easy." Then I started to try to make the records better, more polished, more carefully done.

Did you just learn your studio technique as you went along?

Oh, yes. But what happened was as I tried to make them better and more refined, I started to lose the feel for the market, and my records were now not selling in Jamaica. They were ballad records with people like Jackie Edwards. People would say, "Boy, they're great," but in general they weren't selling. Now and again we'd have one which would sell a good amount. What happened was that in England the import market for them began to pick up until someone contacted me and wanted the rights to press them. So I found that I was, in fact, selling more records in England than I was in Jamaica. Second, the competition in Jamaica had gotten very stiff because lots of people were now making records there. Ska. They were basically ska records at that time. So on one trip I made to England I thought maybe what I should do is start a company there. Now I went to all my competitors in Jamaica and said, "Listen, I'm going to start in England." I made deals with all of them, with the exception of Prince Buster, to release their records in England. Buster and I never really got on too good. Also, he worked with the guy who owned the main record company in England for Jamaican music at the time—his name was Emile Shallit, and he owned a company named Melodisc, which released the ska records under a label called Bluebeat. People used to call it bluebeat music. When I started in England I had to get over this fact that I was like a vacuum cleaner company trying to go against Hoover. The generic name for the music was another person's label. So we really pushed the name ska music, which is what it was called in Jamaica. We really had to get that across.

But there was no difference between bluebeat and ska.

It was the same thing. The difference was that the artists on the Bluebeat label never went on my label. When I pressed my first record in England, I took it around to the shops. I developed a kind of system of distribution which was essentially me. But it was a very efficient system.

What kind of quantities are we talking about here?

I pressed five hundred of the first record in England. It was called "Darling Patricia," backed with "Twist Baby" by Owen Grey. I sold out the first day. I pressed some more. I developed a system of going around to each of the shops in London twice in a week. I carried my stock in my car, a little Mini Cooper. This was great service for the shops. Here I was with the new releases, then while I was there I'd say, "Well, how about this one, do you have enough?" I'd make it my duty to be sure that I sold at least what the last order was. I'd be able to do that all the time. I developed a very good relationship with the shops, and I'd guide them as to what records to buy. If I guided them wrong, I'd take the records back and exchange them. There was no actual exchange thing, I just worked it out so they never bought a record from me they couldn't sell. They loved my service. They couldn't lose. This was essentially what I did from May 1962 until the end of '63.

Then you really hit it big.

At the end of 1963 I brought over Millie Small from Jamaica, who had sung on some of these Jamaican records. She sang on one of the first records we released, called "We'll Meet." It was a boy and girl song. The boy sang the first verse and she sang the second verse. Whenever she came in and sang everybody used to go into fits of laughter because she has this pipsqueak voice. But everybody loved it. So I thought, "I should really bring her over and see what I can do with her in England." Now, before I scratched the labels off the 78s I sold, I used to tape them so I'd have a taped record in case I couldn't get a record again. I had a 7½ IPS reel of these tunes . . . one of them was a song called "My Boy Lollipop." So Millie was over in England and I just happened to be playing this tape of these old records, and I said, "Boy, that's a tune we should record with her." We recorded it and it came out in early '64.

This was really at the height of the girl groups in the United States. Did the popularity of these unthreatening girls make you think that maybe this was a way for a black act to cross over?

Not really. What I thought was Millie's voice just had such a charm to it that you just had to smile when you heard it. Then when I met her she had such an engaging personality that I thought we really had a shot with her. In fact when that record went out the press really went crazy for Millie. She was a dream for English people. She was an unthreatening little black girl, and they loved her. Her record is what put me in the pop music business. I never even knew what the pop business was.

That record was a smash. Didn't it sell six million copies?

Yes. But I didn't put it on my label in England because I didn't think I could handle a hit. I licensed it to Philips, who released it on a label called Fontana. Then, essentially, I left the whole Jamaican business for a bit. I got drawn into the pop business. See, I managed Millie as well. In fact, I was doing pretty much everything for her. In this period I was concentrating specifically on how to promote her. As it became more successful I just became more busy and more into that side of things.

You've said you were never really interested in pop music, and all of a sudden you were this pop mogul. Didn't that strike you as odd?

Well it doesn't happen like that. I was just a guy who produced one pop hit. My main thing was still Island Records, but I got drawn into this because it was widening one's horizon. It was still essentially the same thing. It was still Jamaican music I was promoting, but instead of promoting it on the Island label it was now becoming a worldwide phenomenon with this particular record. We toured the world, basically.

Do you think people recognized it as Jamaican? I remember when it came out; to me, it was just another neat little pop song.

It was recognized as being Jamaican in England because it was a ska rhythm, although a very polished ska rhythm. I think in America there was no knowledge of the Jamaican music scene at all. Whatever existed would have been very underground in Brooklyn. Here in America that record would have been, as you said, like Little Eva or some other pop record.

As you were touring with Millie in Birmingham, England, you first heard The Spencer Davis Group, no?

That's right. I went up to this club with Millie, she was doing a television show in Birmingham. Somebody told me there were these two bands in Birmingham I should really see. I don't know why this person rang me up, but he did. He was keen on one band and he took me to see them first. They were called Carl Wayne and the Vikings. That band became The Move. I didn't really like them. They were dressed in suits, and they were very polished. You know, it was that same era as the early Beatles. They were the band that

was very smart and dressed in suits like The Swinging Blue Jeans
or The Hollies. It was good, but it was pop, and I don't really feel
straight pop music. Then I went to this other club, and this guy
said, "Well, this group draws a lot of people, but they're kind of
rough and ready." It was The Spencer Davis Group, with fifteen-
year-old Stevie Winwood.

Was he singing when you saw the group?

When I walked in he wasn't singing. Spencer Davis was singing,
but it was great. The tune was great, and I really loved that. Then
Steve sang and I couldn't believe it. It was like Ray Charles on
helium [laughter]. Unbelievable.

Did you approach them right away?

Right away. Are you kidding? Absolutely. Right then and there.
I said I wanted to sign them and make a record with them. These
were the days when bands used to go out and play, develop fans,
then try and get a record contract. Nowadays people get a record
contract, buy the instruments, make the record, and then have
videos force-fed to the media. These were real people. I was really
able to sign them because I was able to promise them that I would
be able to get a record out within a month. They were amazed. I
produced the first record of theirs and took it to Philips. It was a
great tune called "Dimples." A John Lee Hooker song. I was really
excited about it. I don't know if you've heard the tune by The
Spencer Davis Group, but I'm very proud of it. If you hear it right
now it sounds great, like it could have been cut yesterday. I really
thought it could be a hit. Then John Lee Hooker decided to tour
England. He essentially took all the shine off it. We had no hope
for our version of the record.

*That is probably the one and only instance in the entire history of
the record business where the black originator came along and
knocked off the white cover version of his song!*

Absolutely. And it wasn't even as if he had a hit with it. This was
1965.

Were there other rock bands you were signing at this time, in '64 or '65?

I tell you who I signed in '64—John Martyn. He has a new record coming out, twenty-two years later, which is his best. I signed a band who was so great, a band that slipped through the cracks— they were called The V.I.P.s. They played the Star Club in Hamburg. That's where I first saw them, on tour with The Spencer Davis Group. They were un-be-liev-able. Energy. Drive. Raw. They were the most exciting band. They broke up, then became a band called Art, then Spooky Tooth. Mike Harrison was their leader. But Spooky Tooth was never as good as The V.I.P.s. The V.I.P.s. were impossible to handle and control. I think now, today, having much more experience in putting these things together, what was needed was really to find the right producer and manager for them. What was needed was somebody to spend twenty-four hours a day with this band and drag out what they had in them. At the time I was running a record company and managing Millie, and I was just overstretched.

What did Philips, which you licensed your records to, then do for you?

They got them on the radio, distributed nationally, and collected. I would never have been able to collect the money for Millie's hit.

What does an independent record company look for from a distribution deal with a major company?

It depends. If you're doing just a straightforward distribution deal, what you want out of them is to be able to give you the records when you need to get them pressed. Also, they can get records into a marketplace when you have some activity in that marketplace in the form of either a band touring or promotion on the radio. The problem is always in motivating a large distribution company. It's very hard in the early stages to get them interested in sending two hundred pieces of something somewhere, because they're geared up for moving hundreds of thousands. You've got to take the time to get the records into those markets in the early stages yourself. If you shout and scream and go crazy, it doesn't really help you because it means that you're not being sensitive to the facts of how the business is run from their point of view. They can't be expected initially to get that excited about sending two hundred records somewhere. That's exciting for me, it's not that exciting for them. Your job as an independent is to get them interested.

When The Spencer Davis Group broke up in '67 Stevie put together Traffic, which became your first big rock act—a real change of direction for a company that had been primarily associated with Jamaican music.

Right. I was always worried about Island as a name. It was formed in Jamaica, conceived in my head, corny as it may sound, as music from "Islands in the Sun." It started just after that movie, *Island in the Sun.* In my head I was always scared—as all our initial records had been Jamaican records—that we would never be able to get over the perception of being an "island music" record company. I tried another name, Aladdin Records, in England. There had been another Aladdin, but it was long gone. That didn't really work. Finally, what I thought I'd do is change the design. I had a pink label and a very sort of pop-image pink sleeve. We started that with Traffic's *Paper Sun,* which was Island's first go at being a pop record company.

What happened to your Jamaican stuff at this point?

The Jamaican stuff continued on a different Island label. Actually, at this particular time, I drifted away from the Jamaican side. Now I was really full-time occupied with the pop mainstream business. During that time there was a merger done with another record company, Trojan Records. Trojan dealt with all the Jamaican stuff, and Island would have very, very few Jamaican releases in that period—from about '66 to '69. I got back into Jamaican music with Jimmy Cliff, *Wonderful World, Beautiful People* in '69.

Was it just automatically assumed that Stevie would stay with Island after the breakup of The Spencer Davis Group?

No. I was also managing Stevie. EMI came up with a really good offer to sign him. I presented him with the offer from EMI, and also said that I felt we could now do it ourselves, because we had this kind of P&D [Pressing and Distribution] type basis with Philips. We'd evolved from a licensing deal to a P&D deal. So I felt we could now handle it. Steve said he would come on Island.

What was he like as a teenager?

He was pretty wild as a teenager. He was like he is now. When I say wild I mean full of life, full of zest for living.

Was he sharp in business dealings?

He was never really involved in business dealings because his brother Muff looked after all his business. He's now one of the main directors of CBS records in England. As soon as The Spencer Davis Group broke up, Muff came to Island to run promotion. It was also because of that connection that Steve decided to stay. So we were really the first independent in England to go out and have the trust of the groups as a [full scale] record company as well as just a label. Andrew Oldham's Immediate label and Chris Stamp and Kit Lambert's Track label also came out approximately the same time, but neither of them had the sort of depth of catalog that we did. They were both just labels. They were in fact very, very good. If those two hadn't sort of disappeared . . . they were real talents in the record business. But Traffic became Island's flagship group, and enabled us to attract other rock talent. Because Steve was the hero of all these guys. He was really adored by all the other musicians.

After Traffic you went on to sign other great English rock bands of the late sixties such as King Crimson, Jethro Tull, and Emerson, Lake and Palmer. Good musicianship seemed to be the link there. Is that what you were after in those years?

Yeah, musicianship and good singing ability were really important to me. I think that's because, as I said earlier, the records I always liked were jazz records.

Let's talk about King Crimson.

King Crimson had a really spectacular use of sound. Their music would really create images. I think they were a real seminal group —a leap forward in rock music. Robert Fripp was really a brilliant musician. What also started to happen in music at this time was more of the well-educated university graduate types were coming in as musicians and band members. So you were starting to have a different sort of input into the music. Robert Fripp really represented that type of new performer.

How did you first hear about the group?

They were just one of the bands that were around that you heard about. They were building a spectacular reputation very quickly. All the different record companies wanted to sign them. Their two managers, David [Entoven] and John Graydon, went to the same school as I did in England. So we sort of got on on that basis. They were both motorcyclists and I was so determined to sign this band that I also bought a motorcycle and nearly killed myself trying to hang out with them on it [laughter]. But I eventually signed the band, and put down the motorcycle from then on.

Jethro Tull?

I would have bands touring—Traffic or Spooky Tooth—and they'd come in the office, and I'd say, "Did you play with any bands or see anyone that was interesting?" Gary Wright, who was one of the singers of Spooky Tooth at the time, said, "Oh yeah, we saw this guy who was really great. He was kind of weird though. He played flute and stood on one leg." That sounded intriguing to me so I checked it out. I found out they were a new band managed by Terry Ellis, who at the time had a partnership with Chris Wright called the Ellis-Wright Agency. So I tracked him down. I made a deal with Terry Ellis. He wanted to start his own label. I told him that was great, I could really show him how to do it and guide him. He wanted to start it right away with Jethro Tull and I said, "No, that doesn't make any sense, Island is really hot now and our name is strong. It will help Jethro Tull to be on Island. What you do is this:

When you have five chart entries—records in the Top 40—on
Jethro Tull or any other acts you bring through on the same deal,
we'll start the Chrysalis label. All the acts will then go on Chrysalis." Needless to say, Terry signed some other acts and worked
them really hard and got five chart entries within a matter of a year.
Then Chrysalis started and it was with us for about ten years. Now
they are one of our main competitors. It kind of outgrew us, and
we made a few mistakes. There came a time when we really couldn't
be of use to them anymore so they left.

Who else was on Chrysalis at that time?

At the beginning it was just Jethro Tull. Then there was Bloodwyn
Pig. Ten Years After, who were managed by Chris Wright, were
on Decca; they only came to Chrysalis later. A group called Clouds,
which never made it. Terry Ellis really liked Clouds. He spent a
fortune on Clouds and they never made it. But Jethro Tull became
a very big band.

Did you ever regret that you didn't keep them for yourself?

Not really. I think it's good for people to grow. If Island grows to
contain their growth, that's great. But if they outgrow us then they
should go on.

How about Emerson, Lake and Palmer?

They came after King Crimson's demise, which was a disaster for
us. There was such great promise with King Crimson. Greg Lake
and Carl Palmer from Atomic Rooster joined Keith Emerson, who
had become a star with a group called The Nice. When E.L.P. first
came on the scene, I remember they had a special show for Ahmet
[Ertegun, head of Atlantic Records, which released the group's
records in North America] and myself at the Lyceum in London.
We watched this show together and it was great. Did you ever see
Emerson, Lake and Palmer? Oh, he used to stab the keyboard with
a knife, then lift it up and throw it against the wall. At the end of
it Ahmet said "Boy, that's the first band I've ever seen play *with*
a piano." [Laughter.] They were great at the beginning.

They were one of the first major bands to use synthesizers. How did you feel about that?

I liked synthesizers from the beginning. I'm very keen on it. I love the new technology in music and everything. The [Pink] Floyd would also have synthesizer sounds. But, it was never used as Emerson, Lake and Palmer used it—in a sort of cathedral rock fashion. Emerson, Lake and Palmer had incredible dynamics. Where I fell out with them—because I fell out with them very badly —was when they started touring with a big orchestra. I felt that the whole brilliance of E.L.P. was all these different textures and colors of sound created just by these three guys on stage. When the audience saw all this sound from three guys they were really impressed. We parted company. They were selling a lot of records, and I just said, "I don't want to deal with you anymore, let's forget it." They were just a huge drag to deal with at the time. We were so rich in talent then that it was easier just to say, "Let's split." Nowadays I perhaps wouldn't feel the same way.

Emerson, Lake and Palmer were presented as one of the first new-generation supergroups.

Yep. Definitely. They really delivered on stage, and were very exciting. It was theater really. I don't think Carl Palmer is a particularly good drummer, personally; he doesn't keep time, which is of the essence. But he looks great—a lot of drums, a lot of flash. Keith Emerson had a lot of flash, and also good musicianship. Greg Lake had good songs, and a great sort of stage persona. They were a great group to watch.

How do you feel about today's heavy metal music?

I'm not a fan of heavy metal music in terms of listening to it. Though I'm a fan of the attitude of it. I think a true spirit of a huge part of rock 'n' roll only exists in heavy metal today—real go for it, flat out, crazed—and it's great that it's there. A lot of this art rock and fashion rock and all this stuff is sickening to me.

How involved were you as a producer with your rock bands in the sixties?

In the late sixties I was involved as a producer with Traffic. No, actually in the late sixties Jimmy Miller was producing Traffic. He produced their really wonderful records: *Mr. Fantasy* and *Traffic.* The one I produced was *Low Spark of High-Heeled Boys.* But producing Steve Winwood is walking in the studio and just being somebody that he can bounce off. That's it, because he's so good. He's such a talent that he just has to play or sing or whatever. I would be involved in what songs would go on the album in terms of would there be X amount of songs. I would work *with* them. I wouldn't say, "This goes, that doesn't go." I would come up with the running order of the album. I'd be working with them to mix it. If Winwood was performing, he'd perform, then come in the studio booth, and we'd discuss it. I was a sounding board. When the other guys were doing their parts, Winwood would be in the booth with me. I'd be the one who actually put into words. . . . I'll tell you the best way to describe how it was producing those groups: They needed somebody to actually say what needed to be said. The group would never really say it because they were the group and I was the record company. See, if one group member was not happy with what another member did, they would never really say it, or they'd spend four hours saying it rather than just saying, "Listen, it's not very good. Do it again."

Right. This was the sixties, and I guess it wasn't cool if you weren't mellow enough to go with the flow [laughter].

Particularly our groups [laughter].

Did you run up some hefty studio time then?

The record that all studios should have up in their reception area, framed, is *Sgt. Pepper's.* That's the record that, quote, took six months to make. So after that, everybody had to spend six months to make a record. Before that, if you were going to make an album, you'd take maybe two or three weeks. Suddenly that was no longer possible. It had to take six months. It got to be so absurd that

Emerson, Lake and Palmer in the mid-seventies spent $2 million making a record in Switzerland. I think the last Foreigner album cost $2 million. It's just out of all proportion. As there are more and more tracks available to record, if you have people who don't really like to make a decision, and they're not prepared to take the responsibility . . . when a group gets big, a producer doesn't want to take responsibility, and none of the members of the band do, and the leader of the band probably wants to keep everything so he can decide later . . . therefore, you'll have fourteen takes of a vocal, and eight takes of this—forty-eight tracks. You spend all this time not making decisions. When I started making records it was in mono, so you made the decision right there, whether it was a good take or not. I still adopt that kind of approach of making a decision right on the spot, and getting it right on the spot. To me the mix shouldn't be something that takes a real long time. Everything should have pretty much been in shape by then.

So you made sure things didn't get out of hand.

They never did get out of hand at that time. If I felt they were going to go out of hand, I changed the structure of the deal so that the royalty rate was increased, but the artist was responsible for the recording costs. For example, Cat Stevens' first album for us cost £4,000, the second one cost £7,000, and the third one cost £5,000. Now those three albums have sold over 20 million worldwide for us. But I foresaw explosions in costs coming. So in the renegotiations we made the royalty rate higher, and he absorbed the costs. In fact, those first three records were his biggest-selling ones. The record after that cost £100,000, the one after that cost £300,000. It just went crazy and the sales fell down. As the act gets stronger and more powerful, the less control you have anyhow. So if you want control you should pay the penalty if you're wrong, and also be able to get the reward if you're right.

Whatever happened to Cat Stevens?

He is now a fully practicing Muslim in London. He teaches in school and spends his entire life in the Muslim community. He's not recording anymore. Well, the last recording he did was a cassette which you could buy if you went into a mosque. It would direct you how to behave in a mosque, and find your way around. He's totally into it. He donates most of his income to schools and charity work in the Muslim community.

That brings up another Island artist, Richard Thompson, who was a sufi for many years. How did you come to sign his sixties group Fairport Convention?

There was this American guy in London called Joe Boyd. He was and is a very, very tasteful person. He was involved in films. He was involved in one of the key clubs of the late sixties where all the new acts would perform—the UFO Club in London. He started a kind of English folk label called Witch Season. On this label, which he had with Polydor, was Fairport Convention, and I think The Incredible String Band. I met him in a studio and we struck up a deal. Then he put all his productions through Island. One of the artists who I initially had, John Martyn, let his contract with Island lapse because the kind of music I was going into wasn't really this kind of music, even though I really liked it. But I didn't really feel I knew it or knew how to make the records. John ended up on Witch Season, then with me again, and is still with me today. John first recorded with me in 1965 or '66. Also Nick Drake came through Witch Season. Nick Drake was at Cambridge and he came to see me and played me stuff. I said, "I love it but I just don't know how to make these records." By chance he ended up on Witch Season. I got very involved in this label and this music. I got to really like it. Then Joe Boyd was offered a job in the Warner Bros. film department. He sold me his company and we inherited all these acts. I'm afraid we weren't really able to continue what he had done. I wasn't that much value to any of those artists I inherited. Like, I don't think I was much help in guiding Sandy Denny, or Fairport, or any of them.

How important is it for a record company to be attuned to a particular type of music? Couldn't you just hire managers and producers who did know that kind of music? I don't understand why that is important.

I think you're right. I don't think it is important. I think in that
period everything would sort of emanate from my tastes. I was the
only A&R guy. Right? An A&R guy is the one who chooses who
should be the producer for these bands. But if you don't really have
the right feel for how they should go you might pick the wrong
producers. Now, I don't think I necessarily picked the wrong producers, because I just stuck with the same ones they already had.
But perhaps if I had a better feel for that music I might have been
able to put them with a producer who could have enhanced what
they had and given them a chance to go to a wider audience. So
I think I failed on those particular acts.

*Is that a problem for Island or any company so closely associated
with the direction and tastes of one man?*

I think it's a problem if you try to sign too many acts, and be too
many things to too many people. I think the key is as an independent company you should be narrow, honestly, in what you're
doing. I don't think you should be wide and have things all over
the place. You can't possibly deal with it. If an independent company has one person's taste, if the taste is reasonably commercial
you'll stay in business. If it's not you'll go out of business—unless
your costs are related to that taste, and to the width of the audience you're going for. To me the great labels are the labels that
have an identity of style: Atlantic, in the early years and in the
sixties and seventies with Led Zeppelin and Cream; obviously
Motown in the sixties, and the album artists, the sort of icons
they built; Blue Note, you knew what you'd get when you saw
Blue Note. Those labels to me are great labels. It's the kind
of label that I always wanted to have. We've wavered at times
backward and forward because one gets lured into one thing or
another. You get lured into signing a few acts in a certain scene
that exists. But in general my philosophy is to try to have a very
few acts that you genuinely like and are in the forefront of your
head all the time, not because you have a huge financial commit-
ment to them, just because they're people that you know well,
and you can represent them in the way they like to be represented.

Couldn't that also be a danger for the artists? I think there are some artists who've been on Island who maybe you got bored with and decided you personally weren't interested in anymore. So because of your singularity of philosophy that was it for them, and they no longer had your support.

That's no more a danger than it is at any other company. The danger that exists in a major company is that the A&R person in charge is an employee, and as such can easily go and work for another company. So the person who sat down with you and said you must come and sign with me, I love your stuff, we'll do this and that, could be working for another company. Or he could get out of favor with his company because he hasn't been successful enough. Therefore, even though he may be championing his bands, he might have lost his credibility within the company, and therefore not be able to get anything done. There's no perfect way.

Did you ever feel that your loyalties were divided in the sixties between your rock groups and the Jamaican music you began with?

The artists from Jamaica I was involved with as artists during this sixties period were Jackie Edwards, Millie Small, and Jimmy Cliff. A little bit Toots [Toots and the Maytals], also. Other than that it was just [distributing their] records. I knew Toots then, but I really wasn't that involved in his career. Nobody really toured other than Jimmy Cliff or Millie. If there was a relationship it would exist between me and [Jamaican producers] like Coxsone Dodd, Duke Reid, or these various characters. When I got involved in the rock side with Traffic and everything I didn't involve myself at all with Jamaican music. I would say over a couple of years I hardly even heard a Jamaican record because I was so involved in the other side.

Did you get bored with the sound?

I didn't get bored with it. It was more a matter of working with artists on the touring side, and management. It was just creatively rewarding to be working with artists in all aspects of their careers.

We did it totally ourselves. Also, rock was the growth side of the company. It was more that *it* took *me* rather than me driving it. If you're successful in something, then people shower you with opportunities.

Let's talk about how you were "driven" back to Jamaican music. How did you become involved with the great film The Harder They Come?

It was partly written by a friend of mine, Perry Henzell. We'd been friends from kids in Jamaica. I'd been involved with him over the idea of doing a Jamaican film, and he always wanted to do it about this famous gangster character that existed in the late forties and early fifties in Jamaica. During the course of a conversation with another friend of ours, Dickie Jobson, a guy who directed another movie called *Countryman,* it was decided to get Jimmy Cliff to play the lead. He was the hottest Jamaican act at that time. He'd just had *Wonderful World, Beautiful People.* Perry particularly liked the look Jimmy had on the album sleeve. I was also one of the major investors in the film.

What was the state of the Jamaican music scene then, in 1970?

The music was selling a lot in England. It was one of its most creative periods. There were lots of producers making records. It was the start of deejay music, all the kinds of music that is in contemporary black music today pretty much started in Jamaica. Dub music. Deejay music. Rapping music. I wasn't really that involved. I was involved a bit with Perry in the selling and market- ing of *The Harder They Come.* Around that same time, in fact, Jimmy Cliff left and signed with EMI. I was very upset at him leaving because with the film I'd now got back into Jamaican music and got excited about it again. I was spending more time in Jamaica. See, if I were to spend a month in Chicago I'd come up with some acts from Chicago. I'd get involved, and see shows, and hear people. I was excited about where we could go with Jimmy Cliff from this film. I'd figured out in my head exactly where one could market and promote him. But we fell out because he felt that I had not done well enough for him at the end of a period. He hadn't earned the money he was guaranteed he would have earned if he'd gone to EMI a couple of years earlier. He felt I'd let him down because I told him, "Don't go to EMI, you'll do much better with me." And he didn't do much better with me in that period. In fact, part of the reason he didn't was because he did the film. If he had stayed, he could have been huge. Really big. I'd have known where to take him from there, and I was going to follow through with exactly the image he had in *The Harder They Come.* Instead he left. His album sleeve after that was a whole different image. Nothing whatsoever from the film, and here was this star created from this film. He should have looked exactly like . . . he should have come out with the T-shirt from the film with the star on it. Remember it?

Anyhow, I was so upset, and I really wanted another act to get into, and then Bob Marley walked in. Somebody told me Bob Marley and the Wailers were coming back from Sweden where they had been stranded. I had released his records in England, but I'd never met him before. Bob came in, and Bob *was* that character that Jimmy Cliff played in the movie. He was a rebel. He was a gangster if need be. But he was a street poet. He, Bunny [Wailer], and Peter Tosh. They all had this fuck you–type attitude, but they were great. They weren't scary, but they had the essence of what any band should have—an attitude. A band should *know.* They should have their fingers on the pulse. They are going to know what the public wants because they *are* the public—much more than anyone in the company. I had always been told you should never deal with these guys [Bob Marley and the Wailers]. This was one of the groups that people didn't want to deal with—just like *Harder They Come*—it was too much trouble. Remember in that film the record company guy would say to the pressing plant guy, "Don't press his record, he's trouble?" That was the reputation The Wailers had. Nobody wanted to work with them. The trouble was that they knew what they wanted, and they didn't want to be treated like gardener boys, which is how the artists in Jamaica were generally treated. So I made a deal with them, and again everybody told me I was crazy. I gave them £4,000, cash, to go and make an album.

Didn't you have to buy out their contract with CBS?

Yeah. They'd gotten to CBS because they were with Johnny Nash, and he had a production deal with CBS. Everybody felt that the £4,000 would go and I'd never have an album. I felt that the only way to work with them was to . . . you know, companies always say, "Trust us, sign here." Sometimes you can get badly burned by it, but sometimes it's good to put the trust out first. I don't say that they necessarily trusted me initially. But I think I had a reputation for being reasonably fair, more fair than most of the other people, let's say. A few months later I went down to Jamaica and they picked me up at the hotel where I was staying. I went to the studio and they played me *Catch a Fire,* the tracks and vocals. I still think it's one of the best records we've ever put out. Because I gave them my trust I knew that every penny of my money was put into that record.

Was it your intention to break reggae music as a big new sound?

No. It was my intention to break Bob Marley initially. You have to start with one particular act to be your flagship. I don't think people would buy a sound in general. I think they will buy an act, and if that act has a different sound they will look for other acts that have that sound in between records of that act. So when Bob was starting to happen, so much of our promotion of Bob was "Bob Marley, *Harder They Come,* reggae music, Jamaica." It made sense then to sign and develop some other Jamaican acts, because if at the same time we were bringing journalists down to Jamaica to see Bob and see and feel the music, then we may as well do an interview with Toots or Third World or Burning Spear or whoever else. Once you have an act and it's working, you get more credibility to break other acts in that scene.

So the negative industry reaction you encountered was specifically against Marley, not reggae in general.

That, and also the fact that I figured that Bob Marley could become as big an artist as Jimi Hendrix. From that first meeting I said I know he can be that big. And one time I said I know he can become as big as Muhammad Ali. I think he would have been. He was somebody who was just growing. The last record he made, which

I basically coproduced with him . . . the album was done and I said,
"Look, I think we need two up-tempo tunes to balance out the
overall feel of the album." He'd never say yes or no. He'd just
acknowledge. I went away to Nassau, and came back three days
later, and he'd recorded two songs: "Could You Be Love" and
"Coming in from the Cold." He probably had had them for ages.
He had so much material in him. He was just becoming bigger and
bigger. And he had no head problems because it had taken ages
for him to get where he was, so he wasn't going crazy or becoming
an egomaniac. Far from it. The tour he did in Europe in 1980, he
was always the first person on the bus in the morning. Unbelievable. Not one scrap of big-star business—except that he was a
disciplinarian. If somebody behaved badly he would get very tough
about it. He was a real person. A real leader in every way.

*You had a distribution deal with Capitol at that point, and I
understand you were not at all happy with the way they promoted
and handled that record.*

I wasn't. But you see, I know a lot more about the record business
—how it works in America—now than I did then. I felt "listen this
record is so great why can't people pay more attention to this
record, and give it all their effort and energy to let people know
about it." But, you know, people have budgets to make, and sales
quotas to meet. People are always going to work the easiest things
to work. They may like it, but basically they've got to get on with
business.

*Did they know what reggae was or have any concept of where the
market for it was?*

No. I felt reggae was the white liberal market. I always hoped that
it would sell to black America, but it never did because the music
was too ethnic-ish. It wasn't smooth enough. Also, it was a foreign
language really. It was Jamaican. The only people who really
related to it were white, liberal, college oriented–type people who
were interested in it because of its sociological aspects as well as
its rhythm. But it was really its sociological side that gave it its
base.

Initially, you didn't intend to produce Marley's records, right?

Right. Initially I intended to work on the mix, which is what I did on all of them except *Survival*. From the beginning I intended to work on the postproduction of the record after the basic tracks had been done. Then I'd come in and get involved and possibly suggest that another vocal be done, or to overdub some instruments. Bob basically did all the tracks, and the vocal arrangements. What he would do is fill up the music completely. He would have horns and backing vocals all the way through. He would produce all the parts and ideas he had, then let me mix it. Then I would send it to him and he would say, "Oh, you left out a good part here," or whatever. Then I'd remix if he wanted me to. On *Catch a Fire*, which is the most rock one, I worked a lot on that on the production side. I put the synthesizer on a couple of tracks, and a rock guitarist called Wayne Perkins on a couple. I felt the first Wailers' record needed to have musicianship in it, rather than just have rhythm and vocals. Reggae never had solos. You see, reggae music up until The Wailers was seen as a kind of novelty music in England. They'd have semi-comedy records. There was never any respect for the music, or its musicianship. I felt that the musicianship was so extraordinary. When I signed the group they were called Bob Marley and the Wailers. But when I put out the first record I called it The Wailers. I've been blamed for changing The Wailers name to Bob Marley and the Wailers. It wasn't like that. Then, when there were problems between Peter [Tosh] and Bunny [Wailer], I put it back as Bob Marley and the Wailers.

Peter accused you of making Bob the star.

That's true. You see, I could never get on with Peter because he would say something and then not do it. Whereas Bob and Bunny would really live up to their word. So once I felt and saw how it could really happen, I realized the problems with Peter and Bunny . . . the fact that Bunny didn't want to tour, and the fact that Peter was erratic . . . I pretty much decided to make it Bob Marley and the Wailers, and then drop The Wailers and really go after Bob Marley. I was fed up with that entity because that entity wasn't going to work. Yet there was some real genius there.

*As I remember the reception of reggae, there seemed to be an
initial surge when* The Harder They Come *came out. Then it
seemed to come back again very strong in the late seventies. Is
that how you remember it?*

Bob really broke strong in England in 1976 or '77. He did a concert
in London that really broke him. It was also big in America. That
was around the time of an album called *Rastaman Vibration*. That
was the highest chart entry he ever had. It got to number eight in
America. It was very important to him to do well. He wanted to be
number one. There was no question about that. He wanted to be
as successful as possible, but on his own terms. He wouldn't run
around and over-promote himself. He very much had a sense of a
long-term career.

*Did his increasing involvement with the Rastafarian movement
cause problems for you?*

No. Not really. There were more problems caused by conflicting
Rastafarian sects which were vying for his involvement. That really
caused a lot of aggravation for him in the last few years of his life.

*Do you think he was ill-advised in the last few years of his life,
particularly involving his medical problems?*

Yes. He was definitely ill-advised. But on the other hand . . . In
1977 he had this accident. He was told he had a [cancerous] lesion
on his toe, and it should be checked every three months. We took
him to a doctor in London first, and they said it should be amputated, and a doctor in Miami said it should be amputated. Then
a doctor came up from Jamaica—Babylon doctors you know—they
said, "You shouldn't cut off your foot."

Because it was against the Rastafarian creed?

Or whatever. I don't know. But the Jamaican doctor recommended
that it was not a good idea for him to have his toe cut off. I guess
one is inclined to take that kind of advice. Really, this whole thing
kind of faded from memory for all of us. I heard something about

it, but I never realized how important it was. But I guess if one had chased him up there and had it X-rayed, and had it checked every three months . . . nobody ever chased him or did anything about it. Everybody kind of forgot it. That was really what happened. And he ignored it.

Did reggae lose a lot of its impetus after he died?

Yes. It's a tiny country, Jamaica. It's got 2 million people. Its music scene lost its leader—the leader who was so far ahead of the rest.

Was anyone as good as Marley?

I think Jimmy Cliff is really talented. But he doesn't have the focus that Bob Marley did, he's not as clear. Jimmy's always been a little confused and not sure of which way to go. Toots is classic. But the thing about Toots is he is so real in what he does that he is not really so easy to market and promote. For example, an old blues singer would sing one sequence of nine bars and another of eleven, and it was all kind of screwed up, but it was just real. It was just how he sang it. Right or wrong, it was just how it was. In the same way Toots, if he was in a groove and the song felt right, that song would go on for twenty-five minutes, and he'd lose the audience, and he would not realize that he was losing the audience because it was feeling really good to him. The problem was that whereas his style is sort of in the style of James Brown, he doesn't have the kind of discipline that James Brown has in his shows. Knowing how to pace the show, how to build the show. Toots is so much of a natural, and that also goes for the recordings. His best recordings are his most raw, natural recordings. The ones I and others made with him, when we've tried to organize it, and structure it, and get a good sound, they don't compare with the early records he made, which were all one-take records. I think it's also the band. Early on he had a band who were all enthusiastic and had great life. He has superhuman energy. He sleeps maybe an hour or two a day. He's unbelievable. He's never been able to find a band which has the same kind of enthusiasm, drive, and energy. The other main problem that Toots had in terms of breaking, is that when Bob broke, synonymous with reggae was dreadlocks and the Rasta culture. Now, Toots is a Rasta, but not in the sect which believes in growing your hair. So his hair is really tight, and his style suddenly became a sort of old-fashioned look. In terms of marketing and getting the kids involved in the fashion aspect that exists in the music business, we weren't able to do it. I wasn't able to, and there hasn't been anybody else as yet. But boy, he is a totally true person, too. A wonderful, wonderful person.

Let's talk about Sly Dunbar and Robbie Shakespeare, and what they do as producers.

I got involved with them quite late because they had worked with Peter Tosh, and Peter and I didn't get on. So they were in a kind of alternative camp. It took a long time before I started working with them. But I'd known them a little bit for ages. They had tremendous ambition. They are like Bob in a sense. They want to be number one. They want to work all the time. They don't loaf around, also like Bob. They love being in the studio. They love touring. They love talking music. They would work nonstop. I don't think they ever take a break. They work in England, America, France, Japan, Jamaica. They bring along whatever they pick up and absorb. That's why their music is constantly advancing.

Whatever happened to your attempts to put them together with James Brown?

It didn't work very well. The idea was Jerry Wexler's son's, Paul. He was kind of working with me as my assistant while I was working with this Compass Point All Star Band. This was a band with Sly and Robbie that I put together for the Grace Jones record, *Warm Leatherette.* That's when I started working with Sly and Robbie. It was such a great band, and such an original sound, that we felt that all we needed was for someone to come in and we could work with their trip and enhance it and really give it something extra. It really didn't work with James Brown because first he wouldn't record any song unless he'd written it—even if someone else was the writer—he's unhappy about not at least having a piece of the song. From Sly and Robbie's point of view they loved the idea of working with James Brown because he is a hero of theirs, but it wasn't something they were going to give up their songs for. The other problem was that Robbie and James Brown didn't hit it off at all. Robbie is a very tough guy. He's a lot like Bob, a sort of street fighter. It just didn't click. We tried some sessions and they were no good. We gave the tapes back to James Brown. I think it came out, I'm not even sure.

While your main interests in the mid-seventies were in reggae, you also signed Roxy Music at this time.

Roxy Music was brought to us by the managers of King Crimson and Emerson, Lake and Palmer. We'd been working well, and had a successful company with them, so it was natural that they'd bring us their next act. When I first heard the Roxy Music tape I must say I wasn't that crazy about it. When I saw the album sleeve I became very crazy about it. I could see the concept of what it was. I became friendly with the band later on. I suppose the one I became most friendly with was Brian Eno. I know Brian Ferry a bit, but I don't know any of the others. I can't say I was involved in their careers at all. This was going to be a major band. They left eventually because they got a fat deal at Polydor. That's one of the problems of being an independent record company—competing against a major at the end of a contract.

When did you sign Robert Palmer?

I went to see a band called the Allen Bown Set. I guess it was about 1970 or '71. Robert was the lead singer. I was really impressed with his talent and presence. I didn't really want the band, but I signed them because I wanted him. Unfortunately, he left the band a couple of weeks after that. He told me he wanted to join another band called Vinegar Joe with a girl singer named Elkie Brooks. I told him I was much more interested in him as a solo act. However, he didn't feel ready to make a record on his own yet. Finally, about 1974 he came to see me and said he was ready to do his own record. He said he really wanted to do a record like [the New Orleans group] The Meters. So we sent him to New Orleans to work with [performer and producer] Allen Toussaint. He cut the first album there with the New Orleans musicians and some of the people from Little Feat. That was *Sneaking Sally Through the Alley.* It was one of the more successful first albums we've ever had. He did six or seven more albums until this current one, *Riptide,* which is his biggest so far.

How would you characterize him?

His records have been varied because he's really almost a musicologist. He collects records from all over the world. All kinds of outlandish records like Bavarian folk songs, Japanese music, African ju ju music. He draws his ideas from that music. Whatever he finds that he's interested in is how he wants to direct his current projects. He's been a real influence on me. He is really more of an A&R man than an artist, and that's been a problem for his career. But he's constantly in search for what's happening that's new, and he wants to go back to the roots of the music, too. He doesn't think in commercial terms, really. He doesn't think in terms of a career artist; he wants to follow his instincts into what he likes. In terms of developing a trademark sound for himself, he's never tried to do that. He changes with each record. That's part of the reason why he's never been as big as people expected him to be. But on the other hand, from his point of view he's been really happy with how everything has developed for him. He doesn't want to play the music business career game.

Let's talk about Compass Point. Why did you set up that studio in Nassau?

Because at the time Jamaica wasn't stable politically. Also the communications in Nassau are a lot better. And that's where my home had become. I thought I could spend time working in a comfortable environment. I like to have a studio anywhere I'm spending time where I can work or go and see who's recording there. I go through phases. Sometimes for a couple of years I'll work in the studio all the time. Other times I don't go near a studio.

Can you describe the setup there?

There are various accommodations. It's right by the sea. There are two studios. Twelve different apartments, one-bedroom apartments. Some three-bedroom houses, one 2-bedroom house, and one 5-bedroom house. People who come out can either stay in any of those accommodations or in a hotel, or rent their own house. What's good about Nassau is when you take a break, you really have a break. There's nothing really happening there. The only thing you can do is lie in the sun. The place has very little personal character as such. If you were to go and make a record in Jamaica you're going to tend to try and make the people in the immediate vicinity react. If you make a record in England, it's the same thing. The good thing about Nassau is it's like painting on a blank canvas. It's totally neutral. You can try any idea there, and you have a better shot. You'd probably reject it in any of the other places. It's got the best equipment: Studer, SSL, all outboard equipment—a top-of-the-line studio.

Under what circumstances is it available to other non-Island artists? I know The Stones have recorded there, and Talking Heads, AC/DC. . . .

Anybody can book there. It's a custom studio. It's not a big money-maker for us. It's at best a break-even. It allows us to experiment, and if you can break even and experiment it's, to me, profitable. Just being in the studio business on its own is not something that really interests me. But to have a studio which we can use for our own recordings, for experimenting and working without the strictures of time for each particular project, is very valuable to have.

Let's talk about some of the artists you signed when you branched out from reggae in the late seventies. Grace Jones, for instance.

I saw her in New York at the Russian Tea Room. Nik Cohn, the writer, was having a drink with her, and I think he invited me to meet her. She'd made a record already, "La Viё en Rose," and I loved it. A classic record. We put that out, then the album that went with it. I didn't like the second album we did that much, and I liked the third one less. It was stuck in a disco queen–type rut. I really felt that Grace was a black New Wave act. So I wanted to put this black New Wave band together. That was the Compass Point All Stars. Reggae was essentially New Wave black music at that time. The only new black music that was happening was reggae. In fact, before we started recording I pinned up the album sleeve because it showed the image we wanted. Jean Paul Goude had taken the photograph of her in a G.I.-type haircut. I blew it up really big, and I said, "We've got to get a record that sounds like that."

Did you urge her into movies? She's a celebrity now from Conan *and* James Bond.

Definitely. That's where her future is, her strength is—as a visual artist.

Let's talk about Marianne Faithful.

A guy called Mark Miller Mundy, who I'd known around the place and was a good friend of Steve Winwood's, came to me with the idea of recording her, and I told him I thought it was completely nuts, and a waste of time. He then brought me a track called "Why Did You Do What You Did?" It was full of bad language and stuff, and I thought it was great. So I said, "Okay, I'll make you a deal for it." I was doubtful how the rest of the album would be. But he delivered the album [*Broken English*] and what can I say? It's fantastic. I think it's one of the five best albums we've ever put out. We worked the record very hard. That was another of the ones like Bob's ten years earlier: I felt, "That must sell immediately, it's so good." But we didn't sell anything much in America. Sixty thousand or so. But I'm going to release it again now. She's in good shape. Fine.

Was she off drugs and rehabilitated when she was working on the record?

I wouldn't go as far as to say that. But Marianne is a survivor. She is one of the stronger people you're likely to meet, in a sense. Certainly she's also very frail, in a sense. There's an undercurrent of incredible strength. We'll hear a lot of Marianne. I think she has a bigger future than the past.

*The B-52's? Were they signed originally by Jerry Wexler at
Warner Bros.?*

No, they were not. I signed the B-52's in New York, and later on
Warner Bros. signed them. One of the reasons they signed them,
I think, was that I signed them. They weren't that sure. Then when
I signed them . . . I signed them for the world, excluding America
and Canada because for some reason I didn't want to take on the
responsibility of America and Canada. I'll tell you why: I didn't
think they'd sell at that time in America and Canada. I didn't really
figure out how I'd market them. So I only picked them up for the
territories I felt sure they'd sell. In fact, I was completely wrong.
They sold in the territories that Warner's had, and not so well
where I was. I produced their first record in Nassau. They are very
serious in the studio. They're very shy and retiring. But they had
a very clear idea of what they wanted. With them the kind of record
I wanted to make was something that sounded like a live group.
I think first records of new groups should not necessarily be incredibly refined. I think they should be more raw in feel. The songs
should be good, and played well, and have an excitement to them.
Even if there's a mistake, if the mistake enhances the excitement
that should definitely be left in there. The main thing is to feel some
excitement coming off the band because then you want to see the
band. When you see the band, if the band is strong, you can start
a career. If you start your first record with a group and it's beautifully, perfectly produced, there hasn't really been a chance for
people to develop a credibility for the actual band itself. They're
buying a record more than the band. I think then a group almost
had to recover from that. Frankie Goes to Hollywood is a classic
example of this. Their first record is sensational. It's so good, but
then there's a serious question as to how good the band is. The
band then has to spend the next period of their time getting credibility as a band.

Did you really dig Frankie Goes to Hollywood?

Yeah. Definitely. I did. A lot. I wish they had been better-advised
and everything. The whole thing happened so quickly. There were
a couple of keys missing. There wasn't strong management at the

beginning. There wasn't somebody who had experience and knew how to deal with this who could advise the band, record company, and producers, and could keep everything on course.

They seemed to be asking for it, coming into America with this gigantic hype. How did that come about?

It wasn't a hype. What can I tell you? The thing is, the record came out and sold a huge amount in England. It was the fifth or sixth best-selling single ever. Then it was followed by the seventh or eighth best-selling single in England. So it wasn't really hype. It was there. The records were sold. They were incredibly exciting records. With that came all the T-shirts, which again came right off the street. They just happened. It was genuine. It wasn't a hype. People just would kill for those T-shirts. Now in America you suddenly have all this attention, in a country that takes a long time to absorb something new like that, which doesn't fit into black radio or AOR radio or whatever—something which has got a sound of its own—and it was very hard. So it was perceived as a kind of hype and they walked right into it.

I saw their debut gig at the Ritz in New York, and my reaction, as well as the reaction of many people, was that they were the revamped Village People.

Yeah. Yeah. I agree. The Village People sold a lot of records. Fifteen million. But there was no conscious attempt to recreate them. That's just how they were. We'll have another record soon, and it'll be great. They're actually very good. The problem is they're recovering from starting so strong. Most bands that start that strong have a very tough time.

Let's talk about one of the best bands to come along in many years, U-2. Were you the original person to sign them?

No. They were sort of brought into the company by Rob Partridge [Island's publicity head] in England. He's got a very, very good ear for whatever is new. He put the person who is in charge of A&R on to them, and he went to Ireland and signed them. He rang me and said he wanted to sign them. I loved the name. I thought it was great. So I said it sounds good to me. We began to negotiate with them. I went to see them in London. I thought they were great. I met them and their manager. They were clearly winners. Again, they were people who were thinking about their careers on a long-term intelligent basis. They don't want everything now. They're in for the long run. They are exceptionally loyal people. They're the most loyal group of people you're ever likely to meet. Just about everyone who has ever worked with them in one capacity or another is still involved some way. If they outgrew what they had to offer, the band would find some other kind of space for them. They've kept everyone, including the first fans.

Whose idea was it to put them together with Brian Eno?

That was their idea. I was violently against it. I went to see them because I felt that this was a time to have a commercial hit record. Brian had never cut such a record, as a producer. He cut some great records but never ones that were . . . multiplatinum. I felt the group was ready to go multiplatinum. I met with them in Ireland to try to talk them out of it. Their approach, and their logic for why they wanted to use him, and all their reasons made sense to me, in the long run. I still didn't walk away feeling that they were going to make a record that was going to sell three million copies. But on the other hand I felt that in the long run it was a wise move. They wanted his intelligence. In the end, I loved the songs, but I was not that crazy about the sound of the record. I like their live performances of all the songs better. I think they've grown considerably as a band since they've made their last record, with all the touring they did. By the end of the touring, I loved every number much more on stage than I did on the record. Four or five of their classic songs are on that record.

Now for something completely different, Malcolm McLaren.

Malcolm is a true . . . I don't really know how to describe Malcolm. Malcolm defies all description. I love his records. I think they're brilliant. The last one we put out [*Madam Butterfly*] . . . how people can't buy that record, it makes me so sad. Brilliant. The first record,

Duck Rock, brilliant. But it's too varied. You see, I like ideas. I like literally all kinds of music. So when a record like *Duck Rock* comes out which has all kinds of music on it, it doesn't bother me at all. I love it. The problem is that most people don't. Most people like a certain type of music. That's why they tune into certain stations. It wasn't news to me that *Duck Rock* didn't sell. I knew it wouldn't sell a lot. His records are like bits of theater.

Many people think he's a great charlatan.

I don't think he is. I am a big fan of his in spite of the fact that the vice versa doesn't exist. He's written very negative things about me in the press. However, I'll put up with all his shit because I think he's extremely talented. His ideas are unbelievable. There's nobody around as talented as he is in terms of their ideas. Ideas are what everything is about. If you're somebody with a lot of ideas as he is, plus the energy, and gift of gab, and drive . . . if you're the manager of a group [McLaren created and managed The Sex Pistols and other bands], you don't go on stage. So at some time you're impotent. You can't do anything. So I can understand Malcolm calling himself an artist, as he does today. Why not? What he really is is a conductor. He puts all these things together and releases them under his name. He talks a bit on the record, and maybe tries to sing. But you're not really buying him as an artist. He's really saying, "What do you think of this as an idea?" I think he's got superb taste and style.

So he's not a con artist?

I think a con artist is someone who says he's going to sell you something, and doesn't deliver the goods. I think he delivers the goods. When he delivered [the single of] "Madam Butterfly" I thought it was incredible. When he said he was going to do an album for it I said, "I don't think it's a very good idea because I don't think you're going to be able to sustain it." But I think every track on that album is fantastic. I think what he did with The Sex Pistols and the whole punk scene in England was something that was so necessary. It was a revolution of pop culture which had gotten fat and gross. The essence of rock 'n' roll should be emanating from the streets, and have a sort of revolutionary-type edge to it. It had become these fat supergroups flying around in Lear Jets, and stuff like that. It was about time something came up. I liked the idea, but I never really liked The Sex Pistols because it just wasn't musical enough at all for me.

How did you feel about the first of the New Wave's interest in ska and reggae?

I welcomed it because it gave the music that I'd been working with for ages a street credibility to a much wider market. Before, I was selling this music to Jamaicans and to liberals, hippies, and college students. Now a whole new market became interested in that. It was great.

Let's talk about the terrific reggae band, Black Uhuru.

They're the best. The story is that they don't talk to each other. It's stupid. Egos. Stupid ridiculous egos. Idiots. They're pure idiots. There's such a gap there right now for a band which is black and hard, and almost a little scary. Tough. You just want something with an edge to it. Black Uhuru was that. I'd see it when I'd go into a restaurant with them. Everyone would kind of clear out because they looked . . . terrifying. Their name was scary. [Uhuru means freedom]. It reminded you of the Mau Mau or something. It was perfect. It's what The Rolling Stones were.

Who's coming along now in reggae?

I haven't heard anything recently. I think reggae is now part of world music. When you hear bands from Australia like Men At Work doing reggae, The Police, Pretenders, everybody. Burning Spear and Toots have now become like John Lee Hooker, Muddy Waters, or Lightnin' Hopkins. The originators. But Bob was so strong that afterwards people were a little lost. They didn't know whether they should try to *be* Bob. Before Bob nobody had any direction to follow, and they would be influenced by various bits of music from the rest of the world, and America particularly. Now the new ones are being influenced by reggae artists. The whole strength of Jamaican music before was the fact that they'd listen to country stations, Miami stations, and so forth. They'd absorb all those things, kinda try to play it. It wouldn't come out right, but it would come out as something great instead. That was ska, and then reggae. Now they're either listening to disco or they're listening to Bob Marley's records. So they don't have anything of their own anymore. Now a song with a reggae rhythm is instantly acceptable in pop music. It's good because that was brought from Jamaica. It's bad because one of Jamaica's main exports is floundering at the moment.

When you brought [Nigerian musician] King Sunny Ade over to America, was that an attempt to do for another Third World music what you had done for reggae?

Yeah. I think his situation is very similar to go-go music. It's back to a whole different aspect of music—music and entertainment for partying and dancing and having a good time. It's not music that's necessarily going to put on a structured show, it'll just start and roll.

How did you find out about King Sunny Ade?

Robert Palmer was very much into African music, and he played me Chief Ebenezer Obey. I liked it very much, so I checked out the various African acts. I felt the one I could most likely work with successfully was King Sunny Ade.

What happened to King Sunny? He came in a big flash and then was gone. And he was great, too.

Management. See, it's very difficult to manage a band who are living in Nigeria and travel twenty-five of them at a time—and get their records played on the radio. It's difficult, right? So you're not going to get somebody who's a great, strong manager to get himself involved in something like that. They're going to work on something a little easier. The guy who was managing them is a jazz promoter in Paris. It was something he really did from the heart, and he loved it. But he didn't have the ability to spread the music.

What about Island? Do you think you guys did enough to push African music and King Sunny?

Well, yes. I think what the problem was is that he came in the first time and he was a sensation. The second time, great. Third time, same thing. But there were things missing in his band, elements he should put into his band that I thought would really make it work. That was, simply, women. He should have three great African women singers—in African clothes because the clothes are fantastic. In a second, one would have been able to break that through a whole black fashion aspect. It would have given the band an additional thrust. Because with music like that or reggae, or any music that isn't on the radio, you have to keep the audience going. Unless that cult grows, and at one point crosses—bam! It fades out. I feel I gave it a fair chance. If he had a manager who was together, I would do it again. If he had the girls. His shows are unbelievable. And I love the records.

How about go-go [the black street music of Washington, D.C.]?

That music is not that far away from African music. Being in Washington, D.C., and seeing this music is like being in Africa. It's huge in Washington.

How did you get into it?

I heard a record on the radio. "I Need Money" by Chuck Brown. It didn't get played much. I must have caught it the one time it got played. Then I went down to D.C., saw the scene, and I felt you've got to see it to really get it. The only way to do that is to make a film. That's what I've been doing since September of '84. It will finally come to its fruition in '86. The film is called *Good To Go.* Go-go music is not big anywhere but in Washington. Black radio does not play it anywhere else. It's too ethnic sounding. Too raw and rough. I believe that people want that music, but they don't get a chance to hear it. I believe they would like it if they could see it. I think with all the drum machine and synthesizer music around, people would like something that is real. Now, with Jamaican music the core audience was very small. It was just Jamaicans.

With African music it was even smaller, it was in a foreign language. But with this, firstly, they're more accessible. Plus, Washington kids are not that much different from other inner city kids.

Let's talk about film. You're getting more and more into it. Your company produced Choose Me, *and more recently released* The Trip to Bountiful *and* The Kiss of the Spider Woman. *What's the attraction of films for you?*

If you're in the entertainment business on the music side, you really need to be in films as well because I think they're really joining into one business. You need to have access to putting your music into other people's films, and expanding the horizons of your artists into scoring, performing, or having their songs in films. I also feel that one needs to be in the film business in order to understand it and have access to people who are good video makers. *Good to Go,* in a sense, is a long-form video—some great music linked by a real story. The two industries are merging. It's a good thing. See, Roberta Flack may not have broken had it not been for her song in *Play Misty for Me.* The radio wasn't playing her records. The film came out a year later, and she started selling then. A song can register so strong in a film that you can break an act from that song.

So how's Island Records doing these days?

It's having a hard time at the moment. It's struggling at the moment because we are in the middle of readjusting ourselves and our focus to the fact that I want Island to be a film and music company. But not with a lot of projects in either field. I think we expanded too fast in terms of acts and personnel. We tried to do too much. In fact, the right way is for us to work in close cooperation with a very strong major company, thereby using the knowledge, clout, financial stability, and help of a major company, while being able to offer the time, direction, and style that Island has in the signing and development of the acts. At the moment we're still reeling through the fact the record business economics has changed violently in the last three years. You never used to have to spend the kind of money you now spend for independent promotion. To get records on the radio costs an awful lot of money. It became more expensive because there are fewer stations that are so important. Therefore, it's more important to get those stations. So it's a supply and demand situation.

What's the expense of doing independent promotion. Are you talking about greasing somebody?

No. Not at all. It's like an agent. He will perform a function because he has contacts in that area. They have relationships in that area. You know what I mean? So you hire independent press people. Also videos are a huge cost now. To really go after a hit single and take it all the way, a company like MCA will spend a half-million dollars on independent promotion and a video for one song. That's one song, not one album. It's worth it if the act is right. If the act is right what you're basically doing is spending a half-million dollars on commercials for that act. But you can't recoup it on one single or one album, unless you're incredibly lucky.

You and Warner Bros. parted company in 1982 over the issue of your One Plus One cassette venture. What was the concept behind that?

The home taping issue is not something that can be solved by asking people not to do it, or "give the gift of music" or that kind of thing. There're people who will want their disposable music to drive in the car. They'll want to make their own tape of things they like. That battle was lost when a record button went on the cassette machines. Once that exists I think one should work along with it. Therefore, my idea was to serve two purposes: One, you get to hear all your music on one side of a tape. A cassette normally breaks it up, but you have the opportunity to put all forty minutes of an album on one side. It's a drag to have to get up and turn it over. My idea was to put it all on one side. On the other side you put the same thing. Because if you like it you don't want to have to rewind, you can just play it again. But on one of the sides, you could record over it. Now what that meant is that when that record sort of became catalog to you, you could use the other side for your own purposes. To me it was the best competition against blank tape. If I could have persuaded everybody to go with it, I felt that people would not have bought blank tapes so much. They would have felt, "I can just get my blank tape free when I get this act." Nobody bought the idea. They said I'd been out in the sun too long [laughter]. I think they're shortsighted. It's even a better idea now. I think compact discs are what's going to save the record business —it has all the music on one side, it's very high quality, it's portable, indestructible. It has a perceived value. People are happy to pay a price for quality. See, the record companies were fighting this by reducing the quality of their album sleeves, their pressings, and eroding the difference between what was a quality product, and what was always a paperback product in my mind—the cassette. Once they eroded the difference, why should somebody be a schmuck and buy a record when they could just tape it off somebody else's? Now with CDs, the packaging is great, the quality is great. Fine. If you want quality, you'll buy that. You're no longer a schmuck to a buy a CD, but you're a bit of a schmuck to buy a vinyl record that'll warp on your way home. The record business reduced the value of the album. If the album even had great packaging for it that would have been great because then you'd've got something for your money.

(February, 1986)

Nile Rodgers

Nile Rodgers may be the hottest producer on the pop music scene today. He could probably claim that title simply on the basis of his production of Madonna's smash-hit LP, *Like a Virgin.* But his credits also include a list of extremely commercial yet hardly mainstream hits such as David Bowie's *Let's Dance,* Mick Jagger's solo-debut album *She's the Boss,* which he coproduced with Bill Laswell, and "The Wild Boys" single for Duran Duran. He has also produced records for Diana Ross, Jeff Beck, The Thompson Twins, Peter Gabriel, Debbie Harry, Johnny Mathis, Inxs, Kim Carnes, and Sister Sledge.

In addition to his impressive record as a producer, Rodgers is one of the most sought-after session guitarists around, and in fact he says he primarily thinks of himself as a jazz guitarist. He can be heard on many of the records he's produced, and on others such as Hall and Oates' *Adult Education* and The Honeydrippers' EP.

Rodgers' greatest success as a musician came when he teamed up with friend and producing partner Bernard Edwards to form the group Chic in 1977. The group's first single, "Dance, Dance, Dance (Yowsah, Yowsah, Yowsah)" went gold.

Chic's second album, which went double platinum, contained the single "Le Freak," one of the biggest hits of the disco era. The third record also went platinum, in 1979. Rodgers' solo album, *B-Movie Matinee*, was released in 1985 by Warner Bros.

How did you end up in the house band at the Apollo Theatre?

I was working for "Sesame Street" and Loretta Long. Her husband was Peter Long, and he was the manager or something at the Apollo.

Yeah, he was the PR guy.

Ah, so now I know what he *really* did. When the Apollo was looking for a guitar player who could read, Loretta said, "Hey, why don't you try Nile out, he seems to be really great with the "Sesame Street" stuff, so check him out." I did the first job and they liked me at the Apollo, so I stuck around. I guess I was around nineteen because everybody was going to the Manhattan School of Music. This was the early seventies, right there at the end, when the whole thing [at the Apollo] was starting to wind down. They started booking other stuff in there. It got weird. . . . I'm sure I did some of the last few gigs there.

What kind of music were you listening to then?

At that time it was jazz, basically. A lot of rock 'n' roll. Blues. The thing is, I had been into rock 'n' roll and blues and stuff earlier, so of course I continued to listen to it. But at that time in the seventies I was more fascinated with jazz. When I was working at the Apollo I had money, so I could buy any record at that point.

That's interesting because we're about the same age, and that's when I started to get into jazz, too. In the early seventies rock 'n' roll seemed to be getting pretty boring.

Yeah, it *was* getting boring. Especially after Hendrix, and because of the politics and stuff. It didn't seem to have that color and that flare it had when Hendrix . . . You know, a lot of people died around the same time, too. And even if you weren't a big Doors fan or a big Joplin fan or whatever, still just the impact of it all happening around the same time seemed like, "Damn, this isn't the right stuff!"

You were at the forefront of the disco movement with your group Chic in the seventies, and with your production of groups like Sister Sledge. I wonder if this turn away from rock to jazz had any direct impact on the way disco developed as a sound.

Disco was always a sort of ambiguous category to me in those days. I thought that disco meant anything you wanted to do as long as the drums went [he mimics a fast drumbeat]. That's what I thought. So what we did in Chic was basically play jazz. My first records, my own stuff, my compositions or the record dates where I was in charge, we basically did updated versions of jazz songs. The first formal arrangement I did was "Bess, You Is My Woman Now." Then we did "Air Mail Special." And we got a lot of really great players together and we went in and did disco records, but we were playing jazz. We were playing all the changes. We just changed the beat and the groove around.

So there was a connection between the jazz you were listening to and the disco you were playing?

Oh, absolutely. We wanted to be known as players, so when we decided to play pop music we thought all we had to do was take really great jazz songs—because we loved the melodies, we loved the heads—and just play those and give them a funky feeling and they'd be happening.

You once said you turned to disco out of necessity. What did you mean by that?

Well, disco was the music that was really happening at the time. We were a bar band, basically, Bernard Edwards, Tony [Thomp-

son], and I. We were just doing the Top 40. We were gigging from
place to place. What the Top 40 consisted of then was rock 'n' roll
tunes from Thin Lizzy and groups like that, but the bulk of the stuff
was disco songs. The Trammps and The Bee Gees. This was when
Saturday Night Fever was happening. Cocomotion, Donna Summer,
Silver Convention, that was the stuff that was really happening.
This was what was on the radio and the Top 40, so consequently
this is what was in our repertoire. From doing gigs, you grew to
like it. I've always liked whatever I've played. I'm not anti any type
of music. I used to play in folk bands when that was happening.
Bluegrass, I still like bluegrass. I started to really enjoy playing pop
music. Then I started to try and write it.

Anyway, so we had a rock 'n' roll band or a jazz fusion kind of
rock band, and we weren't really getting anywhere. Everybody
liked our tapes, but when they saw us, because we were basically
a black band, I guess [they thought] the sound was sort of black
because of our vocal sound. When I listen to the tapes now I say
this is total nonsense, how could they ever know? We didn't sound
like a black band. We weren't singing like Earth, Wind and Fire,
we were singing like The Stones. That's where we were coming
from at that time. But anyway, we couldn't get a record deal until
we did "Dance, Dance, Dance." Now meanwhile, we had been
writing songs all along, but they were all rock 'n' roll songs. Power
chords and the whole bit. As soon as we did "Dance, Dance,
Dance," our first disco song, we got a record deal.

*So that's what you meant by out of necessity—they would not
accept a black band playing rock 'n' roll?*

Absolutely not. They definitely would not, there's no question
about it. And they loved our tapes. They used to keep them at all
the record companies, but when they looked at our pictures or when
they'd meet us, they'd say, "How do you market these guys? Who's
their audience?" We would say, "What do you mean, how do you
market us? You market us to the same people who are buying the
records *we* buy." It just didn't make sense.

*You've said and others have said that the white New Wave groups
now and in the recent past are just doing disco.*

Yeah, it's true. It's funny because it's actually hip now. A lot of the bands that I meet, especially those who came out of the whole New Romantic phase, they love the word disco. They think it's a cool thing. When they're sitting down writing a song they say, "I want something that's a real disco kind of record." They're into it. It's a great thing to them. I can just remember when they had the whole backlash, the Disco Sucks campaign. This is very funny. We went to a party for *Record World* or *Cashbox*, or one of those magazines. It was in a club, a restaurant in the front and a disco in the back. Because at that time disco sucked—it was the funniest thing you could ever imagine—nobody would go to the disco. They were all afraid [laughter]! We were dying. Bernard and I walked in and everybody was packed in like sardines in the front part because they were so terrified to walk into the disco. It was such a bad word. Meanwhile, the number-one record was "Funkytown." It was the funniest thing I'd ever seen in my life. I said, "Damn, these are the people in *my* industry. These are the *hip* people. These are the people who grew up with rock 'n' roll. These are the rebels. Look at them, they're fucking cowards! They're afraid to go into the disco!"

Wouldn't you think this battle had already been fought in the sixties by the Motown people? This stuff about white music and black music.

No, no. It seems like it's always going to be an issue, unfortunately, or at least for a long time. You know, when I did the Bowie record, I must say David is a pretty hip guy to take a chance like that, because everybody around was saying, "Oh, that'll never happen. How can you mix somebody who's great like David Bowie with somebody like Nile who does disco records? And disco sucks, everybody! Right? I mean, it's not happening." When we sat down and talked, he realized I was into a lot more. And I don't mean to say that disco is not happening. Take it from a guy who has played everything. I mean, I used to be in blues bands for years and I know, man, when I was playing in blues bands we were *looking* for new ways to play changes. I loved it when somebody turned me on to a progression. Like, if we had a couple of minor seven chords in there, wow! This is happening! In fact, disco music employed much more sophisticated chord changes than any other type of pop music that I ever played before. To me, I was playing jazz, just with a cool beat, basically. You know, with good hooks.

All that's to say that when I started talking to Bowie, we started talking about other forms of music. We even started talking about opera. He realized, I guess he probably knew it beforehand, but with musicians it's just communication. You want to extract from all different styles. Stevie Ray Vaughan did all the solos on the *Let's Dance* album, and he's a very strong blues stylist. It worked because the different things just mesh. You use somebody's ears to talk to you through their concept. I mean, so what, was Stevie Ray Vaughan playing black music? Is he a white guy playing black music? Yeah, you can argue the roots, but there are a lot of great white guitar players who play blues, and they play fantastic. When I was a kid—and I grew up in basically a serious jazz household—I remember my uncle, who was a great arranger, always used to say to me, "Man, when I was younger I used to think that white cats couldn't play, but half the guys in my band are white guys." That's ridiculous. All the great horn players I use now are white guys, and they're all young, too. So where did they learn? I even feel stupid talking about it, actually. In my lifetime I know that that's so ridiculous. And I know that nobody—or at least I hope nobody—is hiring me because of the fact that I'm black. I know that when I call guys, I've never heard anyone say that.

The weirdest person I've ever had work on a record with me is Anton Fig, because he's from South Africa. He comes in and everybody goes, "Yo, man!" He hears all the South African jokes, poor guy. Everybody goes, "Hey, whoop, I guess this is the first time you ever played with black people, hey Anton?" I guess it's some sort of issue. We seem to be chipping away at the iceberg a little bit now. Now you see these great collaborations. I don't think anyone even thinks about it. I don't think, if somebody calls me up, that they were sitting there talking to their manager saying, "Let's call that black guy Nile to come and produce the record." I don't say, "Hey, let's get that white guy Daryl Hall to come and sing backup."

Was that whole "death to disco" thing racial?

I don't know. Of course, I'm sure that it was some sort of weird, blue-collar movement or something like that, people who were saying, "Where are The Stones?" Because those types of bands really did suffer during that period. I'm a pro now, I know what record sales were doing in that time. A lot of these total unknown people like Silver Convention, who were they? They came out of nowhere and were topping the charts. Donna Summer and stuff, just out of nowhere. Stars were coming. I guess that happens with any new movement. Where did groups like The Thompson Twins come from? Or Duran Duran and Culture Club? Out of nowhere. So what happened is that these new groups were coming and doing a lot better than the established bands. During those days I couldn't even *find* an Elton John record, and he was my favorite. The disco stuff was really happening. Everybody was doing disco, Frank Sinatra, Dolly Parton, everybody.

Was disco music really a producer's medium?

More so than any other type of music?

Yeah.

No, no. The only thing that happened was that for the first time it was a little bit more honest. . . . I guess it was the techno stuff, that's what changed it around. The fact that drum machines were introduced, and sequencers and things like that. So if one person could do all the jobs, he would do it. In the old days it was very rare that you'd find somebody like Stevie Wonder or Steve Winwood. Those people were unique. You wouldn't see albums where one guy played bass, guitar, and the whole bit. But since synthesizers came of age, one person could go play the whole thing. So when disco was popular, one or two people could do the whole thing. I guess that's where that came from.

But also, weren't a lot of these disco groups just manufactured groups that some producer put together in a recording studio?

Oh, well, come on! That's the history of rock 'n' roll! Come on! How many bands have you had where they really couldn't play? They'd

leave the studio and the producer would come in at night and play
the parts right. Or else the band would just look great, and they'd
put them out there anyway. You'd see them live and go, "What?
That's the same group?" Come on, that's records, that's not a bad
thing. It's not an everyday practice, but how about The Monkees?
They had great records. Still some of my favorite records are
Monkees records. Who knows how that stuff was done? I never saw
The Monkees live. The Archies. Big novelty records were all production records.

I suppose you could say the same thing about The Sex Pistols, too.

Yeah, right. There are a lot of bands like that. A lot of groups can
have weak links in the chain. Usually somebody else in the band
can cover the part for a record. We all know about the famous
Troggs tape. They couldn't even get the rhythm track down. I don't
know if it's a joke or whatever. . . .

What's the famous Troggs tape?

You don't know about that?

No.

Everybody in the recording business knows about that tape. After
they had "Wild Thing" these guys are supposed to be out in the
studio doing their next record. They couldn't even get the rhythm
track together and they broke out into a big fight. Most recording
studios have this Troggs tape in their library. You put it on and
you hear the guys trying to rehearse the song and they can't get
it together. Finally they start having a fight and they're cursing
each other out. They're going [with English accent], "Oh, you
fucking asshole, you played the thing right the first time! You went
do, do, do, do, do! Just do it again!" Who knows who ended up
really playing the drum part? I think that's a real minor issue.
That's like saying, when you look at a movie, who did what? Who
knows what you do to get a movie made? Anything that's recorded,
the magic should be in the recording, in the product itself. A record
is different from a live performance. That's what you're buying;

you're buying the record. I saw the movie *Diva*, and they were asking the woman who played the diva how come she'd never done a record. She says, "Because in *my* concept of music, music is a fleeting moment. It's only meant to be enjoyed while it's passing because tonight I may sing this and tomorrow I may sing that. It's only important while it's happening. It's not important sitting on the shelf." That was sort of cool in a way. But records *are* important because you want to enjoy what was captured that moment, that night, to be *shared* with everyone. There are a lot of things you can do with a record that you can't do on stage.

So making a record sound like the artist does on stage is not an important factor for you?

Nah. Totally not. When I first heard Hendrix's *Axis: Bold as Love* and I heard them do that tape flanging thing, who knows who thought of that? All I know is that I bought a Hendrix record, and that thing went [he imitates a tape flanging sound]. Who cares who thought of that? I was listening to a record. It knocked me out. I bought a Sly Stone record the other day because I want to cover a song. This thing had this extreme stereo stuff, the whole band over here and a tambourine on the right side. I thought, "What dodo came up with this?" Obviously it was hip in those days. I thought it was the greatest thing, because basically we just wanted mono. We wanted two mono speakers.

Let's talk about electronics a little bit. You're a believer in electronics, technology, synthesizers.

Oh, to the highest order.

You never worry about losing musicality or soul in the larger sense?

Never. Absolutely never. As a matter of fact, on my album—and I play guitar—a friend of mine came in; he had some programs of guitar sounds that we put into a drum machine that I was absolutely in love with because of the sound. I didn't care that I wasn't playing the guitar. It was the sound that was great to me, and I was making a record. I came up with the ideas and concepts, and when this record comes out it's going to say Nile Rodgers. So on one song I did some guitar programming, and some bass programming. Who cares about that stuff? That limits your art. It's all just paint, right? You just have to grab all the colors you can get. If somebody introduces these new metallic colors that have bits of metal flake in them and gold leaf and stuff—all of a sudden you're starting to get a texture to your work that you didn't have before when you just worked with these primary, oil-based paints with no other textures in them. Somebody introduces a new thing and you say, "Damn, look at this great stuff I can do." Other people develop styles around materials. You can see certain artists who develop styles around just what they use. Technology just allows composers especially to be more creative than they have been. I mean, I can't play the French horn but I have some great French horn sounds in my Synclavier. It allows me to interpret the French horn the way I hear it. In the old days when I had Chic, sometimes it was damn frustrating to write out the arrangements and listen to them played poorly all day. I mean, I'd just sit there for hours and hours and hours. And I'd say to myself, "Damn, I wish I could play cello because *I'd* have it right."

Of course, the other side of the coin is that sometimes you get an interpretation from a musician that *you* would have never thought of in a million years. You can write out a chart for somebody, and you're listening to the section, and somebody in the back makes a mistake and you go, "Wait a minute, what was that again?" You say, "Wait a minute, that's all wrong," and you look at the paper and the copyist copied it wrong, but it sounds hip and you use it. Of course, you lose that spontaneity.

And musicians lose jobs too, right?

Not that I know of.

I mean, if you don't need a string section, that string section is out of work.

Yeah, but hell, all my life I've always been in the . . . You know I went to classical school. Hell, how many jobs did I get, you know?

I never heard the concertmaster sitting around saying, "Damn, you know, we need to find some more pieces for classical guitar players. Man, I sure miss that guy who used to play in our orchestra." No way. Hey, come on.

Are people just going to have to adapt to electronics? Is it like when sound came into the movies? There were a lot of people squawking about how horrible it was, and it would change everything, and it would cheapen everything. And, of course, ultimately it didn't.

Well, initially it did because you had to get used to the new. You were only accustomed to the old. You were accustomed to these great mime artists, these people who could emote and make you laugh without saying a word. So we just had to get used to the people talking. Some of them had terrible voices and we couldn't stand them any longer. A lot of them were great and they continued on.

Is that where we're at now with electronics in the record industry?

I don't think so. I don't think that it is such a major issue at this point. I personally think that recorded music and live music are two different things, I, for one, when I go see bands nowadays and I see them playing tapes and things like that—I don't come from that school—to me that's the funniest thing I've ever seen in my life.

You mean like Frankie Goes to Hollywood?

Sure. There's a million of them. Big ones. Good ones. I'm sitting there going, "What is this?" I see the drummer go and flick on the tape of a bass drum going boom, boom, boom. That's totally ridiculous to me. I didn't study all these years to go play a tape when I'm doing a live show.

So that's jive?

To me it is. I believe in playing. But to me a record is a record. The thing that makes me fascinated with records and films is, I'm blown away with technology. I don't want to see a film that's washed-out black and white like the old days, and subtitles on the screen and no talking. I want to see more and more technology. When they improve the sound in the theater to sound like the sound in my home, then I'll even love it more. I like new things. I want to see more innovation. And personally, as a composer and as a writer, I like the freedom of being able to do my own horn parts myself on a synthesizer, and use my interpretation and know that the damn thing is going to be right when I get finished playing with it. I think that's a great thing.

What's the cutting edge right now in technology, and what are the things we can look for in the next few years?

Right now it's fascinating to me. This is the most stimulated I've ever been in my whole life. I can't even keep up with all this junk I'm buying. To me the most fascinating thing, and I know to some people this is going to sound like a drag . . . We're working on systems where if somebody who lives in England, say, has a system similar to what I have, and he's got a track and he wants me to play on it, well, he can send it to me over the satellite to New York. My system can pick it up. It will go down on tape. I can listen to it, put my guitar overdub on it, send it back to him, and it'll all be digital information. It will sound exactly the same as when I played it. And it'll be clear as a bell and it'll be dynamite. Right there in his home as if I were playing it with him. We just transfer the messages to each other digitally. The quality is perfect. Now, a lot of people would argue about that, but to me that's great, that's efficient. Now I don't have to go there and move into a hotel, and raise the budget $20,000 or even hassle with England! I think that's a great thing. In fact, that's *more* communication, not less. I can play on your record if you're anywhere.

It sounds like the music industry's "global village."

Yeah. It's all just communication.

Is that system something that is really imminent?

Absolutely. Maybe in the next year or two. Oh, yeah, it's going to be happening in a big way.

How did you make the move from being a performer and producing your own records to producing other people's records?

To be totally honest. Chic was only a production to us. Chic was not the band that we were going to be in. It was like what you were talking about before, disco being a producer's thing. Well, yeah, we were producers, we were songwriters. We also sang and performed, but we didn't feel that we had to go out and represent it. Quite frankly, we didn't know if it would be a hit or not, because we had so many bad things happen to us, plus we really wanted to be rock stars. We didn't see ourselves just playing in clubs. We wanted to be like, all right! [He mimics the sounds of a huge crowd, and laughs.] That sort of thing. We didn't basically want to assume responsibility for Chic. We didn't really know what this disco thing was all about. We were just writing songs that sounded good to us, that made us feel great, that made us want to dance to them.

But right from the beginning you produced the group yourself with Bernard Edwards. There was never any question of bringing in an outside producer.

We were Chic. But the thing is, we weren't necessarily going to be Chic forever.

How did you also decide you wanted to be a production whiz for other recording artists?

That was purely an accident. Other producers were producing us before we were Chic officially. And no one could get a record from us because we were overplayers. We wanted to be *players!* We were musicians. Jazz, man! So when a producer came in he could never communicate with us and make us understand that we were making records. Now, this was us; we didn't want to be seen as The Monkees, we wanted to be like Return to Forever, that's where we were coming from. No producers could get records on us. They got records, but they were like son of Mahavishnu.

These were records that never actually came out?

Absolutely never came out. They were tapes; they never actually became records. No record company signed us. We decided to cut our own stuff. It started off as jazz, then progressively became more commercial. The first proper disco record we wrote—it's funny to say proper disco record—was "Everybody Dance," which was the most jazzlike song in our repertoire. When we realized that, we did it for ourselves—we did this not as a musical representation of ourselves, but as what we could do if we wanted to make a commercial record. We thought we could . . .

. . . produce this product.

Right. When you're actually there doing it, you think it's something special, and something really heavy. So once we did it for ourselves we said, "Damn, we could probably do this with anybody." That's really how cocky we were. This was our first record, and we went to the head of Atlantic Records and said, "You know, we could make your secretary a star." This is really funny [laughter]. We were twenty-something years old and we're in there telling the president of Atlantic Records that we could make his secretary a star because we thought that we had really lucked onto something. Not realizing that all we had found was songs, and people who could play the tracks, and people—us—who could make them into records. But we didn't know that. We thought we had done something *magical*. We didn't realize that all we were was just producers, and we just happened to be songwriters and musicians as well, and also I did the arrangements.

So when did you figure that out?

It took a while, because we had all these big records. And we didn't realize that all we were doing was what people like Quincy Jones or Phil Ramone do. I don't really know how they produce records because I've led a very sheltered life. I've never really worked with other producers outside of Bernard Edwards.

Did it take a stumble or two on your part?

Yeah, it took working with Diana Ross on *Diana*. That's when we realized that we didn't understand why things were going so well for ourselves. We had no idea. We said, "Damn, what did we do? We wrote a song. We cut a track. We went in there and sang it." We didn't think we were the greatest singers in the world, so why did that work? Because it just did.

So what happened with Diana?

See, we had never worked with stars before. We didn't realize that there was a communication thing. We didn't realize what producers did. We thought that whenever we produced a record all we did was sit at home and write all these songs. Once the songs are written, we go in and cut the tracks. Once the tracks are cut, we go in and put the backgrounds on. Then we sing the lead vocals. That's how we produced a record. So it was no different for anyone. Sister Sledge, Diana Ross, we didn't care who it was. Diana Ross walks into the studio and says, "Well, how do the songs go?" We said, "What do you mean, how do the songs go? We're going to go home and write them. We don't know how they go. What do you want the songs to be about?" "Well, my life is here in New York and I don't want any of the old life. I don't want to talk anything about California or my past relationships." I said, "Great, so you're coming out with a new bag." We wrote that down and went home and wrote "I'm Coming Out." That's how it worked to us. That's it. That's how you produce a record. So Diana said, "I'm going to have to hear the songs." We said, "Sure, you'll hear them when it's time to sing them." We had no idea. We thought *everybody* did it that way. We really did. So then we got pissed off. We said, "What do you mean? You mean you have to hear the songs? Oh, so we're *auditioning* for you? What do you mean by that?" She says, "Well, I've never just walked into the studio and somebody tells me to sing, 'I'm coming out, I want the world to see.'" We said, "All these big records you've had, what do you mean you've never done that?" We honestly didn't know. We never rehearsed. Rehearsal? I'd never heard of such a thing. "Oh, we got to *learn* the songs first and then record them?" I said, "I'm a pro, you can teach the song to me in the studio and I'll play it." I mean, I survived like that at the Apollo. You learned the show that morning and you had to play it that afternoon.

But that's not the way records are made, you found out.

But *I didn't know that.* We had a big fight with Diana Ross. She left the studio and we didn't see her for months.

Really? Over this . . .

Over just the way that we worked. This whole thing of, "Well, you come in and we'll tell you what to sing, and when you finish singing it we'll tell you when you can go home." And we're, like, twenty-five years old, and this is Diana Ross! Well, we truly didn't know. I mean, we weren't trying to be crazy or tough, we honestly didn't know any other way. If somebody had proposed a different sort of way to us, we couldn't guarantee that the record would sound right. Because I didn't know how to do it if it wasn't *my* song. I couldn't imagine what the record would sound like.

She actually remixed the record herself without your approval, didn't she?

Absolutely.

And that's the way it came out?

Shee, boy, did it ever. But, you know, what happened is that a really great friend of ours, Bob Clearmountain [an engineer and producer], listened to her version of it and said, "You know, Nile, these are great songs, man. You can't keep a record like this down. No matter how bad this sounds to you, believe me, to the people it's going to sound dynamite." I said, "Bob, listen to it, there's no bass, there's no nothing. My guitar doesn't sound like that. That's the worst guitar sound I've ever heard in my life!" [Laughter.] He said, "Nile, trust me, man. It's cool. That's how Motown records sound. It's cool." He was right. I really was afraid. I was terrified. I thought the record was going to be a huge flop, just because of the sound. It shows how paranoid you can get about something like that when really, like people say, "If it's in the groove, it's in the groove." It's hard to mess it up.

You still don't like it, huh?

No, well, I have the original at home so it sounds great to me!

You play the original?

Of course. Of course! I have the *real* one, with the real big horn sound. Oh, they made a mistake because they didn't know that was going on, they didn't know how we did the record. We built a composite trombone solo which is *fantastic* on my record. On their record . . . the guy made a lot of mistakes—which wound up being cool, ultimately, in the end, because they're good players. He didn't make a total jerk out of himself. But on mine he's really wailing. He sounds *fantastic.*

We'll never know. When should an artist produce himself, and when should he go to an outside producer?

That's a very difficult question to answer. But let me say this to you as an artist finishing my own record: It makes you incredibly anxious. I don't know if I'm as objective as I'd like to be, even though it's a very subjective medium. I don't know if I can say, sometimes, if I want to go with this thing because it's best for the record or because I want to appear hip. Do you know what I mean? I might want to take this lyric out because I feel stupid talking about, say, Kellogg's corn flakes, so I put in sushi instead to sound hip. . . .

Even though Kellogg's corn flakes might be better for the disc?

Right. Whereas if it were *your* song I'd say to you, "Come on, give me a break, Kellogg's corn flakes is happening, *everybody* knows about that. So what if your snooty, cool New York friends know about sushi, big deal!" That's the difficult part because when you're producing yourself, you're like an actor. Now that I've been working with films and stuff I see how actors are very conscious about

how they're coming off. So they're looking for scripts and saying,
"Damn, when so-and-so says that line he really comes off heavy,
that sounds dynamite." And they go to the director and say, "Can
I have that line?" You start doing that to yourself. You say, "Wow,
when so-and-so gets that part it sounds really cool; maybe if I put
that on a guitar, I'll have a cool part." It may sound really petty,
but I'm sure a lot of people get into that sort of thing. Because you
are talking about yourself, and you're molding yourself to the way
people are going to see you.

*Do you think there are a lot of people who are producing
themselves who shouldn't be?*

Yes. But then there are also a lot of people who produce themselves
who do great work. Also, some of the people who I think are great
artists allow themselves to be produced well. Certain people are just
fabulous artists, and whoever they're being produced by, they'll
always shine through. The artistry is always there. Bowie is like
that. David Bowie will never *not* be Bowie. He'll always be Bowie,
there's no way you can change that. Or somebody like Jagger. Oh,
even a better example is Madonna. She'll always be Madonna, no
matter what. She is one of those really special, unique artists
that. . . . I swear, I wish a lot of producers could work with people
like that. She's the kind of person you dream about. The kind of
person you know will work on it until it's right. And what's right
for Madonna is the same kind of thing that's right for Bowie—the
question is whether the feeling is right, not whether they sang it
perfectly. If the story is being told properly. When you hear their
records you know just what they're talking about.

*Does a Madonna or Bowie know what they want when they come
into a studio, or are they just very receptive to a good producer?*

I think they have a very good idea of what they want, and they're
also very receptive. What governs this stuff? What's wrong?
What's right? Who knows what can change it from day to day? I
can wake up in the morning with a very clear picture of how a song
is going to be, and I get to the studio and it just doesn't work. You
don't like it, even though you were clear on it. It's just not happen-

ing. So if somebody suggests a better way to do it, sure, you can fight it and just insist that your way is happening because you wrote it. Or else you go along with it and try and develop it with him. It's having very strong editing powers—that's what I think a good producer is, a person who can take their ideas and stop them, like that, in an instant, and let their minds be free and listen totally to what somebody's got to say. Something new. That's what makes a person a good, receptive artist or producer. That you can stop your idea and totally grasp what another person is saying and either develop it with him or make the decision right on the spot, "Nope, it's not happening, let's move on to another idea." That's *my* payoff in this business. What I get out of the record is the enjoyment of those moments when that happens. And it happens every day, twenty or thirty times a day. To be able to stop and create something out of just a shell of something that was there.

And you have that power to say, "Nope, it's not happening," even with a Bowie or a Jagger?

Yes. I think that's my greatest asset or my greatest value to a person, the fact that I'm a songwriter. I write melodies all day. So if you come in and you have a song, and you say there's some part that just doesn't make sense to you, I can give you a thousand suggestions, I hope. Some days I can't, but those are the days we just go home early.

That happens from time to time?

Oh, man, it happens all the time.

Do you consider yourself a good technician on the board in a studio?

Oh, no. Heavens no. I mean, I know how it works, and I can work a board if I have to. But I'm not an engineer/producer. I didn't go to engineering school. This would be Greek to me except that I've been doing it so long that I know what it all does now. Plus, I have a little studio at home, and they're all the same. I truly believe in great engineers. *That*'s the thing to me. Dig this, I'm really simple when it comes to music. I think that first you have a song. Then everybody connected with that song has to make the song better, no matter who it is, whether it's the assistant engineer, the singer, the bass player, the guitar player, everybody's got to make it better than what you did at home by yourself. If I come in and think I have a good song, rehearsing with my band, when I come in and play it you got to make it better than what I just did. *I* can make it as good as I made the demo at home. Anybody can do that.

Let's talk about some of the people you've worked with as a producer. Let's start with Jagger. You did three cuts on his solo record. How did that come about, and was he a little nervous about making his first solo?

Outwardly, no. Inwardly I'm sure he probably was nervous. If he says he wasn't, then I like him even *more* than I like him. I think he's great. How could you be in The Rolling Stones and be Mick Jagger and not be nervous about making a solo record? Damn, if he isn't nervous then he's *really* hip [laughter]. *I'm* nervous!

Were you nervous working with him?

No. I'm never, never nervous working with people. No, I mean I was nervous making my own solo record, so I know Jagger had to be nervous.

Did the songs come together relatively easily?

Well, you know, we had a feeling-out period of him starting to understand my sounds, and me understanding his sounds, and his technique and my technique. Finally, talking worked everything out. When Mick Jagger said, "Nile, get the hell out of the studio and get in the control room," I said, *"Now* I know what you want!" [Laughter.] Then I understood. I said, "Right, Mick. Gotcha, pal!" And then I really dug it. As soon as he said that to me it was very clear. But for two weeks it was like boxers trying to feel out. . . . I got that punch in. Great. Well here's a couple more. After that we were cool. I realized he wanted a producer-producer. He wanted me in there working on *sounds.* He wanted me to capture the moments, these fleeting bits that would go by and he'd say, "Whoops, that's it—hold on to that thing." I couldn't do it if I'm out in the studio jamming, because my music is fleeting too. And I'm hanging out with all the guys, and we were losing stuff. That's the way he makes records, whereas I make my decisions right on the spot. On every record that I do there's only one copy. I don't have two versions of *anything*. Either it's happening or it's not. With Mick, he's from a different school, sort of like Bryan Ferry. They want you to play everything possible and then they'll figure out which parts are hip, and then ask you to refine that.

Do you like being a session musician? I know, for instance, you played guitar for Bryan Ferry.

I love being a session person. I have a philosophy about that too: I don't learn my own songs and I don't learn your songs, either. I don't rehearse. You give me the chart when I get to the studio. Either you give me the chart or I'll learn it with the band or whatever. I play my best guitar on *your* record.

Let's go on to some others you've produced. Jeff Beck—was he a hero of yours as a guitar player?

Serious hero. Jeff, he's the man to me. He's the greatest guitar player alive today, in my opinion. He plays what I would like to hear more than any other guitar player. When I worked with Jeff I had a different concept in mind. I wanted to make a record with somebody like that very accessible. I want other people to enjoy Jeff Beck's guitar playing as much as I do, and the way to get that out there is to have him on a *song*. Not just great fusion records, which I'm sure he can do forever without me. I wanted to give him songs that people would sing. So that's what I tried to do. I tried to say to him, "Like 'Beat It.' " The reason why Eddie Van Halen's solo is so great on "Beat It" is not just because it's great—it is, and he plays great solos all the time—but because of the fact that it's on that *cool song!* That's what makes it really happening.

Was Beck there for that? Did he understand that?

Oh yeah, sure. We talked about it a lot. He likes my songs. We had a good time.

That's not a problem for someone who came out of the sixties, the long-guitar-solo era?

Well, I let him play long guitar solos [laughter].

How about Duran Duran?

Duran Duran is not quite the same as these other people. First of all they're a group. It's a completely different relationship than with a solo artist. When you're dealing with a group it's almost like first you have to be the den mother, like a Boy Scout troop. You have to gain the respect of everyone, which is cool. I don't have any problem with that. Duran Duran were fans of mine before I worked with them. They loved Chic music, so that was great. Plus, there were a lot of Duran Duran songs that I liked as well. Bands are a very different animal. You have to deal with the personalities collectively and individually. And I work best on a one-to-one basis. I just grew up working with individuals. There's a lot of psychology that goes into production because these people are stars and you absolutely have to respect that. I always feel that I work *for* you, not that you work for me. I don't even feel like I work *with* you. I'm employed by you. And I think that it's your record, and you got to give a person that. So when it's five people and you have to give them their records individually and collectively, it's rough. But I get along great with Duran Duran.

Do they make records as great as their videos?

They make great videos. They make good records too. I mean, some of their songs I like more than others, but that's true of any artist. I guess Duran Duran probably falls under more criticism because of the audience they appeal to. If they appealed to older people like Bryan Ferry does, I guess they'd be really hip. Their songs are cool. Like "Don't Say a Prayer." When I saw them live I was crying when they did that song. I was standing on the side and I heard this [he mimics the rhythm] and it sounded so beautiful to me the tears started streaming down my face. Madonna looked at me and went, "Yo, brother, where're you coming from?"

And Madonna?

Madonna is the greatest, I don't care what anyone says. Madonna is so cool. I said this to Diana Ross, too. I said, "I wish everybody were like Madonna, in a weird way." I like the fact that she's the hardest-working person I've ever seen in my life. She was here in the studio before me most of the time. She'd swim like miles every day before she came to sing. That kind of dedication I don't see too often. It makes you feel proud. It makes you feel dedicated. It makes me say, "Hmm, maybe I'm getting a little fat here around the middle. Maybe I should go practice."

Is she a great singer? Does she really care about being a great singer?

I don't know if she cares about being a great singer. I think she cares about being a good singer and being a good storyteller, and that's what singing is about to me. That's *all* that it's about. I mean, is Bowie a great singer? What's a great singer? I mean, yeah, *Aretha*'s a great singer. But Bowie is a great songster. He tells the story and he means it. He delivers the story. To me, I'd rather work with somebody like that than a great singer, because I make records. I'm not really capturing what I consider in my head great live performances. I'm making a contrived thing for a specific type of artistic statement—a record. So even if you sang the same part five times, who cares? If the fifth one is right, that's the one that goes on the record, not the first one. Because this is captured forever. You want it to be *dynamite*.

(March, 1985)

Index